The Spark of Fear

The Spark of Fear

Technology, Society and the Horror Film

BRIAN N. DUCHANEY

McFarland & Company, Inc., Publishers
Jefferson, North Carolina

LIBRARY OF CONGRESS CATALOGUING-IN-PUBLICATION DATA

Duchaney, Brian N., 1977–
　　The spark of fear : technology, society and the horror film / Brian N. Duchaney.
　　　　p.　cm.
　　Includes bibliographical references and index.

　　ISBN 978-0-7864-9511-5 (softcover : acid free paper) ∞
　　ISBN 978-1-4766-1982-8 (ebook)

　　1. Horror films—History and criticism.　2. Technology in motion pictures.　3. Motion pictures—Social aspects.　I. Title.
PN1995.9.H6D78　2015
791.43'6164—dc23　　　　　　　　　　　　　　　　2015013971

BRITISH LIBRARY CATALOGUING DATA ARE AVAILABLE

© 2015 Brian N. Duchaney. All rights reserved

No part of this book may be reproduced or transmitted in any form or by any means, electronic or mechanical, including photocopying or recording, or by any information storage and retrieval system, without permission in writing from the publisher.

Cover image: *Frankenstein* (1931) © Universal Pictures/Photofest

Printed in the United States of America

McFarland & Company, Inc., Publishers
*　Box 611, Jefferson, North Carolina 28640*
*　　www.mcfarlandpub.com*

For my wife, Emily.
Thank you for your advice, guidance
and sick sense of what's funny.

Table of Contents

Introduction   1

Part I—Classic Horror and Establishing the Horror Film

1. The Origins of the Horror Film: From Page to Screen   11
2. The *Frankenstein* Cycle: Film as a Method for Reconciling the Mind/Self in Society   25
3. Horror from Beyond: Social Anxieties, Dystopias and Outsider Threats   42

Part II—Modern Horror and the Fear of Progress

4. *Psychos*, Civic Unrest and Refining Horror   63
5. The Mainstreaming of Underground Horror: Shlock, Special Effects and Slashers   80
6. Us vs. Them: Modern Horror and the Horror of Complacency   96
7. Science Fiction or Science Horror? American Dystopia and Cinematic Frontiers   115

Part III—Contemporary and Postmodern Horrors in a Tech-Savvy World

8. Virtual Terrors: Modern Technologies and the Assumption of Horror   137

Table of Contents

9. Exhibitionism, Technique and Establishing Modern Horror	155
10. The Future of Horror	173
Suggested List of Films	181
Chapter Notes	185
Bibliography	193
Index	201

Introduction

> The moral life of man forms part of the subject-matter of the artist, but the morality of art consists in the perfect use of an imperfect medium.... No artist is ever morbid. The artist can express everything.—Oscar Wilde's preface to *The Picture of Dorian Gray*

When I was about seven years old, I remember the excitement and joy that our family shared when my parents finally got a VHS player. I don't remember when they brought it home, but I remember that it was *expensive* and *not a toy*, meaning I couldn't play with it. Not that I even knew what a VHS player was at the time; all I knew was that it showed movies. So when my brother brought his friend over to watch a film, it only seemed natural that I would be curious as to how it worked. So, allowing them to get into the movie (ten minutes or so), I walked into the room to see what they were doing. As I proceeded to nonchalantly paw at the movie's rental case, my brother paused the movie. It was there on the screen that I saw a group of people hunched over a corpse, happily gorging themselves on his insides. My brother, not realizing that a seven-year-old might be terrified, proceeded to happily show me that "you can even watch it in slow motion! LOOK!" Then, in a ghastly performance, the corpses fed themselves frame by frame, slowly looking up to the camera and coming face to face with a scared little boy. It was years later that I discovered that they were watching a comedy: Bob Clark's *Children Shouldn't Play with Dead Things* (1972). Maybe this explains a lot.

I grew up with horror. Having older siblings meant that I acted as

Introduction

a suitable companion for watching all sorts of horror because, well, let's face it: they liked to watch me squirm. But I adapted quickly. This was the 1980s, when the slasher film was in its heyday and Hollywood effects were a realistic (if not a tad overdone) array of puppets, latex, and blood. It was the ideal childhood. I grew up in front of the TV, alternating between rentals, HBO, and a local station that showed classic horror films, affectionately called "The Creature Double Feature." One week it was *Godzilla vs. Mothra* (1964), another week *Die, Monster, Die!* (1965). Also, I grew up on Elm Street. Maybe it was our shared street that led me to embrace Freddy Krueger as the best of the slashers, but in all likelihood, it was how he attacked his victims: in their dreams.

Freddy exhibits a crucial aspect to understanding horror movies, that of the role of the imagination in accepting horror as real ... at least real in our minds. We rely on suspension of disbelief, or letting go of the outside world in order to occupy the onscreen world. But in order for us to do so, the imaginary world needs to seem plausible. This is the problem with the *Nightmare on Elm Street* franchise (1984–2010), but it's also part of the fun. No one believes that a charred, smart-alecky pedophile corpse will attack us anytime soon. But we shouldn't be so easily fooled—horror films are quite cerebral, and many work among a series of conventions and reinventions in order to keep us running scared, if only to return to the madman to be scared again. Something is at work, telling us to react in such a manner that we keep being scared of the same clichés. For me, that working component of horror is change, specifically changes in technology.

I've always been drawn to times of change and chaos. Maybe it's a way to explain the current world when we can go back and study the past. But horror is a continuous example of how we revisit the past in order to make the present both explainable and foreign. Like other mediums, the horror film is a reaction to outside influences. Directors like Hitchcock, who pioneered thematic lighting in his films, exemplify another development of technique used to illustrate a state of mind that cannot be easily replicated without specific examples. In the famous shower scene in *Psycho* (1960), Norman Bates (Anthony Perkins) is backlit as he approaches the camera, presenting a shadowy falsehood to viewers. Similarly, Marion Crane (Janet Leigh) discovers Mother Bates in a corner as a swinging light bulb illuminates the room. Such effects apply a new standard for film. As film developed into a medium capable of

Introduction

portraying real emotion and not simply a record of a performance, the film genre grew to encompass both a performance *and* a state of mind. For Gina Wisker, this means that "horror explores the fissures that open in our everyday lives and destabilizes our complacency about norms and rules.... The comfortable dismissal of horror as merely entertainment or silly, scary monsters avoids its well-established, politicized role as exposer of social and cultural deceits and discomforts, deriving from the Gothic."[1] This explains the evolution of science-fiction, a medium that was capable of presenting alternate (and sometimes future) realities:

> The mid-fifties ushered in the race to space of the Sputnik era, along with films about disembodied brains that overpowered human will and invasions by brains (and aliens) from outer space. *Donovan's Brain* (1953), *The Brain from Planet Arous* (1957), and *Fiend without a Face* (1958) deal with alien intelligence that takes control of earthling's consciousness, and other variations of this theme. Intense inter-country competition goaded scientists to send men to the moon and stimulated production of low-budget sci-fi films—and the magician turned movie maker [Georges Méliès] foresaw these events in 1902 when he made *A Trip to the Moon*. Horror and sci-fi films of the 1950s were also reactions to the horrors of Hiroshima, and they often expressed fears of another bomb.[2]

This is no different from today's films exhibiting an awareness or consciousness of societal action. In fact, many of today's features employ the same techniques regardless of the genre. Both *Saving Private Ryan* (1998) and *The Blair Witch Project* (1999) employ a "shaky-cam" to represent mental chaos, while detective work and fact finding are essential to both *The Bourne Identity* (2002) and *The Silence of the Lambs* (1991). What distinguishes one from the other is not what is shown, but how the audience reacts to it. This isn't to suggest that war films cannot also be horrific; *Schindler's List* (1993) is a great example of horror brought to life. However, our expectations as an audience change the experience. We don't watch dramas to be horrified, *per se*; we go to relive our troubled human history from the safety of the present. But the modern horror film as we know it derives its core reaction from its contemporary approach to exploring the modern world.

In order to keep current attitudes of horror relevant, the genre must continually reinvent itself. In *Friday the 13th* (1980), the horrific depends not on what is natural, but what is unexpected. Specifically,

Introduction

this film works by showing us our dependence on modern conveniences, in turn making a familial tradition—the escape from society—a living nightmare that now resides in our consciousness. Annie, the heroine of the film, tells us that there should be no worries should Camp Crystal Lake be hampered by darkness: "Steve taught me to use the emergency generator. Town power lines are supposed to be really lousy." The resulting chaos is a psychological adventure, where "probability" is replaced by "possibility." The film heightens the drama of a world that is at times unreliable and removed from the very comforts introduced by men like Edison and Tesla. By returning horror to a seemingly simplified state, *Friday the 13th* gives rise to the basest of horrors, where the natural, the security of society, becomes unnatural solitude and isolation. In many ways, the film echoes one character's commentary on an impending storm, that "this is no dream." The scenes that follow are constituted as parallel realities, where Jack (Kevin Bacon) seduces another counselor in a dark and secluded cabin while the rest of the counselors engage in a game of "strip Monopoly," drinking beer by a roaring fire and engaging in the most stereotypical manners' complete removal from society. Of course, the film cautions the audience about everyday dangers of progress. As iconic as Kevin Bacon's character's death is for future viewers (being stabbed in the throat while reclining with a post-coital joint), the film ushered in a new brand of horror—the slasher flick. But even slasher films, as evidenced in Adam Rockoff's book *Going to Pieces: The Rise and Fall of the Slasher Film, 1978–1986*, has experienced a decided decline:

> By mid-2001, the slasher film had once again reached a crossroad. Critics pronounced that films in which much of the terror was left to the imagination, like *The Blair Witch Project* ... and *The Sixth Sense* ... heralded an end to the graphic violence of the slasher. To them, that the two forms of horror could exist in a symbiotic rather than antagonistic relationship seemed impossible.[3]

But perhaps this signals a new tradition, not for just the slasher film, but for the entire horror genre. Watching horror films will always be a way to deal with life's problems, as Gothic science-fiction stories have not eroded from existence but have become classics. Not only are we able to embed an idea in film, but we can use film to portray apparent "red herrings" in the same manner as early Gothic horror, which exposes our own assumptions, and yes, fears regarding the unknown.

Introduction

And most of what we don't know is due in part to technological advances. Like the films of the 1950s, which reasoned through societal developments and changes, there have been numerous horror films that do very much the same thing: *Flatliners* (1990) explores medical students who bring themselves to near-death, only to have waking nightmares and serve afterlife penance while still living; *White Noise* (2005) depicts Michael Keaton's ability to use EEG (or electroencephalogram) technology to capture conversations of the dead while seeking to communicate with his own deceased wife. Then there are the horrors of an even newer technology. *Untraceable* (2008) explores a serial-killer who posts videos of his victims on the Internet, while the popular *Saw* franchise (2004–2011) exploits technology in order to exploit viewers who watch others exploit others.

There is no denying that reading is taking a distant second place for horror's most loyal followers. But that does not mean that the effect of horror has any less significance as it is ultimately based on the same conventions as early Gothic tales. We believe the axe-murderer, serial killer, or monstrous figure as possible not because they don't exist, but because we have yet to be proven wrong about the possibility of something monstrous happening to us. The Gothic story has not changed, nor has our ability to read into a storyline and come away with a tangible sentiment. What has changed is the presentation and how ideas generated by pictures, and not words, influence our psyche. And it will continue to change. As technology improves, the need to exhibit new forms of horror becomes a necessity. However, what we should realize is that terror in any form is equally awful for those experiencing it. What has changed is not the type of fear, but how we respond to it.

This text builds on the work of others by exploring technological advancement and its effects on human consciousness as represented by the legion of horror films that continually develop a vision of the world with which we are unfamiliar. By reinventing horror through our lack of awareness, the horror film progresses the horrific idea of social advancement through technology as a way of abusing our sense of safety in the modern world. In the discussion that follows, I explore the ways in which technology supplants our idea of self, specifically by showing that horror films manipulate our sense of safety in a technologically advanced world.

I've divided the discussion that follows into three parts, each trac-

Introduction

ing specific developments of social progress through advancing technologies as sources of horror indicative of the times that they encompass. In Part I ("Classic Horror and Establishing the Horror Film"), I trace the origins of horror through the burgeoning film industry and how classic horror films develop the idea of a technological society through our distrust of modern advancement. Chapter 1 discusses the transition of horror as a figurative metaphor on a page to a fully realized figure that stands before us. By looking at the horror as a method to reconciling social fears, I trace how pictorial visions of horror adapt Gothic conventions that set the stage for our modern conception of horror. In Chapter 2, I show how the *Frankenstein* cycle of films embodies reinvention of a singular idea of horror based on technological innovation, tracing the Frankenstein myth from inception to present interpretations. Chapter 3 discusses the prospective reaches of technology as envisioned by the fears of the pre-technological world, in which science fiction and the world of possibilities manipulates social fears of technological progress. Furthering the idea of the Frankenstein dilemma of progress over lost knowledge, this chapter focuses on the social anxieties of scientific advancement beyond the reach of modern thought.

In Part II ("Modern Horror and the Fear of Progress"), I develop the idea of horror through a technological world, exploring the loss of individual control as society began to embrace a technologically advanced world. Chapter 4 centers on the explorations of social discord that arose from a world that was now capable of moving beyond the ordinary conception of society into the much darker and undiscovered reaches of a society that was on the outskirts of modern progress, in which the outsider was defined as a source of horror. Eschewing established ideas of progress, this chapter launches the idea of youth culture and innovation, breaking from Gothic norms of found horror to socially manifested horror through purposeful disenfranchisement. In Chapter 5, the discussion centers on the growing fascination with the taboo, specifically in how technological advancements brought to life the visual aspects of horror that were largely unseen in modern society. Tracing the evolution of shock value from comic books and underground sources, this chapter helps to explain the foundations of modern horror and its entrenchment in showing the forbidden aspects of the human body. Building on Chapter 4's idea of progress at all costs,

Introduction

Chapter 6 looks at the modern world as a manifestation of our own complacency, specifically a society that, once having achieved a technologically advanced world, ceased to question the impact of it and grew complacent in its benefits. Chapter 7 revisits popular science fiction of The Other, building on the discussion of technological fears as shown in Chapter 3 as a source of horror, in which mankind, fully in command of technology, realized the potential to bring about its own destruction by reaching out to forbidden horrors of the unknown.

Part III pulls together the previous two sections by discussing "Contemporary and Postmodern Horrors in a Tech-Savvy World," establishing the modern horror film as a reaction against the progressive reach of the previous eras. In Chapter 8, the discussion explores modern society in a technologically advanced world, showing the reaches of all-encompassing knowledge from the Internet and virtual presence as a failed substitution for personal experience. In Chapter 9, I trace the modern vision of horror as a genre built on speculation and distrust, exploring the establishment of horror as a dystopian vision of American life, where our awareness of horror is blinded by the sublime promise of technological ambivalence. Finally, in Chapter 10, I speculate on the future of horror as a reaction to what we have thus far witnessed in the horror film. Building on that legacy, I trace how our modern iteration of horror is built on expectation and progression. What we will ultimately see as horrific must necessarily be the combination of what we have seen and what has yet to be shown.

If there's anything to take from this book, it will be that horror is an evolutionary process, not only from the sources, but from how we can perceive the horrors of progress to invade our lives. As we reach forward to further society, we will realize that each benefit comes with a cost that has yet to be established in the modern consciousness. For the horror film to speak accurately to our fears of technology and social change, we must continually reassess how innovation and introspection challenge our notion of modernity and the costs that our advanced world has on our perception of safety. In the blurred vision of technological and social freedoms, we will find that our greatest fears lay within a world that changes exponentially beyond our grasp for understanding it.

Part I

Classic Horror and Establishing the Horror Film

CHAPTER 1

The Origins of the Horror Film

From Page to Screen

> Who shall conceive the horrors of my secret toil, as I dabbled among the unhallowed damps of the grave, or tortured the living animal to animate the lifeless clay?—Dr. Victor Frankenstein realizes the horror in his creation of a living monster in Mary Shelley's *Frankenstein*.

Dr. Frankenstein's question is not simply that of a scientist questioning the motives of a deranged pursuit in scientific experimentation; it echoes the question of the author: how far can scientific achievement lead us to understanding human consciousness? When she wrote *Frankenstein*, Mary Shelley helped usher in a period of self-awareness, a period that harnessed the possibilities of horror fiction. While *Frankenstein* follows what we would generally consider Gothic fiction, the novel moves beyond traditional elements of horror, for it was Mary Shelley who popularized the awareness of a growing potential that was beyond the realm of ordinary understanding. In other words, making the unimaginable a visualized—and ultimately human—reality, Shelley brought external fears of scientific discovery to the imagination.

Few works of literature capture the prospects of scientific horrors as does *Frankenstein*. While other works explore scientific achievement as a means to deepen understanding of human consciousness, almost all of them resort to tawdry scenes of test tubes, grotesque transformations, and evil henchmen. Yet, two centuries after its publication, *Frankenstein* is still able to produce chills, not from the monster's disproportionate figure, nor from the terrors that he enacts in order to plague his creator. What we fear in the Monster is his existence beyond the text; that is, we fear the possibility of his existence.

The story of *Frankenstein* began in 1816 just outside Lake Geneva, Switzerland, where a group of friends entertained themselves on a dark and stormy night by telling ghost stories to one another. As a guest of Lord Byron, and accompanied by her husband, Percy Bysshe Shelley, and several other companions, including John Palidori, Mary and the group found themselves lacking entertainment, becoming housebound during an unusually cold and dreary summer. After time spent entertaining themselves with a collection of German supernatural stories (*Fantasmagoriana*), Percy suggested that the group write their own stories: Palidori completed *The Vampyre*, Percy likewise penned a short vampire story, and Mary began work on her masterpiece. Though this story has been retold many times as the inspiration for *Frankenstein*, the group produced a range of stories that played upon old conventions. Equally, the scene is common; but what Mary produced that night was perhaps the greatest influence to modern horror since the invention of the ghost story itself.

However unique Shelley's investigation of scientific progress, her story still includes the basic elements of horror fiction: dark scenery, obscured figures, and a deep investigation into the inexplicable and often absurd notion of human consciousness. Goethe's *Faust* includes a similar theme regarding the evils of pursuing knowledge; or at least in the case of Faust, knowledge that goes beyond ordinary human understanding. Both texts, *Frankenstein* and *Faust*, display a common theme through early horror literature, where the protagonist seeks knowledge beyond the natural realm, to which we typically refer to as the "dark arts." But this is not inclusive to horror fiction alone. Similar themes regarding the possibilities of the depths of man's depravity have been explored over the centuries: Sophocles's *Oedipus* trilogy explores the aspect of man's greed by exposing criminal activity as a means to an end; in a similar fashion, Dante's *Inferno* categorizes the levels of man's sin through the exploration of the worst of horrors—Hell. Coleridge's *The Rime of the Ancient Mariner* explores the darkness of the human mind through the mental anguish of an isolated fisherman. These may all be called versions of horror, but Shelley was among the first (and surely the most popular) authors to explore a condition that man brought upon himself through experimentation with external aid. Thus, it was science that first brought about man's ability to commit acts outside of what are purely humanly possible.

Before there were horror movies, there were written or spoken horror narratives, fables handed down from one generation to the next. The Babylonian *Epic of Gilgamesh* (c. 2000 BC) and Homer's *Odyssey* (c. 800 BC) both pit man against monsters and immortals. In the ancient method, man is at the peril of gods, in that man still sees himself as a pawn. It wasn't until man discovered the idea of free will that he could start really getting into his own head. Dante's *Divine Comedy* (1346) explores the humanistic side of man's quest for salvation. These embryonic horror stories are rooted in the traditions of early folklore. These early explorations largely revolve around religious attitudes toward life after death, evil, and demonic embodiments of evil (notably Satan). However, even in the earliest incarnations of horror, man told of witches, vampires and other cannibalistic beings, creatures (such as centaurs, chupacabra, man-beasts, etc.) and, of course, ghosts. These early superstitions would eventually give way from didactic or moralistic versions of life to becoming an art form in their own right, allowing storytellers the ability to balance human inquest with good old-fashioned storytelling. This would lead to the first main stream adaptation of horror as a fan culture—the Gothic novel.

Gothic Fiction

The inspiration of the "Gothic" novel is one based on features that are relatively outside the Gothic time period, originating in 12th-century France and lasting until about the Renaissance. The Gothic manner of writing dates to approximately 1790–1900 (likely coinciding with the Gothic revival in architecture), after which it apparently fell out of fashion because of changes in the horror genre. While the Gothic is itself a subgenre of both the romantic and Victorian eras, the literary Gothic is established in several ways, for our purposes I will look at two which carry over to and influence the horror film: (1) setting, in which horror is created from localized dangers, and (2) mentality, where the existence of horror resides chiefly in a psychological, non-corporeal form. The influences of setting and mentality rely on cultural assumptions in order to translate the horrific, albeit in different ways. This is what gives the horror genre its gravity, both internally and externally.

Horror is built around the assumption and the breaking of cultural norms. Norms are simply the laws that govern society; more broadly, they are the social forces that impel one to act in a repressed manner. Norms modify behavior. In this regard, horror is built upon the demolition of internal forces of control, resulting in conflict. In the horror genre, conflict is the impetus of the story. Keeping in mind the aspect of mentality that we discussed, the fear of change in real society is reflected in the fictionalized changes of the horror story. Without resolution that conforms to our set of social norms, we directly experience anxiety because, even though we are not taking part in the story, we are expecting an outcome that is recognizable.

In his 1919 essay *The Uncanny*, Sigmund Freud (most notable for his theories about infantile and unconscious desires) questions the psychological or visceral drives from our earliest existence, specifically through the problems that stem from calling forth and identifying that which seems out of the ordinary.[1] What Freud contributes to literary understanding of the Gothic is the idea of the repression of desire and mentality, better shown through French critic Julia Kristeva, who argues that horror in the form of "ghosts or grotesques" are abject forms of mentality[2]: "What we 'throw off,'" she suggests, is all that is "'in-between … ambiguous … composite' in our beings, the fundamental inconsistencies that prevent us from declaring a coherent and independent identity to ourselves and others."[3] Like Freud's view of the uncanny, Kristeva represents the "in-between"—the known and unknown world—as the "the multiplicity we viscerally remember from the moment of birth, at which we were both inside and outside of the mother and thus both alive and not yet in existence (in that sense *dead*)."[4] So, this raises a question for us: are we simultaneous living *and* dead? Or, is our human fascination with death borne from our attempts to connect with the unknown—our "dead" selves? Perhaps it is that we are only living for a short period of time, or that we have no experience of death with which to identify. But, more important for us to understand, is where horror fits into the idea of life and identity.

Horror as a Way of Life

Horror is part of the life cycle that we use to describe events and emotions that consist of the whole of the human condition (or what it means to be alive). Classically, the idea of horror has been described through several manifestations, namely those of folklore and religion as mentioned above, where parable and allegory are the primary modes of storytelling. Doing so allowed authors to subvert the problematic subtleties of right and wrong within the context of everyday life. However, removing the confines of society doesn't always show morality in its best light; society is necessary in promoting healthy values and the ability to co-exist peacefully. As a result, authors employ the use of horrific elements or characters to show how damaging behaviors or attitudes negatively affect society. One Biblical example is that of the Prodigal Son (Luke 15:11–32).

Returning home after wasting "his substance with riotous living," the prodigal vows, "I will arise and go to my father, and will say unto him, Father, I have sinned against heaven, and before thee, And am no more worthy to be called thy son: make me as one of thy hired servants." But his father lavishes him with clothing, slaughters a calf for a return feast. The other son, who stayed on the farm to help his father, complains: "Lo, these many years do I serve thee, neither transgressed I at any time thy commandment: and yet thou never gavest me a kid, that I might make merry with my friends: But as soon as this thy son was come, which hath devoured thy living with harlots, thou hast killed for him the fatted calf" (a reasonable complaint). The father replies, "Son, thou art ever with me, and all that I have is thine. It was meet that we should make merry, and be glad: for this thy brother was dead, and is alive again; and was lost, and is found." The story explains the concept of forgiveness, but at the same time deals with the aspect of redemption and compassion (sentiments echoed in *Frankenstein*). However, within the story is a crucial piece to understanding horror: that of loss and its psychological torment. In Hawthorne's short story "Young Goodman Brown," the title character meets a figure (a stranger) who entices him into the Salem woods. Young Goodman Brown literally loses his Faith (the name of his wife), and he must find the return path back to redemption.

Classical mythology and the stories of the Bible all explore the concept of psychological danger. For instance, a short list may include:

- The Temptation and Resurrection of Christ (literally, rising from the dead).
- John Milton's *Paradise Lost*. Walking with the poet Virgil, Milton is afforded the chance to report on the conditions of Hell (and the aftermath of man's soul) by chronicling the fall of Satan as leader of the Damned.

- The story of Pandora's Box. Made by Jupiter, Pandora is sent to Prometheus and his brother to punish them for stealing fire from heaven (I couldn't resist including this one). Pandora, who was made beautiful, was sent with a box of gifts, and cautioned to beware of these gifts, housed in a jar. Pandora's curiosity gets the better of her, and taking a quick peak, lets out a vast array of plagues on mankind. She is only able to save one gift in the jar: hope.
- The Sirens in Homer's *The Odyssey* sing beautiful songs in order to lure men to sail to them. Unable to resist their temptations, they are lured to their death, sailing into and crashing upon the jagged rocks upon which the Sirens sit.
- The punishment of Prometheus. After making man from clay, Prometheus felt sorry for man and brought fire to man to assist our well being. After being caught for his Olympian heist, Prometheus is sentenced to an eternity pushing a boulder uphill while an eagle devours his liver, which grows back nightly so that Zeus may punish his rouge Titan for eternity.

While this list is far from complete, each story explores a concept that all men face in regards to their everyday lives: death, evil, curiosity, temptation. We could call these sins, but horror stories are often rife with sin and characters behaving badly. This is one of the troubles of classifying horror as we do, because horror often includes two sub-classifications: fear and terror. Before we delve into finding a definition of horror, let's first look at what makes horror attractive to so many people; as an inspiration or as a way of clarifying the mental process.

The Aesthetics of Horror

In criticism, aesthetics refers to the study or philosophy of the beauty in nature, art and literature. It has a philosophical dimension (What *is* art? What *is* beauty?) and a psychological dimension (How do we recognize beauty?). The same is ultimately true of horror in that what makes a "good" horror story is largely a matter of personal taste. My idea of "good" horror is probably not your idea of good horror, nor should it be, especially when we consider that there are multiple levels of personal consciousness. However, the question of "What is horror?" can generally be agreed upon because of our understanding of social norms. For Joanna Burke, the idea of horror is universal in that it opens avenues of talking about the human condition: "Horror stories and films [are] 'not nightmares transcribed, but fears recast into safe and communicable forms."⁵ To appreciate a horror story or film, we needn't experience an identical horror as the author; we need only appreciate the *sensation* of horror. In order for horror to work, it must speak in a manner that connects beyond visual images. So, how does horror transcend ordinary human discourse?

As we now know, horror is built around a mental construct. This can first be traced backwards toward the end of the 1750s. Philosopher Edmund Burke's *A Philosophical Enquiry into the Origins of Our Ideas of the Sublime and Beautiful* (1757) "presented imaginative transport not only as desirable—one rhetorical option among others—but as a necessity, mentally and even physiologically."⁶ In other words, we need to rely on the imagination for our well-being, and, sometimes, we need to literally transcend our natural reactions in order to (in essence) repair our cognitive faculties. In aesthetics, *the sublime* refers to a sense of grandeur, an impressive or exalted state that rises above other (ordinary) human qualities. Following Burke, Kant writes of the sublime (in his *Critique of Judgment* [1790] as a link, where beauty is with the finite (or limited by sense of taste) and the sublime with the infinite. From this vantage point, we realize that the sublime is capable of opening a sense of understanding beyond human capabilities. We've all had that moment where the world becomes ultimately clear and, for some reason, we're unable to articulate the exact specifics of the moment—that's the sublime. In horror, it is often presented visually through extreme close-ups and a cacophonous score. However, in written depictions, that sense of feeling can often only be spoken of; it is up to the reader to identify with, *not* share in, the experience. This is because we cannot translate or transcend the imagination through oral communication. Similarly, we cannot articulate fear as we can happiness. Happiness, while joyous and whatnot, can be transferred. We can have other people join in with us while we experience happiness. Rarely are we able to do so when relaying a horrible event. Here are two short examples:

"John, I just won the lottery!"
"Oh! Diane, I'm so happy for you!"

"Megan, I just had a dream where I was being eaten by a grand piano. It was horrible."
"Oh, Amy, that's so ... odd."
"You don't understand! It was mocking me. I woke up in a cold sweat at two-thirty, and never fell back to sleep. I'm exhausted and, for some

Part I—Classic Horror and Establishing the Horror Film

reason, I want to skip my piano lesson today, even though I know that could never happen. Right?"

"Yeah, Amy ... right."

While this may seem odd (and even silly), it makes sense when we understand the situation personally. Reading the above, you can almost feel your face tighten into a confused mass. Why? Because the horror of being eaten by a piano doesn't translate. We may be able to have facial expressions that convey fear or terror, but unless we share in a horrible event, we won't have the same experience. This is because we have a safety mechanism: our minds are built in such a way as to make horror less horrific. Smiles are contagious. And, sure, we can have empathy after a horrific event. We may want to donate to disaster relief, or we may even tear up. But even then we're not feeling the same emotions connected to horror. We're feeling fear, or sadness, or some other emotion, right? This may explain the ongoing popularity of horror.

It's true that many horror stories are built around archetypes or models, and thus become parodies of themselves (much like in the 1996 movie *Scream*). However, films are continually breaking ground in that they are able to exemplify horror in a manner by which we have yet to experience. The same is true for older stories and novels. We've all seen a couple fall in love (and this, according to *Beauty and the Beast*, is a "tale as old as time"), but how often do we get to enjoy a psychopath cause a young Johnny Depp to literally explode while sleeping in his bedroom (*A Nightmare on Elm Street*)? Or how else can we see a nerdy girl exact revenge on her senior class by torching the gym and all her classmates (*Carrie*)?

As we develop our own notions of what constitutes horror, we should keep in mind the different ways in which horror is presented, whether physically, mentally, or pictorially. Are we being described a scene? Are we meant to view the horrific as a bystander? Or, are we supposed to escape the horror we experience on page and screen, only to have it haunt us for hours (or days) after? We could easily spend several pages gauging our reactions to different types of cinematic violence; or simply read "bad horror" and laugh at all the ways we're not scared by it (seriously, who's scared of *The Blob* anymore?). Amusing as that may be, there is arguably more to be gained by investigating the methods by which authors (and, in some cases, directors) use visceral images in order to present us with the universal notion of horror, bringing us to the point where we simultaneously experience and *feel* the same reactions as the story's protagonists. In order to do so, we need to know what we're looking for. This necessitates a new question: How exactly do we transmit horror?

Transmitting Horror

Since time immemorial, little has changed in how stories are told or envisioned. Despite our absence from Victorian parlors, the modern reader can conjure a picture if asked to consider the methods by which early ghost stories are told, and that picture may be quite similar to the original audience. This is because we connect on terms of *setting* and *mentality*. Modern storytellers and campfire horror story enthusiasts use the same surroundings (a fire, dark room, or a stormy night) as an appropriate setting for our own ghostly stories. However, new horrors cannot rely on clichés. Tired or over-told themes lose their original impact. In order to maintain a sense of horror, a story must present something new, different, or altered. It must, in some way, challenge an audience to believe that a new possibility previously unconsidered may become possible. Yet, how we challenge the audience determines what they feel in response. For Ann Radcliffe,[7] this distinguishes the boundary between "horror" and "terror." She writes:

> Terror and horror are so far opposite, that the first expands the soul, and awakens the faculties to a high degree of life; the other contracts, freezes, and nearly annihilates them. I apprehend, that neither Shakespeare nor Milton by their fictions, nor Mr. Burke by his reasoning, anywhere looked to positive horror as a source of the sublime, though they all agree that terror is a very high one; and where lies the great difference between horror and terror, but in the uncertainty and obscurity, that accompany the first, respecting the dreaded evil?

As Radcliffe's definitions of horror and terror are difficult to distinguish, especially when approaching a work based on individual response, distinguishing between the two will be done sparingly over the course of this book (I tend to favor the word "horror" as a means of general understanding). However, it shouldn't be overlooked that the goal of such writing and discussion is to induce a state of reflection and response to a horrific or terrifying situation.

This is precisely what occurs in Bram Stoker's *Dracula*. The last of the great Gothic novels, published in 1897, Stoker's *Dracula* challenged readers to accept a new possibility regarding the source of horror. As cities developed and technology worked its way into the mind of the world, the modern city became a place of light while, slowly, the world of the unknown was dying out. Stoker, realizing that horror depended on uncertainty and surprise, moved his English character to a new location, in this case Transylvania. However, it should be noted that *Dracula* exhibits two types of horror. First is what is mentioned above, the idea of horror challenging the mental picture. However, Stoker combines setting and mentality in order to exhibit a new idea of horror resulting from the ease of modern travel; Jonathan Harker's recollection of the events, first as he convalesces with Mina in the convent, and later, following his return to England, are challenged because of the speed of travel in which the Count returns to England. For Harker, the Count returns, both mentally (as evidenced in the convent scenes) and physically, promoting the psychological fear inherent to Harker's failure to reconcile his well-being in response to modern amenities. The horror is not built upon Dracula's embodiment of night: filmmakers would later develop this in order to heighten the horrific impact in their adaptations. Dracula can walk around freely in daylight in Stoker's original novel. What becomes horror in Stoker's original tale (and perhaps helps kill the Gothic novel at the end of the 19th century) is the beginning of realized horrors of the flesh. Stoker explores the transition from mental terrors to realized and seemingly imminent physical horrors. Central to the novel, however, are the disparities between country and city.

What changed between Victorian and Edwardian Gothic horror and what we would consider "modern horror"? Part of this has to do with pictures, or rather the visual element and how it is presented. For this reason, Edgar Allan Poe's "The Raven" has ceased to be horrific because talking birds and people descending into madness are everyday occurrences. We need only watch *Sesame Street* for a talking bird and a monster giggling in near hysterics. When watching a story play out, we need not imagine the characters. As a result, audiences focus on a generalization as opposed to understanding the character as we would a real person. By imagining visuals (movements, physical attributes, dress, mannerisms), we gain only a brief overview of a character. For instance, Dracula is described as "rather white and fine." This is about

1. The Origins of the Horror Film

what most viewers would physically notice of an actor playing a part, but Harker continues his inspection. Of Dracula's hands, Harker notes:

> But seeing them now close to me, I could not but notice that they were rather coarse, broad, with squat fingers. Strange to say, there were hairs in the centre of the palm. The nails were long and fine, and cut to a sharp point. As the Count leaned over me and his hands touched me, I could not repress a shudder. It may have been that his breath was rank, but a horrible feeling of nausea came over me, which, do what I would, I could not conceal.[8]

As we know, we cannot feel Jonathan Harker's apprehension and dread resulting from his encounter with the Count. Stoker's use of detail is necessary to convey the horrific for the reader. Yet, there are noticeable differences when comparing Stoker's version of Dracula and the later film versions of the great Count. These differences, none of which are subtle, are all concentrated attempts in order to capture an altogether different audience.

Dracula's move to film accomplished two things—first, it embedded a vision or notion of Dracula in our minds, courtesy of Bela Lugosi's portrayal of the Count as an English aristocrat; second, it developed the character of Dracula through presentation. Rather than drawing from a theatrical notion of the character, as Stoker did, modeling the count on Sir Henry Irving, the tyrannical actor/manager of the Lyceum Theatre, the film adaptation negates these little eccentricities of character, specifically the "fine hairs on the palm," which to Victorian London suggests that Dracula certainly had his hands full (what with three wives and all...). But to get to Lugosi (or any of the many actors who would don the cape), we should consider how technological improvements and invention began a transition in the way audiences interpret fact. Science—specifically, the ability to harness electricity—changed the manner by which we read, listen to, and interpret horror. It was this development, recognized by authors like Radcliffe and Stoker, that created possibility and added dimensions to the mind that we are now coming to realize within modern horror, specifically through films.

In his biography *Edison*, Neil Baldwin[9] notes that in the "early years of the motion picture business, as in the early years of the phonograph business, the subjects of the films were initially secondary to their novelty." Audiences would flock to see acrobats, boxing demonstrations, and one *Sneeze* produced by Fred Ott in 1894. This public curiosity was true of electricity as well. Nikola Tesla, one of the first pioneers of alternating current, or A/C current, would hold demonstrations for audiences, first developing an "electric clock attached to an oscillator."[10] Once Tesla mastered electricity, he would captivate men and women who "understood little of the science involved ... and when he seemed to turn himself into a human firestorm by using the apparatus with which he had so often thrilled his laboratory visitors, they cried out in fear and wonder."[11]

Fearing competition from George Westinghouse, for whom Tesla worked, Edison manufactured what were—to the public—unthinkable disasters in order to capture his audiences' unknown sense of horror surrounding the new technology: "As Edison saw it, accidents caused by AC must, if they could not be found, be manufactured, and the public alerted to the hazards."[12] Edison carried out experiments on dogs and cats to warn the public of the dangers of his competition. Staging a traveling show, one of Edison's associates, Harold P. Brown, developed and demonstrated these dangers of alternating current, where "on stage he electrocuted a number of calves and large dogs.... In effect he was asking Americans, 'Is this the invention you want your little wife to cook dinner with?'"[13] It should be noted that Tesla created the modern kitchen, for in these attempts by Edison to demonize Tesla, he sought to capitalize on the unexplained—Freud's concept of *heimlich*—in an attempt to vilify Tesla as a mad scientist.

Perhaps the greatest horror of pure electrical experimentation comes at the expense of William Kemmler, who was electrocuted on August 6, 1890, in New York's Sing Sing Prison. Kemmler was "only half-killed" and the "dreadful procedure then had to be repeated. A reporter described [the electrocution] as 'an awful spectacle, far worse than hanging.'"[14] Responses to such reports leave Tesla a victim, but not for his inventions alone. It was, in part, due to Edison's campaigning of his brand of power. When Edison debuted the country's first publicly lit street, New York's Pearl Street, he "made much of the archetypal struggle between ancient, 'evil' gaslight and his new, 'good' electric light."[15] Of gas lighting, Edison commented that "the result of the vile poison is almost entirely heat and only incidentally a little light. It is a nasty, yellow light, too, and far removed from the color of the lovely natural light."[16] At first, the public was not assuaged. Baldwin notes the following public commentary regarding Edison's new light:

These "lamps that outshine Canopus" were bright as daylight, too intense for the quieter needs of domesticity, where manufactured illuminating gas prevailed. But gas was costly; it could explode; it silently poisoned the ground, and water wells and cisterns, leaking out from the mains through which it invisibly traveled; it blackened walls, and discolored paintings; it devoured oxygen, made you dizzy and gave you headaches; it smelled of sulfur and ammonia.[17]

It is not the intention of this work to debate whether Edison or Tesla was first in bringing electricity to the masses. In fact, Joseph Swan provided "primitive filament lamps and arc lamps" to the London public in December 1878.[18] But it is interesting to compare the effect of this achievement on the crowds. The people who sought an explanation to new technologies and its uses are the same individuals who eventually took control of them. In the long succession of technological innovation, corporations have been struggling to prove the competition inept or as having faulty products. In the middle of this have been the consumers, all of whom are dealing with a changing world that becomes unfamiliar with the technology presented to it. As a response, they are conditioned to wait and explore. For the most part, the mainstream public is skeptical concerning change. This is why "motion pictures, like phonographs and sound recordings, were being defined by the way in which they were exhibited."[19]

Mary Shelley's "hideous progeny," both a reference to the horror of her real-life miscarriage and her invented Monster, challenge tradition. As with all early Gothic horror, Shelley presented a problem to her audience, one that was difficult for the public to reconcile against their own conservative backgrounds. This is similar to the dawn of film projection: "As motion pictures moved into commercial use, exhibitors drew on a tradition of screen practices developed by lecturers.... Film exhibitors were working out of these traditions, and it is not surprising that they influenced the evolution of the motion picture business as projection replaced the peephole kinetoscope."[20]

As audiences grew to rely on a more developed, straightforward production, a new level of consciousness awakened. In order to keep audiences coming to the theater, filmmakers had to develop new techniques, eventually moving past reproductions of stage performances. This may explain how violence became a staple of the horror film. But violence is nothing new to the Gothic tale: "Contrary to popular criticism, violence in the horror film is not gratuitous but is rather a constituent element of the genre. The horror narrative is propelled by violence, manifested in both the monster's violence and the attempts to destroy the monster. Horror is produced by the violation of what are tellingly called natural laws—by the disruption of our presuppositions about the integrity and predictable character of objects, places, animals, and people."[21] As film developed, there was a natural inclination to highlight the aberrations of the mind and exhibit for audiences the pictures that most minds had yet to conjure.

Chapter 2

The *Frankenstein* Cycle

Film as a Method for Reconciling the Mind/Self in Society

> With an anxiety that almost amounted to agony, I collected the instruments of life around me, that I might infuse a spark of being into the lifeless thing that lay at my feet.—Dr. Frankenstein, discussing his apprehension prior to giving life to the Monster in Mary Shelley's *Frankenstein*

It seems that many horror films (especially those that investigate matters of man's advancement) revolve around science fiction. But we shouldn't just look at progress as a matter of science, for often what holds a society in place isn't the technology but the attitudes of society. This can be seen through the characterization of The Other,[1] wherein self-awareness is primarily a response to internalized views of social influences and stimuli. Thus, horror—or what we see as horrific—is built upon the realization of that which doesn't appear as normal or connected in any way to the culture we inhabit. It is this reasoning that dictates horror's dependence on the outcast. Horror largely works against the known universe, often trying to establish norms by offering a competing or alternative viewpoint to a set of standard and accepted norms. Since the advent of the Faust legend,[2] the modern conception of horror has evolved, with supernatural forces and scientific advances all but intertwined.[3] As a result, modern horror often heightens the connection between science and technology that help initiate matters of the world into new (and perhaps terrible) realms.

As a character, Frankenstein's monster served as a warning against unnatural acts of science and the inherent potential of reckless progress. But when the monster moved to film, the possibilities of awareness changed from dangerous omen to fortuitous opportunity. In this manner, the monster—or the version inspired by the novel—can act as a guide for understanding the motivation of filmmakers and audiences, showing a definitive progression of intended (and eventually realized) sources of horror. This is especially true in the case of early horror films, where the landmark release of *Frankenstein* (1931) coincides with a world set in the midst of real-life horrors, as Susan Tyler Hitchcock suggests:

> It is not simply a coincidence of history that the most famous Frankenstein film of all was created during the Depression. World War I had shown the terror as well as the triumph of new technology—its mechanized military maneuvers causing ghastly physical deformations if not outright slaughter. The twenties roared with optimism, but the crash of 1929 left people tottering precariously. They wanted entertainment to take them into a realm of fantasy, to raise their heart rates without reminding them of real-world dangers.[4]

This version of *Frankenstein* happened to combine several elements of technology that ultimately gave audiences the thrill of their lives. Stylistically, it explored the stereotype of the "mad scientist" more effectively than the Faust-like Victor Frankenstein in the novel. Instead of dwelling on the doctor's innocent mistake, as Shelley laments the downfall of both monster and creator, the film moves beyond the premise of a lapse of reason, presenting a title character that has a thirst for something almost Machiavellian, that being the doctor's hunger for control and power.

Shelley writes of a Monster that attempts to communicate his wretched condition, seeking to clarify his identity as a monster and that of his outsider appearance and stature. The Monster himself questions his origins, asking:

> But where were my friends and relations? No father had watched my infant days, no mother had blessed me with smiles and caresses; or if they had, all my past life was now a blot, and blind vacancy in which I distinguished nothing. From my earliest remembrance I had been as I then was in height and proportion. I had never yet seen a being resembling me, or who claimed any intercourse with me. What was I? The question again recurred, to be answered only with groans.[5]

2. The Frankenstein Cycle

This line of thought by the Monster is central to understanding the novel. At this point, recounting his learning of language and rationalizing his existence and benevolent inner nature with his creator, the Monster's appeals explore the internal aspects of evil, and whether we are born evil or become evil as a response to our society. The film bypasses these questions, simply showing a world in which the impossible and unknown *are* possible to those who wish to figure a way to make it so. In other words, the film's heightened awareness of technological advancement creates a barrier between the audience and their own sense of safety. Hence, the Monster's horrific nature isn't that he was rejected by his creator, but the creator's realization of his error becomes the focal point of the film.[6]

At the center of the film's modernity was a conflict made apparent in James Whale's direction, that being the reconciliation of knowledge and social progress. Dr. Frankenstein becomes drunk with power as he reconstructs the possibility of a new identity. This is furthered by the wider setting apparent to the viewer of the film. The monster is not a creation, as Shelley suggests, but is an evolution of human ingenuity: "Pieced together from graveyard, gallows, and medical-school scraps, the monster is brought to life in a machine-age orgasm of crackling machinery. In 1818, Mary Shelley had made a passing reference to 'a powerful engine'; in 1931, her dream-image took on the pop-sculptural reality of the present."[7] The film gives audiences nothing more than a ghastly creature devoid of intellectual or compassionate thought (though his benevolent internal nature is highlighted, especially in the later films. In this regard, the Monster echoes Shelley's concept of wretchedness and victimization). And yet, the impression of the film is greatly enhanced when giving an image to the madness of Frankenstein. As the doctor (Colin Clive) and his assistant, Fritz (Dwight Frye), uncover the Monster (Boris Karloff), the laboratory is full of electrical gadgetry (thanks to electrical special effects creator Kenneth Strickfaden). Subjected to the lightning, his very being thus in danger by the same spark of his life, the Monster's physical essence causes the machinery and circuits to blink and flicker; as the Monster is lowered down the hoist, the doctor notices movement for the first time, signifying to the audience that the monstrous life before them was the result of scientific progress, not the just over-reaching of a madman.

Though *Frankenstein* is innovative in its approach to the "spark of life," it was not a new concept in 1931. Technology was the focus behind many early films, in part because technology and the resulting marvel of progress echoed throughout America, where technology was the essence of modernity and innovation. Behind the perceptions of the public was that Hollywood heralded the future, for "cinema is the only art form that fully depends upon scientific invention: cinema could not have come into being had it not been for science."[8] As the film industry grew to incorporate modern technology, the films themselves reflected an awareness inherent to the business of moviemaking itself— that reality is best displayed when it moves beyond the audience's capabilities for understanding the production of such spectacles. This is why early films with horrific themes were so successful; they presented a reality that differed from the mental picture, bringing to life possibilities beyond the imagination, creating a genuinely surprising and frightening result. However, it wasn't immediately apparent that Shelley's creation could convey true horror to audiences. Indeed, there were no "horror movies," per se, in the silent era; films dealing with the supernatural were classified as offbeat melodramas.[9]

The Making of the Celluloid Monster

Before the modern vision of the Frankenstein monster had been cemented into the public consciousness, he was depicted through stage and film adaptations that presented Shelley's story as a moral problem, one existing seemingly as an exercise in moral curiosity rather than as a horror story. The first production of *Frankenstein* on film appeared in 1910. Directed by J. Searle Dawley, this 16-minute one-reeler, produced and distributed by Thomas Edison's film company, sought to emphasize the mythical and psychological problems facing Victor Frankenstein's monster, virtually eliminating the Monster's humanity and entreaties for a life of equal recognition. In other words, the film was not a horror film but a display of cinematic technique and triumph. The same is true of the lost 1915 five-reel film *Life Without Soul* (dir. John W. Smiley), wherein the Monster is rendered into a dream after someone helplessly releases the beast while falling asleep reading Shelley's novel. (*Life Without Soul* was the first feature-length adaptation of *Frankenstein*.)

In order for the Monster to make a sufficient impact on audiences, there needed to be some dramatic flair. Like the inception of the Frankenstein story, the film medium itself had to undergo change, evolving as a separate entity configured as a sum of its parts. The convergence of science and technology needed to grow and adapt to in order to meet (and eventually exceed) the same degrees of realism as that of the stage (timing, fluidity of human movement, and appearance were all questionably suspect in the days of early film). This level of realism would be achieved through redesign, technique, and, ultimately, sound.

Early sound reproduction on film went through an evolutionary period. The first recordings were harsh, taking away from the audience's sensibilities and deadening the effect of suspension of disbelief. The same was true concerning synchronization, where speech did not match the characters' lips on the screen. In order to present a unified and distinct aspect of realism, studios partnered to redesign the theater experience, transforming a well-established medium through trial and error. Eschewing the spectral characters of silent films, studios sought to unify the experience of sound and film, because "filmmakers could not take for granted … the sound transition, when the technique could function to expose the flatness, the lack of color, and the lifelessness of the filmic world and its inhabitants."[10] The coming of sound film actually resembles Dr. Frankenstein's trials with animation (symbolically, a fitting use of the word when we think of what film captures) and attempts at bestowing language to actors and actresses, those playing parts themselves.

Soon, silent films were replaced by sound films (colloquially called "talkies"), and by the late–1920s sound had become a staple of modern films. Sound revolutionized the film industry, but a fortunate byproduct for Shelley's imaginative tale was that it would become utterly terrifying by attempting to give the monster a voice of his own, providing a realistic appearance of man transformed into monster, first through the utterances of unintelligible grunts, eventually progressing to the eloquence that the monster displays in the novel. Further, it was through sound that Frankenstein's monster became legitimately humanized; specifically through the rationalization of Dr. Henry Frankenstein's[11] efforts to build a working human being in the first sound film depicting the Monster. Henry's declaration of "It's alive!" is not only widely recognized, it is both a cry of exultation and awfulness, for both doctor and viewer simultaneously. For early audiences, namely those that first meet the Monster through the pages of the novel, the recognition of the Monster's life acted as a jarring realization of the Monster's otherness, and was symbolic of a changing world. Once that feeling was combined through the still mysterious depiction of the moving image, the result was a phenomenon that helped usher in a change in audiences tastes and appetite for the uncanny.

Released in 1931, James Whale's *Frankenstein* debuted in November, at the end of a year that saw the birth of the horror film genre, thanks in part to the previous February's release of Tod Browning's *Dracula*. Though *Dracula* was a major achievement by a major Hollywood studio (it was a full-length horror film with no comic relief or twist ending, thus relying solely on a story of terror), the film's success was downplayed in the wake of Whale's *Frankenstein*: "*Frankenstein* surpassed *Dracula* at the box office and with the critics. Many reviewers hailed James Whale's film as superior to Browning's, finding the film not only artistically more impressive but also scarier and more shocking."[12]

So, where did the fear come from? By this time, studio tactics, such as reports of people fainting and awaiting ambulances did little to affect audience reception of either film. In fact, they didn't need to: the image on the screen (courtesy of the great makeup artist Jack P. Pierce) surpassed the imagined reality. Nöel Carroll writes that horror is meant to be cathartic, in an Aristotelian sense,[13] where we purge our fears by bearing witness to tragedy: "Our responses are supposed to converge ... like the characters we assess the monster as a horrifying sort of being."[14] However, the problem with reconciling Shelley's Monster with Whale's depiction is that there are two different villains and two corresponding reactions. Shelley writes of a tortured soul, in which the audience empathizes with the monster, whereas Whale shows a monster that is out of control, an outsider seeking to destroy that which is familiar. And yet, that is how the public felt at the time of *Frankenstein*'s release.

According to Julia Kristeva, horror gets its power from the idea of the outsider:

> There looms, within abjection, one of those violent, dark revolts of being, directed against a threat that seems to emanate from an exorbitant outside or inside, ejected beyond the scope of the possible, the tolerable, the thinkable. It lies there, quite close, but it cannot be assimilated. It beseeches, worries, and fascinates desire, which, never-

theless, does not let itself be seduced. Apprehensive, desire turns aside; sickened, it rejects.[15]

With the questions of scientific advancement looming over audiences (furthered by the talkies' surprising realism), the subject of *Frankenstein* was both realized cultural monster and as an impression for monstrous ideologies. The horror of the abject is central to the evolution of the monster as a symbol for world-wide anxieties about forbidden knowledge, or what Shattuck explains as an demonstration of ancient angst:

> We can probably tolerate a good deal of anxiety over the image of ourselves as ancient monsters and over the prospect of knowing how to modify the fundamental givens of human existence. But our ambivalence about traumatic changes in our lives caused by science leads us to consider some constraints on that immense and growing international institution.[16]

Humanity is built on a sense of freedom, and any constraint on individual liberties manifests a sense of revolt, often punctuated by physical responses, where criminal acts or violations of well-being demand a hands-on assault. This portrayal on film ranges widely, from the extremes of lynch mobs with torches and pitchforks, to the simplest accusations assumed by pointing a finger (as evidenced in *The Invisible Man*: "It's *him!*"). Especially in the actions of the horror film, revolt is central to the idea of social transgression, where concern is directed to those who are different or foreign; the idea of the abject figure is not one of cathartic pity. Instead, the figure is monstrous, a source of revulsion, incapable of redemption: "The abject is not an ob-ject facing me, which I name or imagine. Nor is it an ob-jest, an otherness ceaselessly fleeing in a systematic quest of desire. What is abject is not my correlative, which, providing me with someone or something else as support, would allow me to be more or less detached and autonomous. The abject has only one quality of the object—that of being opposed to *I*."[17] For a story like *Frankenstein* to have the biggest impact for audiences, then, it makes sense to have a monster that is an archetypal terror, one that society can clearly see as a social Other, though it is clear that this was never Shelley's intent.

The novel's complete title, *Frankenstein, or The Modern Prometheus*, calls to mind a very clear distinction that should be made. First, the "hero" of the story is not the Monster but Dr. Frankenstein. Though the Monster is eloquent and sympathetic (as opposed to the tragic, inarticulate figure in the 1931 film classic), it is the doctor whose suffering is greatest, similar to the Greek Titan Prometheus. The legend of Prometheus is emblematic of a struggle for providing assistance, perhaps the Titan's own catharsis at witnessing the struggles of early man. Prometheus was the originator of man. Making humans out of clay, he saw humanity as his to fulfill. After watching them struggle in the cold and dark, Prometheus stole fire from the gods in order to protect his creation; he is subsequently punished by Zeus for his theft and must live for eternity having his liver pecked out each day, only for it to regenerate and live in an endless cycle of torment. Our understanding of the horrific in *Frankenstein*, then, should be the overreach of knowledge and the subsequent hell in which Victor exists. He is tormented by his cathartic struggle, having to engage in the horrible act of creating a mate for his tortured Monster, only to have to suffer the consequences of his repeated mistakes. However, Whale's adaptation (unlike Dawley and Smiley before him) emphasizes the abject nature of the being, that of an outsider created by "evil" science.

Inherent to this retelling of the *Frankenstein* story, Whale emphasized the idea of human progress in conjunction with the darkness of humanity. Therefore, it should be seen that Whale's *Frankenstein* is equal parts horror and drama, but it is clear that Whale's monster lacks humanity (in all ways, he is inhuman). This is to heighten the impact for audiences. Leaving the Monster without redemption, he is a source of outrage and, ultimately, horror, one produced by the social progress come to light, the very same manifestations that Shelley herself feared. Though not a literal monster, he is brought to life by the "godlike science" of the motion picture industry. Therein lays the drama of the original, where the audience must reconcile not the nature of the beast, but the nature of man, presenting the unimaginable as lifelike terror. This foundation has since been a central component of the horror film into the modern age.

For years, filmmakers relied on drama in order to tell the story of the horrific, exploiting suspense and withholding terror until the final revelation. These films, such as F. W. Murnau's *Nosteratu: A Symphony of Horrors* (1922), Wallace Worsley's *The Hunchback of Notre Dame* (1923), and Rupert Julian's *The Phantom of the Opera* (1925), highlighted the struggles of the human condition, in which the protagonist is a disfigured outcast. Combining the dramatic movements and actions of characters with the advancements of cinematic makeup and set design, the early silent films were able to give a clear presentation of right and wrong or good and evil. This is what makes Browning's *Dracula* so dramatic. The Count preys on victims through mind control and cunning, and is thus exhibited as a symbol of evil. However, *Frankenstein* was a different type of monster, not existing but created, therefore symbolizing a new and deeper level of evil and distrust. But where is this distrust rooted, and how can that concept be replicated for audiences first seeing monstrosity as a seemingly living creature?

Returning to the concept of the abject, it is clear that this distrust is caused by questions of identity. Fritz Lang's silent film *Metropolis* (1926) explored questions of progress by depicting the struggles of the German working class. Lang presents a futuristic dystopian society that is awaiting the coming savior. That savior comes in the form of a robot named Maria (Brigitte Helm), a technological advancement and false prophet that urges the citizens of Metropolis to destroy the machines of progress that stifle their existence. *Metropolis* is well known as the first feature-length science-fiction film, however it is aptly recognized as a film depicting social struggle in the wake of modern industrialized life. Despite the clear-cut political message of the film, Lang objectifies the existence of the working poor by highlighting the social striations, pitting the character Freder (Gustav Frolich) and his idle upper-class life of privilege against the backdrop of Marxist theories of the working class. The film clearly espouses the aspects of Otherness, one built on the identification of personal goals tempered by social responsibility. Humanity, in *Metropolis*, loses freedom as it is possessed by the will of the greater society.

Lang's dystopia is not just metaphorical; it has a clear connection as a source of defining the abject in society. Kristeva suggests that Otherness is itself revealed by the cathartic nature of abjection: "I experience abjection only if an Other has settled in place and stead of what will be 'me.' Not at all an other with whom I identify and incorporate, but an Other who precedes and possesses me, and through such possession causes me to be. A possession previous to my advent: a being-there of the symbolic that a father might or might not embody. Significance is indeed inherent in the human body."[18] In this regard, the

Frankenstein Monster is similar to Maria in *Metropolis*, the character of which arrests viewers in the panic of social upheaval. The Other captures the spirit, embodying the very essence of abjection and fear, causing distrust and doubt for the audience.

The European approach to the supernatural was another type of abjection, often centering on the psychological aspects of social failure, as opposed to personal harms exhibited by monsters of the early sound era. The Hollywood monster, specifically Whale's interpretation of Frankenstein's Monster, traces its roots to Robert Weine's *The Cabinet of Dr. Caligari* (1919), which highlights the psychological elements (specifically those of Freudian interpretation) of distrust bred from the social anxieties of a modernized world. The psychological foundations of Caligari are explained by Packer as something bordering on the demonic: "Dr. Caligari was evil incarnate. He was as evil as the devil but was divested of past centuries' superstitions. Dr. Caligari was a real person, rather than a supernatural entity, even though he proved to be an imposter. [Siegfried] Kracuer[19] thought that Caligari was a man of his times: a mortal man who could kill without conscience, who could turn other men into killing machines. That had happened during World War I, which had raged just before *Caligari* was filmed."[20] Like Whale's *Frankenstein*, Weine's *The Cabinet of Dr. Caligari* exhibits a change in identity, one that invites critical inquiry into character and the nature of man.

Caligari lends itself to the study of technology not for what elements cross over into modern horror films by technique or cinematography (although there can be no denying the influence that the German film had on Hollywood filmmakers). Instead, the grounding is in that of denial and doubt, or that there is always a seemingly "rational" explanation to phobias and distrust that plagues the mind of modern man. There's no coincidence that Freud's theories were popularized during the shift from postwar Germany and the rise of the Weimar Republic, where *Caligari* was meant as a commentary on the past, not as a harbinger for future evils. This sense of dialogue established *Caligari* as a landmark, proving that film was an adequate method for the conveyance of ideas, specifically through the cathartic experience of the audience. In the filming of *Caligari*, Weine employed a philosophical approach in discussing the nature of evil, namely existentialism. Existentialism, the philosophical field popularized by Søren Kierkegaard and Martin Heidegger as a belief that individuals are capable of determining their own free will, is clearly exhibited in the morality of early horrors, often leaving the audience to decide the nature of evil, despite the existence of evil residing in the body of man or monster.

Like *Metropolis, Caligari* invited a social response to realized horror, where political commentary seemed to mesh with the dynamics of evil presented in the film. However, rather than focusing on suspension of disbelief, Lang and Weine made films that expressed the popular artistic movement of expressionism, which displayed subjectivity reality, favoring exaggerations of character and objects, such as through grotesque distortions of makeup and scenery. Additionally, the expressionist movement resorted to jarring the audience into realizing the not-so-subtle references of onscreen action, employing distorted and violent representations of reality. Combined with expressionism, existentialism influenced the modern horror film, suggesting less than literal interpretations, moving films into a realm bordering on the fantastic. As adopted by Hollywood filmmakers, the removal of reality "locks the viewer inside the perspective of a single character in order to examine the nature of traumatic memory, using striking, often alarming imagery to suggest two alternate realities."[21] By this reasoning, the expressionist movement contributes greatly to modern horror, offering a distinctive viewpoint between audience and action. Onscreen, the possibilities often move beyond the intended realities, creating a gap between viewer and subject, enabling viewers to believe the onscreen action as an extension of their own reality. By this reasoning, *Caligari* isn't just another film about a mad scientist, but a stepping stone into the legacy of horror and how it invites viewers into the experience. Yet, the experience isn't simply absent watching, but progressing the idea of audience awareness through suspension of disbelief.

The Frankenstein Cycle of Films

The Frankenstein cycle embodies all of the changes in horror, in that it encapsulates the monster as a necessary agent for the changing times. Whether horrific, comic, scientific or political, *Frankenstein* signifies the cultural awareness of horror to capture the imagination of society. However, Frankenstein's monster is symbolic, reflecting the questions of science at the time of his creation and beyond, being adapted time and again with each interpretation, be it page, stage, or film. He is not a creature of existence like humanity, but a creation born of our anxieties, through which he symbolizes an entirely new level of evil and distrust. The concept of the outsider (the Other) is taken further in *Frankenstein* than any other monster story to this point; the story of the creator's refusal to accept his labors, however nefarious they were, forced the audience (both reader and viewer alike) to reconcile the concept of humanity, coming face to face with their own Other through the Monster's curious and benevolent nature. The differences of interpretation lie in what the audience sees, which only had been visually accomplished through Whale's mute and destructive avatar. Despite his onscreen appearance, the Monster's muteness is a curious decision, especially at a time when sound was essential to marketing the future of the Hollywood film. But this was no doubt a conscious decision, one necessary on bridging the gap between the Monster's inception and what he had come to symbolize for modern audiences. Aside from the vocalization of the Monster's humanity, which itself would be too horrible for contemporary audiences, the Monster had to remain an "old world" monster, a transitory figure of past fears amid a new and vibrant technology. By the time Whale brought the Monster to the screen, Shelley's simple fireside story had evolved through the machinery of political, sociological, and technological change.

Whale's film is evidence that, by the time Universal released *Frankenstein*, the film industry had figured out how to capitalize on the way in which audiences grapple with the uncanny, and thus kept people coming back for more by serializing productions. With the overwhelming success of James Whale's *Frankenstein* (1931), in which Boris Karloff cemented the public perception of Shelley's Monster with audiences, there were two successful sequels: *Bride of Frankenstein* (1935), also directed by Whale, and *Son of Frankenstein* (1939), produced and directed by Rowland V. Lee. All three films were critical and commercial triumphs, however something curious happened after the wildly successful production of *Son of Frankenstein*: Karloff, feeling that the character was becoming the brunt of jokes, left the franchise. With the loss of the star actor,[22] Universal severely cut funding from future sequels. As a result, further *Frankenstein* films lacked star power, relegated to the status of B-movies,[23] and for many years Shelley's Monster endured through adaptations ranging from the exploitive to the absurd. Among the entries into the Frankenstein franchise:

2. The Frankenstein Cycle

- *Bud Abbott and Lou Costello Meet Frankenstein* (1948)—comedy team Abbott and Costello act as freight handlers, retrieving the shipments of Frankenstein's Monster (Glenn Strange), the Wolfman (Lon Chaney, Jr.), and Dracula (Bela Lugosi). Chaos ensues.
- *I Was a Teenage Frankenstein* (1957)—Professor Frankenstein (Whit Bissell) steals the remains of dead athletes from the site of an airplane crash to build a Monster, which subsequently goes on a killing spree.
- *Frankenstein: 1970* (1958)—Tortured and disfigured because of his refusal to cooperate with the Nazis, Baron Victor Von Frankenstein (the now-elderly Boris Karloff) leases out his castle to a film company documenting his ancestors activities for television. With the money from this enterprise, Victor buys an atomic reactor to create a Monster of his own.
- *Frankenstein Conquers the World*[24] (1965)—a Japanese retelling, where a human heart from Dr. Frankenstein's lab is irradiated following the bombing of Hiroshima. The heart mutates, growing into a complete body, turns feral, and terrorizes woodland creatures (when he's not eating them, he throws trees at them). He eventually grows 20 feet tall and battles a lizard-monster in the same fashion as Godzilla.
- *Frankenstein Created Woman* (1967)—Baron Frankenstein (Peter Cushing) is resurrected by his assistant in order to prove that the soul does not leave the body at death. Brains switch bodies, and death is avenged through recollected memory in a different body.
- *Blackenstein* (1973)—a blaxploitation[25] film centering on a Vietnam vet who is mutilated after stepping on a landmine.
- *Flesh for Frankenstein*[26] (1974)—a querulous concoction that follows Baron Frankenstein's wish for a super-race. After building a perfect female specimen, the doctor accidentally implants the brain of an asexual aesthete into the male specimen. Crises of fidelity, sexual identity, and revenge fill out the subplots.

Despite the multiple adaptations and a search for identity, the Frankenstein franchise was ultimately resurrected by Mel Brooks, who produced and directed *Young Frankenstein* (1974). Wishing to pay tribute to the original, Brooks breathed new life into the seemingly overwrought clichés of the franchise. The relationship between *Frankenstein* and *Young Frankenstein* is paradoxical; in the former the technology and science is a sign of distrust and fear, whereas in the later the stylistic choices represent absurdity and comic effect, almost asking the viewer, "Can you believe this was scary?"[27] And, as a further nod to the original, Brooks chose to film the picture in black and white, returning the narrative to its Universal roots.

In *Young Frankenstein*, the grandson of the great doctor, Dr. Frederick Frankenstein (Gene Wilder), himself a neuroscientist, doubts the veracity of his familial legacy, which has brought him great shame. However, upon inheriting his grandfather's castle, along with a skeleton crew of servants,[28] he finds his grandfather's journals. Intrigued by the experiments, Frederick resorts to robbing graves, implanting an "abnormal" brain into the corpse of his criminal body after his assistant, Igor (Marty Feldman), accidently drops the "good" brain that Frederick planned to use. The new Monster (Peter Boyle) reenacts the scenes of Whale's original. Following the same format, the Monster is met by a mob; however in this retelling, the Monster learns some degree of intellect from his creator, and is able to persuade the townspeople to set him free so that he may live out his life with his willing concubine (Madeline Kahn). In this instance, the creator and his creation live happily ever after.

Frankenstein's move to comedy signaled a shift in audience perception of the Monster. Where in 1931 he proved to be a source of controversy,[29] by the 1950s he had evolved into a pop-culture powerhouse. As a member of the Universal Studios "classic monsters," Frankenstein's Monster has often been grouped as a member of a clan, as in *Monster Squad* (1987), *Van Helsing* (2004), and *Hotel Transylvania* (2012). This isn't to say that there haven't been several serious and well-made adaptations, such as *Mary Shelley's Frankenstein* (1994), with the film's director, Kenneth Branaugh, in the eponymous role, and featuring Robert De Niro as the Monster. However, there has been a dramatic shift in the poor adaptations, as evidenced in *I Was a Teenage Frankenstein* (1957).[30] Once directors realized the power these monsters had over audiences, they realized they could exploit the influence. Ironically, the transformation of the Monster is central to the modern conception of the creation, leaving behind a cultural legacy on the meditation of horrific possibilities envisioned by Shelley. Like the sum of his parts, the Monster is continually being reimagined and reborn for new societies.

The Monster has since become recognized as a symbol of otherness rather than monstrosity. In *May* (2002), the story is reimagined as that of a lonely girl, whose only companion is a strange doll named Suzie, given to her on her birthday. May (Angela Bettis) grows to be an isolated and strange outcast who works in a veterinarian's office, assisting with surgeries, eventually volunteering at a school for disabled children. When the children attempt to free Suzie from her glass case, the case falls and shatters, cutting the children and leaving the doll blood-

2. The Frankenstein *Cycle*

stained and destroyed. In a murderous rampage—on Halloween, no less—May exacts revenge on her human friends. She then endeavors to build a new companion, using scraps of fabric and the remains of her victims to build a life-size Pollyanna. *May* is both a gory example of modern horror and a meditation on the original story's quest for recognition, finally reconciling the horror that couldn't be shown in Whale's adaptation with the pathos of Shelley's vision of the monster. The reconciliation of the abject is carried forth by the outcast, who is seen both as a monstrous being and a sympathetic foil to social Otherness.

Taking a cue from *Young Frankenstein*, *The Frankenstein Theory* (2013) explores the veracity of the legend as a source of truth. *The Frankenstein Theory* takes the science-fiction horror story a bit further, offering the possibility that the original *Frankenstein* was a factual account of science. Professor Jonathan Vankenheim (Kris Lemche), seeking to redeem his academic reputation and his family name, takes a documentary film crew to the Arctic Circle in order to exonerate the legend that has cursed his family. Opposing the comedic elements of failure embodied in *Young Frankenstein*, *The Frankenstein Theory* is a story of vindication, using modern technologies as a source of proof through photographic evidence. *The Frankenstein Theory* explores the depths of the Frankenstein story for a new, tech savvy audience. Prof. Vankenheim is initially presented as likeable, until his aptitude is questioned. Jonathan is a genius from a privileged background (both of his parents were diplomats) that afforded the leisure of study and personal inquest. His fortunate upbringing is also a conscious decision, signaling the same social problems plaguing modern society that were brought to light through the existentialist foundations of the original, depicting the life of leisure against the workers he employs to assist in finding his ancestral Monster.

Vankenheim is in possession of letters, these being the very same letters that have been dictated by Walton to his sister. In an interview, Vankenheim states that Shelley's novel is actually a work of nonfiction, and that his letters, passed down through generations, are the proof that Shelley merely recorded the events of a very real and horrible time in human history—a direct nod to the original chaos that engulfs the turbulent times of social growth beyond ordinary human understanding. (The film seems to mirror the same horrors as the novel, as much as the film imitates the actions of *The Blair Witch Project*, where the horror of realization is largely viewed through night-vision camera effects. However, the fact that the Frankenstein story is still relevant for modern viewers is a telling artifact in our discussion of horror cycles and the realization of horror.) Vankenheim explains that the process, the notes of the experiment, were purposefully destroyed, so that it could never be recreated. This is a mirror of modern horror. Horror can never be duplicated—once we've seen it firsthand, the source of horror fails to be equally as horrifying. We become inured to the image, the thought, of the horrific idea. This is why we must continually recreate horror, exploring the differences and nuances of each story and façade that breaks the walls of our safety.

Vankenheim explains that the Illuminati[31] were founded at Ingolstadt University (the same school Victor attended), where their work focused on the origins of life, which "they felt was the key to immortality," passing on information in the efforts of producing knowledge, thus "building upon each generation's work." This is no different from the method by which modern horror films have evolved, where the story of *Frankenstein* is part of a cycle.

Progressing even further, *I, Frankenstein* (2014) shows a creation with compassion for his creator. The Monster (Aaron Eckhart) buries his creator, only to be attacked by demons. He is then rescued by gargoyles. The queen of the gargoyles, Lenore, renames the Monster "Adam"[32] and asks him to assist in the battle between the rival clans (literally distinguished in the film as angels and demons). Preferring isolation, Adam remains secluded for 200 years, returning from his solitude to find a modern society being torn apart by the rival clans. Here, Adam becomes an Everyman for humanity, an action hero[33] for the 21st century. Based on the graphic novel by Kevin Grevioux, this latest entry in the cycle shows how far the monster has progressed, returning full circle to his roots as in inspiration for page and screen.

If there's something to take away from these numerous films, it's that ideas concerning humanity evolve in much the same way as the film medium. As technology improves, we're forced to look at how those improvements impact our lives (for better or worse). The cultural impact that one simple vision has had is easily charted; in fact, it has been already been done. Susan Tyler Hitchcock traces the myriad ways that the legend has been adapted, beginning with Shelley's anxieties over her lost child[34] and the social changes experienced throughout England and continental Europe. Her study, which traces the almost–

200-year history of the Monster, shows the expansion of the Monster as a cultural phenomenon. She explains that the story "speaks of an eternal conflict in the human condition. It is the tension between what we have and what we desire, between that which is firmly within our grasp and that which we can dream but not materialize. The story summons the universal dialogue between what our culture now calls red and blue, conservative and liberal, traditional and progressive, authoritarian and libertarian, conservative and radical."[35] The obvious parallels signify an ongoing struggle of give and take.

Despite the often-polarizing effects of progress, the Monster has grown to signify anything representing assembly through the combination of parts, specifically those reaching toward genetic modification. Frankenfoods, or genetically modified foods, are demonized by environmentalists and whole-food advocates who decry scientific encroachment on the natural world of agriculture. In 2012, Hurricane Sandy, which ravaged the East Coast and devastated the Jersey Shore, plagued society once the media and meteorologists began referencing the storm as a Frankenstorm, after the small category-one hurricane merged with a large inland storm. Hurricane Sandy transformed into a powerful behemoth that caused approximately $68 billion worth of damages. Because of the cultural significance of the Monster, he has superseded even fear, achieving the status of a cultural icon, instantly recognized regardless of age group or nationality. He appears in cereals and vitamins, on T-shirts, is the basis of children's books and toys, and is the affectionate choice of name for Eddie Van Halen's guitar, one that was assembled from other guitars. The "Frankenstein" guitar, like the Monster, has inspired clones of its own.

The Frankenstein cycle of films is, in almost every respect, based on the interpretation of one director and the makeup of one actor. Yet, the initial image of fear, as predicated by Whale's 1931 film, spawned a franchise that, for the most part, misses the point of the original novel. Shelley wrote the Monster with a voice, one capable of speaking out against incomprehensible scientific progress. But, perhaps, the modern interpretation of the Monster has achieved the same legacy as a symbol of progress. Time and again, he is recreated to speak—whether through unintelligible grunts or the eloquence that has since developed over multiple interpretations—about the victimization of isolation through technological progress.

CHAPTER 3

Horror from Beyond

Social Anxieties, Dystopias and Outsider Threats

> Ethics, morals, codes of conduct, are the stern rules which in the past we needed to survive—as individuals, as groups, as nations. Now, although we give lip service to survival, we are embarrassed and beginning to be smothered by our own numbers.—John Steinbeck, *America and Americans: Americans and the Future*

> The future of science—nay more, the future of mankind—depends upon whether it will be possible to restrain these various collective hysterias until the populations concerned have had time to adjust themselves to the new scientific environment.—Bertrand Russell, *The Science to Save us from Science*[1]

While *Frankenstein* toiled amid serialized spoofs, Hollywood swelled with Gothic-inspired monsters (such as *Zombies on Broadway*, *The Picture of Dorian Gray*, and *The Body Snatcher* (all 1945). Following the conclusion of World War II, and the devastating end to war with Japan, America began its new existence in the Atomic Age. Veterans came home to a society they did not recognize; attempting to fit in became a struggle in itself, as exemplified in William Wyler's *The Best Years of Our Lives* (1946). This Academy Award–winning film may be the first to show how the war transformed modern society into a place of psychological horror.

3. Horror from Beyond

The bomb was evidence of power beyond the natural ken of the American imagination. In the place of safety and national identity, the dropping of the bombs in Japan opened up a new age of possibility. Despite the conveniences of the modern age, "Americans had learned to live with the bomb and with the legacy of World War II in all its understated terror and overstated triumph. Fears and insecurities were shunted aside, restricted to a covert culture that nonetheless brimmed with the allusive, iconographic, and amorphous images of the moral corruption and communal insanity, the death and violence, that accompanied life with the bomb."[2] It was during this period, leading into the Cold War,[3] that the American consciousness was growing, reflecting a changing state of awareness from that of the days before the war, or what David J. Skal implies as the changing façade of innocence in American culture: "The torrent of technology and science-driven socioeconomic change in the 1950s also spurred a desire for the return of protective parental moral and religious values seemingly swept away in the postwar tide of transformation."[4] The drive was to find a "new normal" in a world that possessed the awful power of technology that could destroy all of mankind. However, the dream of a prosperous society came at a very large cost—the cost of freedom.

Following the bombing of Hiroshima and Nagasaki,[5] America cultivated an age of prosperity, largely seen as the growth of the American Dream. But it was not immediately realized, held back as it was by worry and paranoia. As the Cold War deepened, evidence of America's transformation promoted a succession of films that put man against a growing siege of outside terrors. Audiences were treated to a host of threats, from alien visitors to mutant ants. However, each threat represents a challenge to previously held ideas of American identity. Similar to the way in which *The Cabinet of Dr. Caligari* was a response to fascism following World War I, Hollywood films followed the current postwar era by exploiting the cultural impact of film as a method to speak of societal trouble—and capitalize on moviegoers' tastes as a way to help the struggling film industry, which was growing stagnant in the wake of television's mainstream acceptance.

In this new era, the Hollywood horror film was in a state of dormancy; like a monster in hiding, waiting for the moment to re-emerge and begin a new reign of terror. But, during this transitional period, something needed to happen to breathe new life into the way we interpret horror. Ironically, how we achieved that feat was through a combination of methods that set horror back several years. Horror films still existed, but they were fully rooted in the fears of the day, specifically the impending threats of atomic bombs and alien invasion. This is, in part, due to the way the war ended. With Germany split into two pieces, the final conclusion of the war was a tentative peace that never restored balance to the world. There was no conclusion, only another chapter. In a battle of technological supremacy, the United States and the Soviet Union embarked in a progressive arms race, building ballistic missiles in order to protect against attack from one another. Both nations amassed a collection of weapons, building on the knowledge gained through wartime developments. Scientific progress, specifically atomic advancements, created a gap between those seeking a return to life "before the war" and those seeking the brighter horizons promised by a progressive society. This was clearly evident in the United States, and, as such, was reflected in films that showed social pressures as the catalyst for a failing America. Alongside McCarthyism and the growing distrust of outsider influence, the American public was becoming increasingly aware of coming dangers. But beyond the troublesome problems of social harmony, the country still pushed forward, trying to reconcile the old ways with new ambitions.

The science-fiction film of the 1950s is a reflection of social horrors, in that the duality of invasion (outsider threats) and the resurgence of mad scientist (namely those modeled after the frenzied and secretive minds that worked on the Manhattan Project) created a singular source of fear that resounded in the minds of Americans. This served as an inspiration for horror films that spoke directly to their audiences about real fears, even if the destructions implied by such films had yet to be fully realized. However, the motivation behind science-fiction horror films of the 1950s has been the cause of some debate. Mark Jancovich summarizes this as a way to ground interstellar fears of invasion within the confusion of life after World War II. Citing Peter Biskind's claim that America "pulled together" in the wake of World War II and the subsequent Cold War, Jancovich notes a distinct difference between invasion films and those dealing with mutant or radioactive beings: "Science is dominant and the military is presented as a mere functionary to be ordered and controlled by the technical expertise of scientists.... For this reason, Biskind challenges critics such as Susan

Sontag who have seen these films as the product of anxieties about nuclear weapons. He argues that these films 'are not primarily worried about the Bomb; they loved the Bomb, or at least the technology that made it possible.'"[6] On the other hand, atomic scientists create problems that are reflected in postwar American society because they work to both progress advancement (nuclear power) and destruction, in which "the scientist literally did increasingly possess the ability to bring about apocalyptic destruction."[7] Separated by what appears to be two distinct types of films, the underlying message is ultimately the same.

Refining Our Fears: Distinguishing Between Horror and Science Fiction

The major studio productions veered off into two paths during the 1950s. The proliferation of science as a source of horror grew, by which filmmakers eventually found two inspirations: the horror of society and the horror of scientific progress. Unlike the early films that attempted to resolve the scientific debate as a cure for social anxieties, the modern science-fiction film exploited this divide as a unique source of horror, which eventually materialized into an entirely new genre, building on the fears of scientific progress and technological advancement as a source of horror within itself.[8] Meanwhile, the horror film grew to encompass social advancement of technologies symbolic of a changing way of life. Aside from these two subgenres, the film industry progressed with technology itself, using modern technologies as a means to produce new horrors for viewers. This division of genre is important to understanding how we perceive technological progress as a source of horror. Initially, science *was* a source of horror, as seen in the Universal films of the 1930s that exploited the mad scientist as an outsider. But modern society is built on the foundations of progress through technological means. Together, the two could not co-exist. With science and technology enveloping everyday life, horror had to evolve in order to survive.

For Kevin Heffernan, this was a process that was not only necessary, but instrumental in making horror films what they are today: "I trace the horror genre's evolution through its two phases. The first is the refinement phase, characterized by the increasing psychological complexity of the characters and by technological innovation, such as in the color movies of [England's] Hammer Films."[9] Indeed, the Hammer horror films humanized the Gothic story, moving the monster from a type or form to a fearful presence. They exhibited a knowingness (albeit rather tongue in cheek) of horror's ability to speak across boundaries—both geographically and chronologically. Reinventing the horror film as a psychological fear rather than simply one of manifested fears of the mind, Hammer's product did more for modern horror films than is readily apparent when taken out of the context of social progress.[10] Hammer recreated the films of old, substituting social terrors for graphic realism—in color and in depravity. By today's standards, however, they are rather tame.

The second process Heffernan notes is that of refining the movie experience, or the technological advancements that cemented the horror film as an innovative method for social commentary. He cites "drive-ins and auditorium 'hardtop' theaters" and "double bills" (also known as double features) and film distribution as motivating forces behind the "changing industry during this volatile period," one that eventually reduced distribution of major films, leading to an increase in second-rate and exploitive films reaching a greater swath of mainstream America.[11] Through this refinement process, we can trace the advent of modern horror films by exploring the establishment of social and moral codes as they grew out of the 1950s Cold War horror film. At its core, the Cold War horror film is an exploitation of a technologically advanced society. But for audiences, technology played a large part in the enjoyment factor. Director William Castle was a key player during this period, a creative man who sought to make horror fun, often traveling to theaters to greet fans in person. Using gimmicks, he would promote films that gave audiences physical sensations as opposed to playing on purely visual fears. One such gimmick, "Percepto," was made possible by wiring theater seats with buzzers for his film *The Tingler* (1959). For a while, Castle's gimmicks worked, but they ceased to be more than novelties before long.

For horror to maintain its relevance, the genre had to make use of one of its stock components: the psychological adventure story rooted in social anxieties. The viewing experiences underwent their own changes—drive-ins and walk-in theaters upgraded sound systems, thus transcending films as a substitution for reality. But with the inflated costs of film production, quality languished. Horror films became repetitive, seeking cheap thrills in order to produce revenue. Soon, audiences began to adapt to the stereotypes of the horror film.

3. Horror from Beyond

To combat this, filmmakers changed the perception of the films themselves: "The formulas, superficial knowingness of horror films and their playful manipulation of audience expectations provide the predictable pattern against which the moments of excess, the visual shocks and violent shifts in angle, can be staged: anxiety and anticipatory desire are heightened."[12] Therein lies the pattern that horror enables—we become pawns to the staging of the film itself. Modern horror films exploit our knowledge of perception, which works in favor of the audiences' preconceived (and often false) perspectives. In these early forays of perspective, horror was manifesting itself as a genre built on disappointing expectations, providing shock value instead.

Filmmakers (led by the major Hollywood studios) responded by capitalizing on the appeal of horror as a subgenre and as a form of spectacle, which sought to enhance the appeal of the theatrics of horror as they are exhibited on the large screen. However, the downfall was that fewer films were seeing the benefits of this technology: "The major companies, now focused on maximizing profits through fewer and costlier releases, began an aggressive move into new technology like widescreen projection, stereo sound, and 3-D, both to compete with television and to profit from the sale of equipment to exhibitors. The Production Code, which had depended for enforcement on studio ownership of the premium theaters, began a decades-long weakening."[13] Even though horror films were being produced, their overall capabilities for capturing the social imagination was waning: "Universal's B picture output was the studio's mainstay, and the filmmakers had no arty illusions about their products. According to Reginald Le Borg, who directed several horror films and melodramas for Universal in the early 1940s, the intended audience was 'factory workers and blacks.' Angry and alienated, often voiceless and beleaguered, the monster characters had clear appeal for the socially and economically marginalized."[14] But, these monsters were types, suffering through an endless barrage of modification and retellings.

While many films of today depend on the same social awareness depicted in the horror films of the 1950s (and early 1960s), it would be a long while for these films to take root in the consciousness of viewers. For many viewers, science fiction films were plain enjoyment. We marveled at the possibilities, but we were never removed from safety. But within the ongoing split of science fiction and horror, what is largely determined to be the psychological fear that is deeply embedded within the thematic are largely eliminated in favor of moral and philosophical statements of scientific merit and possibility. While new questions of identity were raised, it seemed that there were fewer answers amid the turbulent era of the Cold War. As a result, some films explored the problems of the Cold War, while others—those that eventually led to our notion of modern horror—sought to explain the dilapidation of society as a whole. Eschewing outsider threats, these films looked for the enemy within.

Science Fiction and the American Nightmare

Horror alone is incapable of showing viewers fear. For horror films to resonate, there needs to be an identifiable influence. If we had yet to witness the nuclear attacks on our own soil, or the mad scientist propagating mutants, then where could Americans look to find horror reflecting social upheaval? Monsters existed, but they were not the monsters of old; they were the offspring of social tensions that were reflected in a changing society. Several changes, stemming from government action to modern technological amenities, created a schism in the social fabric of ordinary day-to-day life, including: the Immigration and Naturalization Act of 1952 (removal of ethnic and racial barriers to citizenship); television; the 1954 legal case, Brown v. Board of Education; and the introduction of domestic airline flights in 1958. While Americans were largely unaware of the Manhattan Project, there was an idea that society was unified in keeping alive the idealism that pervaded the return to life after World War II. But change was afoot, stemming from the growing youth culture and the simple need to forget the past and move on. Psychological in nature, the science-fiction film is a breed of horror; however, it is nothing like what we expect psychological horror of today to look like. Rather than progressively looking forward to impending threats, the science fiction films of the 1950s bore a striking resemblance to modern horror films in that they actively look at the world in its current state. Though the fears may be future or alternative, they are rooted in the realities of the present, where ultimately, we learn to cope with the source of fear and wait for the next threat. Cyndy Hendershot suggests, "As taboos were emphasized more and more in 1950s America, the allure of transgression was heightened. The horror film expressed the interplay between taboo and transgression."[15] Through the films of the later 1950s and the early '60s, the America vision of itself was turned into a society waiting for the next catalyst of destruction. The period following World War II and The United States' direct assault on communism in Vietnam would ultimately be centered on how we recapture the idea of the American Dream. Technology had a large part in determining that direction.

For the modern viewer, science fiction films are now largely relegated to a cult status, enjoyed by those seeking to point out the logical flaws that time cannot hide. But, like the human monsters that came before them, the mutant races and aliens of the 1950s speak to another audience. The 1950s marks an era of self-awareness at the growing prospects of world annihilation, but the rising science-fiction horror films lack the clear and unabashed social commentary of their predecessors. Underneath all the rubber costumes and gadgetry of scientists gone awry, the science-fiction era had little impact on horror as a mainstay beyond the '50s. But, taking into account the culture in which they were made, these films had a definitive impact on how society viewed their given state of affairs, namely by the process of influence. Without such films as *The Thing From Another World* (1951), *Invasion of the Body Snatchers* (1956), *Forbidden Planet* (1956), The *Fly* (1958), *Them!* (1954), or the more absurd science-fiction films like *Creature from the Black Lagoon* (1954), *The Blob* (1958), or *Plan 9 from Outer Space* (1959), and countless others that let audiences confront fears of the unknown or otherworldly, the entire genre seems like a footnote to the Golden Age horrors of Universal and company. But, the horror film is largely an amalgamation of types, never more evident than by its assumption of science fiction. The science-fiction horror film of the 1950s is a statement against society, in which technology began once again to creep into the public imagination. But, unlike the classic monsters, where one madman unleashes a terror that society must fight, the modern source of horror is the unseen. In horror films of the postwar era, humanity is seen as a pawn to outside forces, awaiting the fatal blast of sirens as a last harbinger of our impending doom.

"Who Goes There?": Aliens and the First Invasion Wave

It isn't by accident that the air force is a central component featured in what can largely be considered the birth of the science-fiction genre. Directed by Christian Nyby, *The Thing from Another World*[16] centers on a United States Air Force regiment sent to the North Pole, seeking evidence of a crashed ship of unknown origin. An "aircraft of unusual type" is, in passing, thought to be Russian by Captain Hendry (Kenneth Tobey) is dismissed by the general, who orders the captain and his men to investigate the matter firsthand (a subtle sign toward verifiable intelligence or data). The ship's lone inhabitant (James Arness) is taken back to base, still frozen within a block of ice. While on watch, to avoid looking at the alien, Corporal Barnes (William Self) accidentally covers it with an electric blanket, thawing the block and releasing the monster. Science is further shown in terms of ordinary power; when wondering if the plane would melt the ice, Dr. Chapman states that "one of our own jets generates enough heat to warm a 50-story office building." Science is the thrust behind information, the hopes of communicating with the alien a symbol of unlocking vast secrets withheld from humanity. The story is rooted in the *Frankenstein* mystique of forbidden science and the goal for social progress (the alien a hulking, eight-foot-tall figure), but the story adds to the zeal behind discovery in that it excites the entire crew, not just a lone madman. Realizing the ship is perfectly round, the airmen exclaim proudly that they've "finally got one!," excited for the prospects of interstellar contact and firsthand information.

Ned "Scotty" Scott (Douglas Spencer), a reporter, is censured, his scoop being withheld from the world because it is "air force information," covered up until Scott is given clearance to share the material with the public, something he repeatedly threatens to do.[17] But while the public is kept in the dark, the airmen themselves are shown as lacking the necessary knowledge of protocol. According to a military document released by the Department of Public Information—DoD Bulletin 629–49, item 6700, extract 75,131—a suggestion that information within the military is itself difficult to ascertain, "The air force has discontinued investigating and evaluating reported flying saucers on the basis that there is no evidence," citing three reasons: (1) misinterpretation of conventional objects; (2) mass hysteria; and (3) they're jokes. The crew themselves disparage the information, knowing that they, too, are in the dark when it comes to information. Despite the detection of large levels of radiation from a Geiger counter, the airmen are lulled into a false sense of security, forgetting their objective. The

3. Horror from Beyond

film showcases technology, the comforts of American dominance transplanted to the farthest reaches of the planet. The Arctic base replicates a modern world, complete with a quiet transplanted civility that desperately clings to a return to life after the war. Despite the removal from civilization, the Old World echoes in the sentiments of the crew as much as the New World presented by the alien delineates the powerful reaches of technological progress. In fact, this is verified by Dr. Carrington (Robert Cornthwaite), who says, "Only science can conquer him. All other weapons will be powerless." He later attests that "knowledge is more important than life."

Dr. Carrington, in telling of his experiments, is met with skepticism, but his search for answers turns him maniacal. When confronted with the prospect that the alien has come to conquer humanity, Dr. Carrington exclaims that "there are no enemies in science, Professor, only phenomena to study." Ironically, the enemy is subdued by a suggestion from Nikki Nicholson (Margaret Sheridan). When prompted with the question of how to deal with a vegetable, she answer simply, "Boil it." (The logic behind Nicholson's solution lies in the fact that she is the one person in the crew expected—by the film's contemporary audience—to have the means to conquer domesticity.) Practical means finally overcome the technologically unknown. With temperatures falling after the alien escapes through a window (again, it is Nikki Nicholson who notices Hendry and Scotty's breath, a not-so-subtle detail showing her role as "homemaker"), the crew retreats to the generator room. In protest to a forthcoming attack on the alien, Dr. Carrington urges the crew to capture the alien, stating that "civilization has given us orders." He is willing to sacrifice the safety and lives of the crew to further scientific knowledge, but for the crew, survival trumps progress. Dr. Carrington attempts to reason with the monster, but science (in the figure of the doctor) is swiftly pushed aside. As the alien approaches the secluded crew, they electrocute him with an improvised device, thus putting an end to the encounter.

The film concludes with the open acknowledgment of a poorly hidden romance between Nikki and Captain Hendry. Foiling the monster, the crew urges Nikki's suggestions that the captain settle down, leave the war behind and move on. Scotty is finally allowed to file his report once the radio reaches normal voltage, and he triumphantly reports the events of the mission, urging a room of reporters to tell the story of a crew that fought the first alien invasion with an "arc of electricity." Despite losses, Scotty bypasses the mission's leader, who is "attending to demands over and above calls of duty." After being lauded by the crew for his willingness to expose the truth, Scotty ends with a final warning: "Tell the world. Tell this to everybody.... Keep watching the skies." The patriotic nature of the film is pinpointed by the final credits, which end in a Souza-esque fanfare, promoting vigilance against outside threats and belief in the modern world. But the political aspirations of the film were soon countered by another invasion film, this one debuting in September 1951.

Diamonds as money, plastic as strong as steel, a mysterious robot and a flying saucer, both made of a metal of unknown origin: these are the mysteries of the universe featured in *The Day the Earth Stood Still*, directed by Robert Wise. The film centers on an alien visitor—Klatuu (Michael Rennie)—that comes to earth to deliver an urgent warning to the president himself. Surrounded by crowds and a large military presence, he proceeds to exit his capsule. Despite his protests that he comes in peace, he is accidentally shot; when he recovers, he reveals that the object he brandished was, in fact, a "gift for your president. With this he could have studied life on other planets." This is the central premise to the film: knowledge is feared while power and control dominate. This is evidenced in the opening scenes following Klatuu's arrival, when news reports urgently downplay mass hysteria's assertions of invasion as "absolutely false." This is echoed by the residents of the boarding house where Klatuu seeks refuge as "Mr. Carpenter" after he escapes Walter Reed Army Hospital with a pilfered suit. Society is shown amid various tensions; one resident states, "It's the media that spurs social distrust, encouraging the fears of the public, spouting on about destruction and overthrow." Another irate citizen objects, "People my foot! They're Democrats!"

Klatuu seeks intellectual communication, not brash reaction. The film is less about invasion, but a way around the polarizing discourse that centered into the mind of Americans. Aside from the obvious political tensions hinted at throughout the film, the clear distinction between an advanced society such as Klatuu's and our own is the progress of science. At Walter Reed, Klatuu states that he is 78 (despite looking 35), making one doctor say that he feels "like a third-class witch doctor." The inscription of the Gettysburg Address within the Lincoln

Memorial inspires Klatuu. Like Lincoln, Klatuu realizes that earth has become a battleground, where "government of the people, by the people, for the people..." shall keep the honor of the dead (presumably those of World War II) from being vainly discarded in the search for atomic dominance. The intersection of the political objectives of power over progress are largely seen through Klatuu's relationship with a boy named Bobby (Billy Gray) and his mother, Helen (Patricia Neal), both of whom reside at the boarding house. After volunteering to chaperone Bobby for an afternoon, Bobby takes Klatuu to Arlington National Cemetery to visit the grave of his father, who was killed in World War II. Klatuu then takes Bobby to see the spaceship, which, parked on the National Mall, has become a tourist attraction. In his genial and supportive way, Klatuu takes the moment to influence the curious child about the practical uses of atomic power; however, he is mocked by those listening to him explain to Bobby the very real (for him) possibilities of atomic power beyond those of merely destructive means. Their final stop of the afternoon is the residence of Prof. Barnhardt (Sam Jaffe), the man Bobby likens to the greatest mind of his generation. A man of science, Barnhardt is the link between action and consequence. Klatuu sees this man as a scientist, a humanist akin to a modern Lincoln, one who understands the peril of the world and will work accordingly to ensure that society will progress in a rational and practical manner. The professor confirms Klatuu's intuitions when he says that science is to be respected: "We scientists are too often ignored or misunderstood."

Atomic energy and the powers of the atom require both caution and foresight. Even though it is renowned for its destructive capabilities, Klatuu says, "Atomic power ... is for a lot of other things, too." However, the singular mindset of destruction and control is central to the narrative of *The Day the Earth Stood Still*. Klatuu warns us of progress, namely by sending an intergalactic warning: "By threatening danger, your planet is facing danger." By way of a demonstration of the consequences of atomic destruction, and his confederation's willingness to enact safety measures of their own, Klatuu explains to Bobby's mother, Helen, that "electricity has been neutralized. All over the world." Somehow, this includes engines, machinery, and any source of power, except those that would cause harm to humans—hospitals remain fully functional, as do planes in flight. (Klatuu's demonstration brings the world back to the Dark Ages before the time of Edison and Tesla. The result is a shutdown of modern society.)

Professor Barnhardt, after being told of the worldwide shutdown of power, asks his secretary, "Does all this frighten you? Does it make you feel insecure?" When she answers in the affirmative, Barnhardt says that he is pleased—pleased by the ingenious decision to show humanity what's at stake in their modern world. However, at 12:30 p.m. when the machines of society come back to full functionality, the world rushes to simply move forward. Amid horns and engines rumbling to life, no notice is paid to the temporary outage.

The Day the Earth Stood Still is a morality film, seeking to bridge the gap between public fears and practical advancement. Klatuu "isn't a menace," Helen tells her fiancé, Tom (Hugh Marlowe). Instead, he's a voice of reason in a time when humanity is on the brink of destruction. After he is restored to health following the hunt to capture a robot that had been aboard the spaceship, Klatuu addresses the gathered crowd on the Washington Mall, explaining that "the universe grows smaller every day." Citing the wisdom of which the laws of the United States Constitution were drawn, Klatuu tells the onlookers that the universal idea of freedom is necessary to "provide security for all, or no one is secure." The robot, it seems, is no source of evil—it is merely the enforcer of law. At the risk of leaving the earth a "burned-out cinder," it is up to the governments of the world to determine the future fate of the world; as Klatuu says, "The decision rests with you." The onlookers, the world dignitaries that have assembled to hear Klatuu's message, silently ponder these warnings. For now, it seems, the world leaders have listened.

The Thing from Another World and *The Day the Earth Stood Still*, in both of which military dominance and interstellar invasion combine to offer a glimpse into the public imagination of the time, best illuminate the problems of a technologically advanced society. Though both have been adapted into modern remakes, the remakes have largely followed the legacy of their predecessors, only with updated effects and inflated budgets. But the adaptation of Jack Finney's 1955 novel *The Body Snatchers*[18] is a telling reminder of the power of science fiction as a method for speaking about changing attitudes amid technological advancement. Jack Finney was busy writing a modest piece of fiction that, while never topping the best-seller lists, eventually changed the way Hollywood viewed the horror of science fiction. After his book was optioned by Allied Artists, it grew to cult status due to the expert direction of Don Siegel. *Invasion of the Body Snatchers* (1956)[19] explores the prospects of alien "seeds" replicating in the bodies of sleeping people, where they grow into perfect duplicates. Once achieving full maturity, they leave their host (the sleeping humans) to decay to dust. (This, incidentally, is the same effect on many of the victims when exposed to the nuclear blasts of Hiroshima and Nagasaki.)

At the core of *Invasion of the Body Snatchers* is the paradox of social fears, those of which were grounded in a growing distrust of individualism. Dr. Miles Bennell (Kevin McCarthy) realizes to his horror that people are succumbing to their alien hosts, leaving them devoid of feelings or emotions; in other words, to blindly consume and assimilate to the larger culture. Dan (Larry Gates) tells him that the change is all but instantaneous: "Suddenly, while you're asleep, they'll absorb your mind, you memories, and you're reborn into an untroubled world." This is precisely what Americans were realizing about their changing culture, but rather than a dramatic alien takeover, the change happened gradually, from within.

Americans were forced to rely more on capitalism and uniformity: "While the burgeoning capitalist system of the 1950s produced unprecedented opportunities for upward mobility in America, this highly complex system also required, for its operation, an unprecedented level of efficiency and standardization. Thus, if the 1950s represented a sort of Golden Age of science fiction film, the decade was also the Golden Age of American homogenization, as efficiency-oriented mass production techniques pioneered by industrialists such as Henry Ford reached new heights of sophistication and new levels of penetration into every aspect of American life."[20] Therefore, *Invasion of the Body Snatchers* shouldn't be seen alone as a foundation of the sci-fi film; its legacy as a horror film is central to the fears of technology as a standardizing force. By this reasoning, we can envision two types of messages from the film:

> While [director Don] Siegel contends that *Body Snatchers* was intended to be an "entertainment" film with the tepid message being that people were becoming pod-like stereotypes, the film has long been subject of critical debate regarding its underlying political implications.

Considering that it was made during the Cold War, during Eisenhower's presidency, a few years after Korea, when Joseph R. McCarthy was at his peak of power, it seems unlikely that Siegel's film was only meant to tell us that we were becoming identical to our neighbors. Much of the film's cult following is a result of the picture's ability to be interpreted in two quite contradictory ways: as being anti–McCarthy and an indictment of the red-scare American mentality; and as being anticommunist allegory.[21]

Regardless of its original intent, the story is symbolic of American fears as they relate to World War II and the changing nature of advancement as a way of American life.

This may explain the multitude of remakes throughout different eras, each changing the film to explore social fears in a unique manner for the audience of the time. The original *Invasion of the Body Snatchers* brings an end to the debate as to what will be the downfall of American society. Rather than aliens or nuclear war, it was becoming apparent that our downfall will be ourselves. Following Siegel's film, with its blend of the psychological and the scientific, there appeared to be a door opening, showing a new avenue in which horror is able to serve as a criticism for society. In the tradition of the mad scientist, a new character was emerging from the vapors and blasts of the sci-fi horrors of the Cold War. Because of modernization, industrialization, and mass consumer culture, the cultural landscape was beginning to be homogenized. Individuality began to erode, and individualism was presented as a threat to the American way of life.[22] As the culture began to develop into a fractured specter of identity, we found it hard to follow the logic of the McCarthy hearings, and were asked to redefine "American" in the same way that we are asked to redefine "horror" in the era of the science-fiction horror film. This is why there is no closure made by *Invasion of the Body Snatchers*: "it is not entirely clear that this mobilization will succeed or that the invasion can, at this point, be stopped."[23]

Either through depictions of impending doom from above (in the form of aliens or the bomb) or through that of a transformation changing the concept of American identity into something seemingly revolting and shadowy, there is plenty of evidence that "the atom bomb shook the foundations of the physical and psychological universe.... The tightrope that science and technology had long walked was now excruciatingly taut, and henceforth mankind teetered on the brink of annihilation."[24] Each of the above films depict alien outsiders as having a definite influence on the growth of science on the modern imagination. However, interplanetary fears were not the only sources of science-fiction horror. Increasingly, the reality of life in the atomic age would manifest itself into a progression of horrors that melded the possibilities of scientific progress with the ways it would change the everyday world.

Rogue Science and Nuclear Consequences

Amid the wave of otherworldly monsters, a Japanese film exploited nuclear fears as a metaphor for complete social destruction. Like Frankenstein's Monster before him, *Godzilla* (1954)[25] explored scientific ends without consequences, and like his predecessor, became a cultural icon while spawning a legacy of sequels and imitations. And, like Shelley's automaton, Godzilla is less a monster to the public than he is because of his nature, being reborn from his own destruction in order to repeat the cycle for future generations.[26] Likewise, *Eyes Without a Face* (1960) eschews mad science in favor of exploring the evils of scientific possibilities. Director Georges Franju's French-Italian cult classic (gory even by today's standards) is an artful look at humanity. After his daughter is injured in a car accident, surgeon Docteur Génessier (Pierre Brasseur) has a plan: kidnap young girls and restore his daughter's beauty. While there are traces of the *Frankenstein* element of surgery and spectacle, the film doesn't qualify as a pure science fiction. However, it does provide an understanding of how science connects horror with progress. This is most fully realized in Kurt Neumann's *The Fly* (1958), a unique film that is keenly aware of how America has moved past the immediate fears of the Cold War.

By this point, the public had begun to ease its fears about nuclear annihilation. Partly because, by now, atomic bomb testing had moved underground and had thus become a dirty secret in the search for security. But, as Klatuu explained, the Cold War states had finally found an alternative use for atomic energy. In 1954, the USSR's Obninsk Nuclear Power Plant became the first to use conventional nuclear energy for public consumption, with Pennsylvania's Shippingport Reactor becoming the first American reactor in 1957. Thus it makes sense that *The Fly* seeks to explore nuclear energy as a mainstay of modern American society, specifically through atomic mutation. Despite the dangers of genetic mutation[27] by radiation, the promise of the atomic sciences utilizes the mad scientist premise, this one a genteel academic named André Delambre (Vincent Price). *The Fly* "explicitly links André's assumption of the god/scientist role within the Atomic Age. In a conversation that takes place in the laboratory, Hélène [Patricia Owens] expresses fear of the present, commenting on 'the suddenness of our age.' After listing many recent discovers she laments, 'Everything's going so fast.'"[28] Technology, as explained by André, is a promise of something faster, better, and, well, more. With science we are able to achieve results that were only dreamed of, in much the same way that automation and mechanical industry progressed society to the current state of a consumer culture. What, then, would be the next breakthrough for society? For Dr. André Delambre, that comes by way of transportation. Transportation represents technologies of the 1950s, equivalent to microwaves and the modern kitchen. (Tesla's dreams of modernity, while often providing a great social benefit, come with the cost of leaving the familiar behind. The creation of the Eisenhower Interstate System, authorized by the Federal Aid Highway Act of 1956, gave us the highways that we use today. Additionally, Americans were afforded with greater mobility as cars replaced mass transit [this is reflected in *Invasion of the Body Snatchers*, where Miles tells Becky, "Our only hope is to make it to the highway"]. This led to the growth of suburban living in America, but that too came with a price.)

The best instance of how drastically the American home changed in the 1950s was the creation of a small town in Levittown, New York. Named after the firm that envisioned the hamlet, Levitt and Sons built a planned community on New York's Long Island. Targeting returning GIs, the homes were rapidly constructed from prefabricated materials. The system employed cost-efficiency and speed, leaving little (if any) room for personalization. Consisting of homes only, the development became prisons unto themselves; residents had to leave the community to shop, dine out, or find any source of recreation.[29] Suburban lifestyles integrated the daily commute and the automobile into the minds of Americans as a necessity for modern living. This is echoed in *The Fly* by André's experiments. In a typical mad-scientist scene that conveys the progressive style of modern living, André shows his teleportation device to his wife in his basement lab. After showing her a demonstra-

3. Horror from Beyond

tion by transporting an ashtray, Hélène questions the truth before her, pointedly saying, "You're playing a joke on me." But André's response is a vision of possibilities, veiled in the film's questioning of scientific limits as they are viewed as both possibilities and idealism.

> **ANDRÉ:** Take television. What happens? A stream of electrons—sound and picture impulses—are transmitted through the air. The TV camera is the disintegrator. Your set unscrambles or integrates the electrons back into pictures and sound.
> **HÉLÈNE:** Yes, but this is different.
> **ANDRÉ:** Why?
> **HÉLÈNE:** Well, because it's impossible.
> **ANDRÉ:** Fifty years ago, if my father were told he could sit in Montreal and watch a World Series in New York as it happened, he'd say it was impossible. This is the same principle exactly.

This exchange culminates in André's dream for a world that embraces the modern aspects of transportation, which could unite all mankind into a global sphere of commerce and charity: "I can transport matter—*anything*—at the speed of light, perfectly.... Think what it means! Anything, even humans, will go through one of these devices. No need for cars or railways or airplanes, even spaceships. We'll set up matter-receiving stations throughout the world, and later the universe. There'll never be famine. Surpluses can be sent instantaneously at almost no cost, anywhere. Humanity need never want or fear again." André's idealism is central to the problem of scientific discovery. Television, still a relatively new phenomenon at the time, and André's marveling/explanation about it, represents the problem of new technology in that it often moves beyond the realm of ordinary understanding while still providing a useful benefit for society. Most telling is the resulting "error" in this first transmission. The "Made in Japan" marking on the bottom of the plate he's sent through as a demonstration appears in reverse from its original position. "Made in Japan" should be understood as a mark of technological rebirth that flourished in the country following World War II, as well an implicit failure to realize the enormity of his aspirations.

A further consideration is how the mad scientist role has become less an outsider figure and more a part of modern society. In this new position, "The scientist assumes a prominence which elides the other political and cultural forces behind the use of atomic bombs and arms race. As such, the postwar atomic scientist, fashioned after nineteenth-century models such as Frankenstein, provides a site where difficult ethical questions are replaced by a lone individual who bears the blame and the praise for the double-edged continuation of scientific 'progress.'"[30]

Science fiction is a particular brand of horror film, one that seeks to define technology and science by its perceived limitations. As future sources of horror become more evident, we'll see that horror films are always concerned with boundaries, where the expression of horror in these films is the divide between perception and transgression. Science fiction is no different as a source of horror. However, as Chapter 7 will explore, the genre as a source of horror must be reinterpreted, as all horror necessitates updating to present the current problems of society and its potential dangers. For the 1950s, technology was horror, or (at the very least) a bridge to accessing the changing world and the changing mindset of modern America.

Part II

Modern Horror and the Fear of Progress

CHAPTER 4

Psychos, Civic Unrest and Refining Horror

> What's the use? Mr. Boogeyman, King of Blood they used to call me. The Marx Brothers make you laugh; Garbo makes you weep; Orlok makes you scream. My kind of horror isn't horror anymore. No one's afraid of a painted monster anymore!—Boris Karloff as fading movie star Byron Orlok in Peter Bogdanovich's *Targets*

Up to 1960, the horror film was largely devoid of one element that is seemingly essential to the modern idea of horror—gore. That would come ... eventually. But, to reconcile the psychological problems of safety and home as represented in horror of the 1950s, audiences had to first realize what exactly they were to be afraid of. By the time the late 1960s rolled around, society realized that once-rational fears of nuclear apocalypse following World War II were dried up. What was left behind was the lack of promise that the previous generation clung to as a means to a better life. Instead, as society separated into two factions (conservatives and liberals), the evidence of future horrors clearly indicated that we would tear ourselves apart. But the psychological fears of the past were not soon forgotten. Despite the promises of a better future, there was unrest in society. Social norms, as they began to erode and evolve into something new, took a new place at the forefront of the horror film. Behind the shift in social change was the evidence of promise, and the lack of attainment for that promise.

It should be noted that technology and science, the very same devices that drove horror since Shelley's publication of *Frankenstein*, are largely absent from horror films of the 1960s, almost conspicuously so. That doesn't mean that its reach can't be felt through the lives shown onscreen. In every way, the characters, plots, and stories that we witness show a determined struggle of a changing America, one that has to come to grips with a world that is forever changed because of technology. A better standard of living through technology created a world that was equally fearful of technological advancement that few understood, much like Shelley's proclamation of science being out of the reach of ordinary citizens. Few people understood how a microwave worked, or how a telephone enabled communication from miles away, but the desire to have such technologies nevertheless changed the social spheres of American life. As such, the 1960s was a definitive—and important—period in developing the horror film from "classic" horror to "new" horror, where horror would be found within seemingly ordinary individuals, not from mad scientists or monsters. In fact, monsters, aside from the Hammer productions, had faded into obscurity. Instead, horror films of the 1960s delved into reality.

Despite the absence of science as a stimulus for fear, modern life itself substituted as a symbol for a world that was moving too fast, leaving in its place a sense of social unrest. The future, or so it was seen, was based on technological advancement, the greatest being one that would solidify the American legacy of a path to a new future. These hopes hinged on one technological achievement that riveted the nation—the Apollo space missions of the 1960s. The idea was that if we could send a man to the moon, then we would prove our dominance to the rest of the world. Underneath the space race, there was still the lingering notion of external threats, specifically the ideology of the Communist agenda. But internally, there was a resurgence of the individual as having a purpose. There seems to be a stark contrast between the ordinary and the seemingly ordinary, and what unknown terrors lay beyond the horizon. Despite many horror films suggesting these terrors, the time had come when the screen began accurately reflecting the darker side of the human condition. While earlier horror films sought to bring about the tingling feelings of horror as it was meant to be felt, there was little that showed horror as it was meant to be seen. Prior to 1960, with the pervasive fears of war and a resurging sense of identity, America was

4. Psychos, *Civic Unrest and Refining Horror*

beginning to rediscover itself. The problems that persist within society are depicted as a matter of surreal expression in the 1960s. Technology offered promise, but the immediacy that was expected was slow to meet society's demands. There was an expectation that something would come along to make society better and alleviate the general dread of a stagnant society. At the same time, society needed an outlet. According to Charles Derry: "When the horror film returned in the sixties without the science-fiction paraphernalia of spaceships and interplanetary monsters, the traditional horror genre had been transformed largely into one of three new subgenres": the Horror of Personality, the Horror of Apocalypse, and the Horror of the Demonic.[1] Of course, technology will cross these boundaries and types multiple times, but what Derry qualifies is that horror evolved from monsters and scares to a more societal-based concept of fears.

Following the paranoia of the Other, horror films were searching for a villain. People, it seems, were unhappy. The promise of the "good life" was not only unfulfilling, it was, for many, undesirable. The life that so many sought to keep was evaporating, largely because of a heightened sense of progress or of wanting "more." And, given the social struggles that punctuated the 1960s as a decade of progress and change, it makes sense that true horror, as Sartre suggested, was other people: "Thus, in this period, one can see why neither pseudoscientific horror nor supernatural horror was really the concern of the day. What *was* horrible, however, was man. It was a horror that was specific, nonabstract, and one that did not need a metaphor. Since the symbolic schizophrenia of the classic horror film had now become a literal insanity, it was necessary for a whole new basis of explanation to be applied. What seems to have been adopted in the early sixties in these horror films (however sometimes skeptically) was the psychological explanation."[2] While many films argued that the American Dream was in danger from outsiders and scientific progress, there was a new undercurrent of directors questioning the very notion of the American Dream. It seems the question of stagnation lay in the following: there had to be more to life than this.

After the dread of worldwide nuclear apocalypse, people sought to redefine the American experience, returning to a semblance of normalcy simply by living the American Dream rather than trying to build it anew. And, despite the overly cautious attitudes of the 1950s, a carefree sense of freedom engulfed society. Unfortunately, the fear during the 1960s came from within. Americans were learning to confront their own failures, and the progress they so desperately sought had to come from within. Yet, retreating from the national phobia of atomic catastrophe, people began to seek refuge in their own capsules of domestic bliss. The home became a central focus of life, and thus was reflected on the screen as a nightmare of confinement and constraint. What had once been a refuge had now become a source of inescapable fear.

With the advent of violence, particularly the realistic portrayal of blood onscreen, the human body transformed from an extension of human emotions and reactions, particularly the audience's response to bodily harm. As Isabel Cristina Pindedo explains, violence is nothing new to the suspense stories (or those films that mirrored suspense masquerading as horror) that explore personal boundaries: "Contrary to popular criticism, violence in the horror film is not gratuitous but is rather a constituent element of the genre. The horror narrative is propelled by violence, manifested in both the monster's violence and the attempts to destroy the monster. Horror is produced by the violation of what are tellingly called natural laws—by the disruption of our presuppositions about the integrity and predictable character of objects, places, animals, and people."[3]

Amid the changes that took place in the 1960s the most prevalent was that of a changing generation, from one that sacrificed all in order to support the war effort and achieve the American Dream, to their children. The image we're shown is often of a select few white middle-class Americans with something to lose. But, ironically, it would be the inheritors of the good life that would set afire the domestic bliss that was holding American society together. Social progress thus was a determining factor of changes in the horror film, and a more liberal, progressive lifestyle, as it was to be discovered individually, hinged on several factors that helped shape the manners by which horror evolved by the end of the decade.

The 1960s was a period that itself was transitory and remarkable for seeing what was yet to come. The decade was marked by two versions of America, one that looked backward as a way of recapturing the prosperity of postwar America, and one that looked forward as a way of developing the American Dream as a tangible element of success attainable to all. In the midst of the turmoil, four qualities resonate through

4. Psychos, *Civic Unrest and Refining Horror*

horror films of the 1960s, all of which are discernible as a way of testing the psychological and emotional loss of innocence the country was experiencing. These are fears of: (1) isolation; (2) change; (3) loss of innocence; and (4) lack of progress. Not by coincidence, technological progress is at the center of all four of these fears. Technology, specifically automation and machinery which diminished the need for manual labor, enabled the working class, offering leisure and wealth: "With the diminishing importance of work, at least the traditional notions of industrial work, suburban culture defined itself through conspicuous consumptions, the purchase of large, flashy, new products as a means of defining cultural status."[4] Largely, this wealth was a byproduct of factory workers and laborers in northern, industrialized cities, and the beneficiaries were largely the white middle class.

With their wealth and leisure they did their best to carry forward their prosperity to their children by sending them to college, both perpetuating a sense of status and enabling their children to avoid manual labor as an occupation. As a result, a new middle class was born, one that was aloof to the sacrifices of their forbearers and idle in terms of what actual sacrifice entailed. Unknown to them, their good life would create the counter-culture movement: "Familiar with a world of mass consumption, many middle-class white baby boomers believed that an era of perpetual affluence and total freedom of choice was at hand. They were eager, at least for a few years, to forego the quest for economic security and its material tokens that had driven their elders. By the early '60s, youth communities had sprung up on the outskirts of college campuses, often in cheap housing available near black or Latino ghettos.... Surrounded by one's peers and largely free from the responsibilities of career, family, and mortgage, young people could experiment with their bodies and minds in ways that usually shocked and enraged older people raised amid the constricted horizons of the Great Depression and World War II."[5]

One of the resulting horrors, at least to the detriment of the counter-culture movement, was the thought of inheriting the lives of their parents. "A striking characteristic of fifties horror is its ambivalence about the good life, and the tenuous nature of material security and social identity,"[6] but these new perpetuators of the American Dream opened up a rift in who shares in that dream. Living a stagnant life of luxury and suburban bliss was, at least for the counter-culture, a limitation. This would be further explored in the 1960s, with films exploring the nature of personal identity in contrast to social forces. As people sought to redefine themselves outside their patriotic duty and return to living on their own expressionistic terms, the shift in society became more apparent. And it was most apparent in the character of an isolationist who lived at home.

Anthony Perkins's dark portrayal of Norman Bates in *Psycho* is quixotic. As the title suggests, there seems to be no reason for his madness. But, withheld from his childhood traumas, it appears that Bates, with his mother, sets out to cultivate an existence free of consequences. Hitchcock showed Americans the darkness of society, the rough edges that the blissful American Dream sought to hide. *Psycho*, by extension, represents a changing world, one the technological promises of the space race couldn't solve. Despite her protective measures, Mrs. Bates herself ends up a victim, much like the World War II generation who sacrificed their lives only to have their children unravel the standards of society. Hitchcock knowingly eschewed the conventions of previous horrors to display the downside of conformity, so "that from the beginning to the end it [the film *Psycho*] very consciously goes against all the established conventions, and in doing so manages to redefine exactly what horror is by relating it to the modern sixties sensibilities."[7] Hitchcock, and likewise Norman Bates, turns expectations of the Other as a source of horror away from outside influences to a nightmare of domestic breakdown.

In trying to save Norman, Mrs. Bates sets forth to psychologically break down her son. Ironically, Mrs. Bates brings about her own demise by trying to have Norman conform in such a way that he is identifiably conformist. This is paralleled by Norman's victim, Marion Crane (Janet Leigh), whose escape is not only illegal, but championed as a fresh start. Of course, her sin is wish fulfillment. In escaping to Bates Motel, she learns firsthand that, despite Norman's good looks and quaint lifestyle, he, too, feels trapped. It is Marion's (and the viewer's) first hint of the private turmoil facing Norman. Yet, this comparison should act as a parallel for social ambivalence that weighed heavily on the American consciousness:

> **NORMAN:** We're all in our private traps ... clamped in it ... and none of us can ever get out. We scratch, and claw, but only at the air, only at each other; and for all of it, we never budge an inch.

MARION: Sometimes we deliberately step into those traps.
NORMAN: I was born in mine. I don't mind it anymore.

Norman's characterization of an institution (a "madhouse") is a juxtaposition of opposites, "the laughing and the tears," suggesting that the freedom of the American Dream comes at a price. We learn this through Norman's hedonistic wishes to drop away from the cultural status quo. In hearing his "mother," Norman openly wishes for escape, to "curse her, and leave her for ever ... or at least a fire, but I know I can't." Not only is he burdened with expectation, but he is burdened so violently by her expectations that he wishes his mother's total destruction (a fire) in the most benign manner possible. He tells Marion, "I hate what she's become." Since she is already dead, the voice that Norman hears is that of the previous generation, one demanding conformity and progress. By the end of the film, while Norman sits in jail, we learn the true depths of Norman's psychosis; however, this scene also shows the impact of the previous generation in that the voice he hears is equal to the pressures of modern society weighing in on his existence; Norman doesn't have independent thought.

Psycho changed the perception of horror, as much as the baby boomers changed the perception of society. Raising the tensions between the old Hollywood mystery film, Hopkins's portrayal crosses from mystery film to a realistic exploration of Americans' distaste for then-current standards of living. First is the matter of the house as a scene of terror: "Hitchcock uses the very generic house in his film to foil the audience's expectations of having the most horrific act happen there."[8] Where Gothic horrors often showed the home as a source of horror, it seems that modern horror created safety in the home. The rise of outsider threats and modern living created sanctuaries of the home, marking the Bates home as a symbolic center of social downfall. Further, there is the issue of Marion's car, which for many Americans was the ultimate possession of 1960s freedom. Marion is fleeing her past life, her car being her one source of escape. But Norman is trapped in his home, lacking the means by which to see the world at large. Norman displays a keen sense of removal from the world of others, suggesting that despite the mobility and freedom offered by her car, Marion had no escape. The subtle pause of the car's sinking into the mud is symbolic, showing both Norman's apprehension and pleasure of ridding himself of the past.

Part II—Modern Horror and the Fear of Progress

The obvious sexual identification of films such as *Psycho* and *Peeping Tom* (1960) explore horror in the conventional sense, but broaden the depth of horror as a method for investigating society from behind the lens of technological advances. Television opened up a world in which the dark and unseen reality of life blurred with the quiet pleasantries of social norms. On the surface, society was functional, yet the realness of life was often washed away by the situated awkwardness of fictionalized television programs. But the possibility of seeing the unseen (or, at the very least, watching the possibilities of an extant reality that was very real but hidden) drew a curious audience seeking to look beyond the ordinary and explore the darker depths of the human imagination.

While some films sought to explore now tired and cliché sources of horror, a few broke new ground to explore the home, and by extension the promise of an advanced technological society, as a prison unto itself. Norman Bates's freedom is depicted through isolation; it is only when tempted by Marion's arrival and search for freedom that Norman gives in to his baser desires. Likewise is the scenario of Mark (Carl Boehm) in *Peeping Tom*. Mark is a photographer by trade, but a voyeur who is obsessed with the idea of filming his victims at the moment of their deaths. From the start of the film the brief view of the Kodak film lets us know that we are, like the killer, watching and documenting the action. After the first murder (nary three minutes into the film, just prior to the opening credits), we've become aware that we're watching a movie about snuff films, in this case a film about murdered prostitutes. The fact that sexuality is central to the premise is perhaps secondary to director Michael Powell's commentary on observation. Always filming on the fringes of the action, the killer is not one to easily be led into the spectacle; instead, he is more concerned with capturing the surrounding atmosphere. He wants us to believe that we're witnessing his executions, though they take place offscreen. Mark acts as a director, choosing which view to show the audience, and what he permits others to see. This is echoed by his work environment—the chair in his dark room is that of a director's chair, on which his name is printed. Through his films, Mark establishes control. But this control is loosely held. His dark room is located in a basement, the site of his father's former laboratory. In his father's house (which he inherited), he is nervous, seeking ways to establish control in much the same way that Norman Bates did by murdering his over-protective mother.

4. Psychos, *Civic Unrest and Refining Horror*

We observe Mark on a date, in which Powell makes the audience a voyeur as well. By this point, we're fully aware that Mark is not to be trusted, but we're forced to witness the action on the screen through the dual nature of film—we create meaning as much as we witness action. Mark asks Helen (Anna Massey), "Do you know what the most frightening thing in the world is? It's fear." This becomes a cue for the viewer, who, besides being subjected to the obvious red herrings of staging and perception, is now forced to watch what happens, making Mark's question essentially for the viewer.

Powell captured something unique in the redefinition of the horror film, that being the suspense leading up to the kill. By showing Mark's monologue as a source of relief for the killer, Powell makes the audience a participant in the onscreen carnage. Mark explains that his victims became aware of the scene: "I made them watch their own deaths. I made them see their own terror as the spike went in. And if Death has a face, I made them see that, too." Powell has the audience watch as well. In doing so, the audience becomes complacent, resolving the fears of outsider threats by seeing it happen to another. *Peeping Tom* was thus reconciling the problem of horror by showing real-world fears in the safety of someone else's imminent death.

Although the film was too ahead of its time to save the career of director Michael Powell, *Peeping Tom* has an empathetic side, one that captures Mark's all-too-aware sense of self-destruction. The film ends with Mark's suicide, amid a sea of flashbulbs, filmed as though he saw himself as a celebrity in his own alternate reality. Mark's life ends with the echo of his father's voice, saying, "Don't be a silly boy. There's nothing to be afraid of." But of course there is. Mark's fear is built on the prying world of the outside. With every move being captured either on film or audio, Mark is victim to his father's tests of voyeuristic study. This echoes the presence of Big Brother from George Orwell's *1984*, written in 1949. Orwell's dystopian novel is a testament to government surveillance and the watchful eye of the Inner Party elite that control society by limiting independent thought. However, most pervasive in *1984* is the ever-watchful eye of society that condemns individualism. This should not be disregarded when considering *Peeping Tom*.

Mark's goal as a photographer is to capture the world at large. Photojournalism is an exceptionally valid manner in which to "watch" society, providing the documentation through physical evidence as a testimony for actual events. On his date with Helen, Mark cannot give up his camera; it has become an extension of himself, taking the place of "seeing is believe" and replacing it with "believing is seeing." For something to have existed, it must be captured, allowing for it to be relived. *Peeping Tom* was evidence of the growing tensions of reality, where technology provided the means by documenting and thus preserving a state of consciousness. From his earliest recollections, Mark was filmed by his father, continually portraying a character that his father would document. He was both a subject and an experiment for his father to film. Mark states that his father's interests were, in fact, a condition in which he would study "the reactions of the nervous system to fear." In all probability, his father was trying to create a record for the future Mark, exhibiting a soul imprisoned by the fear of a generation. Little did he know that Mark would be the symbol of the next generation.

Powell's *Peeping Tom* was progressive in that it tried to capture the sentiments of the world through the fears it then faced. But as is the case of contemporary technologies, they lack the public understanding or assimilation to fully portray the afterthoughts that are envisioned to be potential sources of horror. Thus, there exists in the world of horror a two-fold nature: first, is societal terror, or those the contemporary society would readily recognize; second, there is progressive terror, that which builds on the current state and theoretically shows the downfall of society as a result of modern complacency. By the end of the 1960s, in order to capture the state of the world, directors turned to brazen plots about madmen and drugs, along with rediscovering the monsters of before and changing them to fit the looser standards of society. However, within the retelling of the horror story, some films sought to answer the problems of social breakdown. For instance, *Wait Until Dark* (1967) is the story of Susy Hendrix (Audrey Hepburn), a blind woman who is victimized by criminals in her own home. *Wait Until Dark* is unique in that it turns the paranoia of the times toward the audience, causing the viewer to feel guilty for watching what unfolds on the screen while Suzy herself cannot bear witness to the events taking place.

The difference is that while Susy is literally unable to witness these events, the viewer is fully aware that horror is in plain sight. Susy, at one point, actually realizes the importance of her isolation, taking in the benefits of darkness, as she thwarts her attackers. *Wait Until Dark* earned Hepburn an Academy Award nomination for her portrayal of the frightened yet brave Hendrix, but the film left too much to be seen. For horror to truly escalate in the imagination of the audiences, it had to portray the psychological terrors of society as a product of its own faults.

Rosemary's Baby (1968) is essential to understanding the psychological problems that struck the 1960s. The story's title character, Rosemary Woodhouse (Mia Farrow), captures the ennui and ineptitude of a society that is too comfortable with isolation and conformity. Despite the obvious references to the satanic and the occult, *Rosemary's Baby* is Roman Polanski's interpretation of a woman as the secondary figure to male-dominated success. Rosemary is a symbol of the successes of her husband, but "no matter what assurances are offered, no matter what charms and preparations she uses or ingests, she is not really safe. One of many indelible images in the film version of *Rosemary's Baby* is the pregnant but wasted-looking Mia Farrow dashing out against the light into midtown traffic, an apt metaphor for childbearing under socio-technological siege."[9] Yet the technological strife is largely a byproduct. *Rosemary's Baby* has largely been interpreted as film about the occult, specifically that Rosemary gives birth to the Antichrist. But what, then, should audiences consider as the devil in society? At the beginning of the counter-culture movement, *Rosemary's Baby* demonizes conformity, where the outsider faces the torments of a society that has accepted the New World Order—in this case technological progress.

Technology had begun to encroach on public perceptions, specifically that, amid the constant recording and documenting of the minutiae of life, we were now helpless. Several films mirrored the voyeuristic aspect popularized by both *Psycho* and *Peeping Tom*. For instance, in *Lady in a Cage* (1964), the wealthy Mrs. Hilyard (Olivia de Havilland) becomes trapped in her apartment's elevator due to an electrical failure. Over the course of the film, she is terrorized by a drunk accompanied by a prostitute and three teenaged accomplices as they torture her and rob her of her belongings. This was followed by *No Way to Treat a Lady* (1967), wherein Rod Steiger plays an actor bent on murder. To accomplish his crimes, he creates an alter ego that treats each victim like a character in a play. To his end, he is enacting a performance. This is precisely the scenario behind John Frankenheimer's *Seconds* (1966), which provided an escape from the harsh realities of the real world. Arthur Wilson (Rock Hudson) is allowed the chance to "go back" and begin life again ... the way he wanted it (or imagined it) to be. If given the chance to escape, *Seconds* shows what the consequences would be. Many of today's horror films focus on young people, but the eerie recognition of *Seconds* is that horror isn't meant for the young. Sure, there are scares and the adrenaline rush of being afraid, but true horror isn't found until there is something to lose. Together, these films explore the rise of onscreen torment. But one film in particular explores the rise of this new subgenre of horror through the method of placing the viewer as a willing participant, an onlooker that, in essence, helped create the monster on the screen.

Fueled by youth culture and hot rods, Peter Bogdanovich's *Targets* (1968) features a young man bent on taking his revenge on society. Bobby Thompson (Tim O'Kelly) is a Vietnam veteran who, despite his outwardly well-adjusted life, turns into a senseless killer. We are given a glimpse into his mind as he writes his farewell to a world from which he, like Norman Bates and Mark Lewis, feel disconnected. Bobby's note reads:

> TO WHOM IT MAY CONCERN:
> IT IS NOW 11:40 A.M. MY WIFE IS STILL ASLEEP, BUT WHEN SHE WAKES UP I AM GOING TO KILL HER. THEN I AM GOING TO KILL MY MOTHER.
> I KNOW THEY WILL GET MAINE, BUT THERE WILL BE MORE KILLING BEFORE I DIE.

At home, Bobby kills his mother, his wife, Eileen, and a boy that had just arrived to deliver groceries. But the motive for Bobby's actions are never revealed to the viewer. Instead, we bear witness to the recklessness of youth gone wild. Once Bobby sets his plan in motion, he becomes reckless, weaving his car through traffic and running red lights, yet cautious of being caught. His mindset is punctuated by the sounds of his radio. Peppered throughout scenes of Bobby's driving are the loud, whining noises of electric guitar music as he commands his Mustang. Like Marion Crane, Bobby is set free in the private world of his automobile and the escape of the rock music on the radio.

Aside from the main plot of a killer is the large subplot about the nature of the horror industry itself. Initially, Bobby sits atop a water tower to shoot at passing vehicles, creating a pileup on the highway of cars and bodies. But, once he is discovered, Bobby retreats to the nearby drive-in, where famed movie star Byron Orlok (Boris Karloff) is scheduled to make a live appearance, before fading quietly into retirement. Along with his appearance, one of Karloff's actual films, *The Terror* (1963), will be screened. In an earlier scene, discussing the film industry with novice film director Sammy Michaels (Peter Bogdanovich himself), Karloff discusses the changing reality of the horror genre: "Everybody's dead; I feel like a dinosaur. I know how everybody thinks about me these days—old-fashioned, outmoded." This subplot of old Hollywood horror against the backdrop of the lurking threat of social breakdown is a crucial turning point, displaying Bogdanovich's awareness of how refinement of the horror genre is necessary: "Bogdanovich created a cinematic elegy for Hollywood's golden age. Largely overlooked in its day and mostly forgotten now, it remains one of the unsung masterpieces of the New Hollywood period: a brilliant meditation on the evolution of onscreen horror and one of the most terrifying depictions of gun violence in movie history. In the end, the conditions proved crucial to the film's success; *Targets* wouldn't be half as effective without Karloff and *The Terror* playing themselves."[10] Interestingly, Karloff displays a subtle humor in his role of Orlok, stating that he gets to play "a human being." The man who made a legacy on playing monsters is, for once, able to play the hero. Perhaps it is this catharsis that signaled the change upon which modern horror is built.

Paranoia was central to the 1960s, mostly because of the feeling of loss that overcame many people. This is the motivating ideology behind *Targets*. Bobby's victims are chosen at random, but their deaths are no less troubling for the audience. Through a carefully directed sequence, Bogdanovich punctuated the violence in much the same way that Mark Lewis captures his victims, by simulating the crosshairs of a gun scope: "Bogdanovich's camera (manned by director of photography Laszlo Kovacs) doesn't simply mimic the perspective of the sniper; it mimics the perspective of his bullets as well. As Bobby fires, the lens zooms toward Bobby's victims at high speed, following the path of the ammunition as it makes its way to its *Targets*. Many films have used point-of-view editing to make the audience feel like accomplices in a crime, and to call into question the audience's own motives for wanting to watch grisly violence. Few have used point-of-view editing to make the audience feel like the actual murder weapon, or to implicate the viewer so directly in brutality they've willingly chosen to witness."[11] Point-of-view is not just Bogdanovich's way of approaching terror; he's also deconstructing society. Bobby is a victim of society, but he should not be championed.

Targets shows the easiness of gun culture and Bobby's willingness to follow convention, despite the costs of his actions. Shortly after its release, Robert Kennedy was assassinated in the kitchen of the Ambassador Hotel, prompting Paramount to add an anti-gun warning to the film. Perhaps this was the problem that Bogdanovich saw as a turning point in society. America now had a culture built on violence and revenge, all the while seeking to establish territory over its own, collapsing reality. What's terrifying in *Targets* is the immediate distrust of others. This is articulated by an aside by Orlok, when he says that it is "strange not to hear the reactions" of the audience, noting the isolation of the audience, since each vehicle is itself free from the distractions of others. The audience itself has become a distant figure in the world of horror: "The shooter picks off one audience member after another, sitting in their cars, ignorant of the horror surrounding them. It was a metaphor of alienation and the ways that moviegoing can dull the senses. Stuck in their own cars, separated from one another, the audience is the ultimate monster. They cheer the violence on-screen, overlooking what is going on right next to them."[12]

As Bobby fires on the oblivious victims at the drive-in (the portable speakers in each car drown out the gunfire), he eventually takes aim at the elderly projectionist who inadvertently raises the volume as he collapses from one of Bobby's bullets. While some in the audience realize what is happening (either victims or those with victims), they shout to communicate the danger, while others blame those around them for the increased volume. Some people, realizing a sniper is on the loose, flee the drive in, while others yell out their windows, admonishing those leaving to shut off their car lights. The confusion escalates with car horns, accidents, and images of Bobby's victims. The scene ultimately becomes one of panic, where it is every carload of people for themselves.

Sammy arrives late to the drive in, only to learn of the carnage taking place. Rushing to the snack bar, he advises an attendant to tell the projectionist to stop the film. Upon discovering the dead projectionist, the lines from the screen film punctuate the chaos, such as, "Let me

4. Psychos, Civic Unrest and Refining Horror

see who you really are," and "Where are you?"[13] These lines, brought to full volume, mirror the chaos of the audience, both onscreen and in reality. Bobby's rampage is a quick and decisive torrent of bullets; he fumbles to reload his gun quickly after spilling them to the ground. As the film is abruptly halted and the bright stage lights illuminate the parking lot, Orlok realizes, quite by accident, that "that man has a rifle." At the same time, word has gotten around to the patrons. Sensing the trouble, the audience fights back; one patron is clearly seen with a pistol, further underscoring the pervasiveness of weapons in society. In a determined attempt to stop the mêlée after his assistant is shot, Orlok heads toward Bobby, an apparent standoff between old horror and new. Bobby is unable to distinguish between reality and fiction, as he shoots at both the real Orlok and the Orlok on the screen, both of whom are determinedly approaching him. He freezes, giving Orlok just enough time to disarm him. New Hollywood might be more frightening, but at least on this day, Old Hollywood still reigns supreme. As he's being led away by police, Bobby says, "I hardly ever missed, did I?" His satisfaction is devoid of any emotional attachment to his victims, just the hedonistic search for acceptance. The film ends with fans beseeching Orlok for a minute of his time, the arrival of police lights, and a wide shot of the empty drive-in as the credits roll.

Targets is not a murder mystery in the traditional sense, but it is still a mystery, one in which Bogdanovich asks the viewer to consider the breakdown of society. That theme would eventually be shown through George Romero's *Night of the Living Dead* (1968), which takes the terror of *Targets* and amplifies the senselessness of violence, this time in the form of mindless, cannibalistic zombies.

Night of the Living Dead completed the statements of Hitchcock's *Psycho*; horror had evolved to suit modern sensibilities of fear and distrust as a socio-political statement on the expectations of progress. Ultimately, we failed. Additionally, these films bookend the trial and error of the 1960s, that horror is a way of looking at ourselves. Romero heightened the reach of the horror film, showing that, despite our best efforts, we were constantly under attack by the social forces from within. However, this isn't to suggest that the zombies were a new monster, or that violence had eclipsed psychological horror; violence, after all, has always been a part of the horror film. But Romero pushed the level of its acceptability: "The American horror film had long been threatening its audiences with the sense that something dark and deadly was lurking at the edges of modern life. *Dracula* threatened defiling chaos, *The Thing* [from *Another World*] initiated an invasion of inhuman monsters, and *Psycho* unraveled the illusions of the American dream. In those films, the threat was always something that was on its way. With *Night of the Living Dead*, the threat to American security and optimism was over. The end had begun."[14]

The film is unique in that it is a reflection of social anxieties that didn't exist prior to the Vietnam War and the counter-culture movement. *Night of the Living Dead* became, like *Psycho*, a marked turning point, finishing the argument begun by Bogdanovich in *Targets*, asking society to rethink what true horror is. These films advance the horror genre from the classic Universal films of the 1930s to new (or modern) horror, which looks at our tendency to avoid the question entirely, instead masking over that which we should really be concerned. The tacitly implied competition of building a better life at any cost was costing some dearly. The continuous barrage of doomsday scenarios combined with the exploration of scientific progress of the 1950s led to a rather skewed view of life as it is presented in the next wave of horror films, culminating in a breakthrough of raw onscreen violence and terror.

In *Night of the Living Dead*, a group becomes stranded in a remote house amid a terrible scenario—the dead have come back to life. While many have focused on the racial undertones of the film and the apparent connection between youth culture and the consumption of American ideology, the real triumph of Romero's zombie epic is the complete and utter failure of social expectation: "In *Night*, Romero's zombies slowly and disturbingly shredded the last vestiges of American hope and optimism."[15] The Coopers, Harry (Karl Hardman), Helen (Marilyn Eastman), and their daughter, Karen (Kyra Schon), are first to arrive at an abandoned house, claiming the basement as their place of refuge. With the arrival of others (Ben [Duane Jones] and Barbara [Judith O'Dea], and teen couple Tom [Keith Wayne] and Judy [Judith Ridley]), Harry insists that they join his family in the basement. A power struggle ensues between Ben and Harry, the white establishment (Harry) against the youthful minority (Ben). More significant, though, is the theme of conflicting information found on radio and television, which resonated with audiences in their similarity to the news reports on the ongoing war in Vietnam. These reports spur the younger members of the house to action: Ben, for example, plans to seek help in a nearby town for the ailing Karen, who is suffering from a zombie bite. Unlike earlier films which showed the automobile as a symbol of escape, Ben's truck explodes in a violent fireball, leaving him (and the group) trapped, and Judy and Tom dead. After gaining entrance back into the house, Ben attacks Harry, who had locked him out. With the door open, the zombies swarm the house and attack the remaining survivors, except for Ben, who barricades himself in the cellar.

The following morning, Ben awakens to the sound of gunshots, as deputies clear the local fields of the living dead. However, sensing Ben's movement in the house, he is shot to death, which some interpret as symbolic of the young men who were dying in Vietnam: "The film's final moments, as the closing credits roll, consist of a series of grainy still photographs of the disposal of Ben's body on a bonfire filled with the now dead living dead. The sequence is made all the more disturbing as the photographs seem so realistic, reminiscent of the innumerable newspaper photographs from the war in Vietnam and domestic civil unrest."[16] Before horror films resorted to exploring violence as a means of expressing angst, there was a buildup taking place, something of an onscreen downward spiral depicting society's losing battle with its own values: "We leave *Night* with nothing but an overwhelming sense that the oppressive, chaotic world around us may be insurmountable. As R. H. W. Dillard observes, *Night of the Living Dead*, "as a whole undercuts most of the cherished values of our whole civilization."[17] *Night of the Living Dead* follows a tradition, finalizing the refinement of the horror genre, bringing audiences a new method by which to visualize the cacophony of social unrest and distrust first set in motion by *Psycho*. Romero's low-budget film centers on graphic portrayals of carnage as a central image showing the horror of society. Singlehandedly, Romero popularized gore.

Chapter 5

The Mainstreaming of Underground Horror

Shlock, Special Effects and Slashers

> You never bring it out in the light...—John Carpenter, on what makes monsters successful for audiences

In 1954, the establishment of the Comics Code of the Comics Magazine Association of America brought about the end of a publication that would both popularize and inspire horror fans for decades to come. EC Comics started out as Educational Comics, publishing *Picture Stories from the Bible* and *Land of the Lost*. But, after founder Max Gaines's untimely death in 1947, the company was placed in the hands of his son William. Bill Gaines, seeking an edge to attract new audiences after a recent rise in readership of comics, changed the name to Entertaining Comics, and with the change established a line of horror, crime, and suspense books aimed at younger readers, offering westerns, romances, science fiction, and, most notably, horror, where one book set the industry standard for occult stories. This was *Tales from the Crypt*. The stories in *Tales* depicted in glorious detail the absurd fates of those who went against society in order to make personal gains, usually through twist endings or macabre reveals on the final pages. In establishing the horror genre of comics, Bill threw out every guideline that his father set forth, including, "Never show a coffin, especially with a corpse in it. Don't chop the limbs off anybody. Don't put anybody's eyes out. No blood or bloody daggers, no skeletons or skulls.... Never show the kill."[1] Given his father's influence, Bill had made a choice, one that entered an agreement with his readers. He knew that what was shown was not for the sake of excess but for entertainment.[2] Fans soon found themselves engrossed in crude, simple humor, written with a subtle sense of wit, at times chastised by the narrator of books for choosing an "inferior" publication. This, of course, helped to establish the fan base for horror comics. In many ways, the stories from *Tales From the Crypt* were lessons in morality, but they were most important in their inspiration for the upcoming legions of horror filmmakers by showing a world that was taboo.

Gaines was ahead of his time, giving readers a taste of their own imagination. Apparently, that was too much for mainstream America; soon, comic books fell victim to censorship. Charged with indecency, Gaines pulled the offending titles from further circulation prior to the enforcement of the CMAA decency standards, which (listed by David Hadju) included:

- No magazine shall use the word horror or terror in its title.
- All scenes of horror, excessive bloodshed, gory or gruesome crimes, depravity, lust, sadism, masochism shall not be permitted.
- All lurid, unsavory, gruesome illustrations shall be eliminated.
- Scenes dealing with, or instruments associated with, walking dead, torture, vampires and vampirism, ghouls, cannibalism and werewolfism are prohibited.[3]

Other conditions demanded that comic books maintain respect for parents, clean up language and exclude obscenities, and uphold the sanctity of marriage. And, though Gaines continued to sell reprints in hardbound form, EC Comics never had the same impact within the comic book industry. However, Gaines and the stories of EC Comics had a lasting effect on horror as a genre.

Horror comics tapped into an audience that was still developing in the early stages following the counter-culture movement: the youth market. Barring an outlet from the conformity of the previous generation's conservative ways, horror comics offered an alternative: "They stood apart from virtually every source of information and entertainment available to young Americans in the early 1950s. Mainstream culture at that time exuded conformity and consensus behind Cold War imperatives, established authority, and white middle-class mores."[4] Beyond escape or fantasy, horror comics provided a glimpse of the world that existed outside the ordinary, but still existed in the darkness of human thought. Central to the depiction of violence in horror comics was the essence of realism. Realism, though, should be seen as a two-fold idea—(1) the realistic portrayal of graphic images, and (2) the realistic portrayal of man. Mad scientists producing overly complex experiments provided a shield for early viewers. To consider the monster evil, be it man, monster, or machine, the audience would recognize that the figure was beyond their ken. For early depictions of graphic violence, the shield was the page. That horror existed two-dimensionally as an animated concept, the belief that horror would spring from the page was virtually eliminated. The same was true with early science-fiction films posing as horror films.

While these films were about inherent dangers, they could not replicate the same feelings of dread or terror that were suggest by the story. This was due to the fact that early films lacked the necessary qualifications to be considered horrible for new audiences. The problem with "monster movies of the fifties and sixties [was that] they are not badly written, badly acted, or badly made—until the monster shows up. And then it's some guy in a stupid suit. The monsters are stupid and the plot is smart. That changed in the seventies when the plots became stupid and the monster smart."[5] In the early EC comics, the monsters were able to take any shape they wanted, provided that an artist was skillful enough to create the image on the page. And playing to the audience's awareness of the page as a reflection of a mindful interaction with the author, the two-dimensional recreation of horror was both safe and pioneering. This could not be translated to film; even though the writing was good, the horror was often lost in a sea of models and unseen intimations of horror that takes place largely offscreen. With limited resources, films were unable to inspire the imagination in the same way as horror comics.

This would change with advances in movie making, specifically through the rise of special effects. Following the decline of the Hayes Code,[6] horror films opened up in terms of their willingness to show violent actions (and, likewise, gory depictions of violence) on the screen. Slowly, films depicted more and more violence, but these offerings were largely low-budget (or B-films), much like the previous entries in the science-fiction staples of the 1950s. These films, pioneered by independent filmmakers, were made for the sole purpose of profitability.

5. The Mainstreaming of Underground Horror

One filmmaker, Herschell Gordon Lewis, discovered that audiences were getting tired of morality. Lewis realized that in order to capture the most attention, he had to show audiences what they hadn't already seen—graphic violence. "As audiences became progressively inured to watching pain and suffering on the screen as a means of escape from their own lives—an escape through indifference to the suffering of others,"[7] they began to find that the screen too often reflected the horrors of the real world. Films became a saccharine depiction of reality with the advent of television. Ironically, it was television that assisted in the move toward more graphic films.

With the sale of classic films to television, youthful viewers were introduced to the classic monsters of the 1930s and '40s. Showcased on such series as *Shock Theater* and *Creature Double Feature*, these films were past visions of horror, completely unreflective of the viewers' own state of being. While fewer mainstream horror films were being produced, the classic films were often supplanted with low-budget contemporary horrors, such as *Godzilla* and *Creature from the Black Lagoon*. It was then that society went through an adjustment period, where Heffernan's suggestion of realization of society is furthered. To combat the reaches of television as an alternative to big-budget productions, "The industry made many changes to adapt to these conditions, including technological innovation, new patterns of distribution, increasingly aggressive advertising campaigns, independent production, co-productions with the film industries of Great Britain and elsewhere in Europe, and the sale of features to television. The low-budget genre cinema of the fifties and sixties plays an important role in all of these adaptations."[8] To extend profits, Hollywood took fewer chances on production, limiting their filming schedules, sacrificing talent and realism for quick release.

Adding to this was the impact television had on public perceptions on violence. The Vietnam War was a nightly source of horror, broadcast directly into homes, earning it the nickname of the "living-room war." As people tuned in for nightly developments, the effect was two-fold. It contributed to the anti-war mentality that pervaded the counter-culture movement, as well as perpetuating the lost values of society, paving the way for graphic depictions of violence and gore in theatrical films. Television, it seems, was what fueled the adjustment that Heffernan suggests was happening during this time. Technology became a necessary part of modern living; fears of flying saucers and mad men were abated, and the world at large became a new source of horror. Society was awash in technology: "Technological innovations—freezers, washers, dryers, televisions, and automobiles—freed the homemaker from the daily grind of shopping, washing, and seeking information or entertainment, but the freedom from daily necessities was limited by the overall sense of isolation wrapped up in the suburban vision. Families achieved their dream of conspicuous consumption—a gorgeous showcase home in an affluent suburb—but the dark underside was a sense of confinement, isolation, and confusion."[9] Underneath the living-room atmosphere of entertainment, something was brewing. Nöel Carroll writes that "horror, a genre which may typically only command a limited following—due to its basic powers of attraction—can command mass attention when its iconography and structures are deployed in such a way that they articulate the widespread anxiety of times of stress."[10]

As evidenced in Hitchcock's *Psycho*, the realization that society was failing itself was evident. Now, after Vietnam, as soldiers returned home having seen the real-life atrocities of which mankind is capable, society had to once again consider the best path forward: "In the 1960s, confidence in promises of modernization coexisted with a distinctly antimodern criticism of contemporary life. Despite economic growth and social reform after World War II, there remained a deep suspicion, voiced by romantic, radical, and conservative thinkers, that dark forces of power and destruction were endemic to modernity. The tendency to see modern life as a catastrophe only gained strength among social critics as the Vietnam War revealed again (for those who had forgotten) the death-dealing capacity of modern technology."[11] Technological advancement came with a price. The modern world was both a window into society and a prison, captivating audiences with a dazzling array of information and insight, but with no release, no finality, and no moral to explain the violence on display. America was in a stalemate with its own conscience.

The Development of Special Effects

While Lewis stumbled upon gore in his films, his films were at a level that mimicked amateur theater—they were bloodfests, little more than hackneyed plots with bad acting. But, they were successful, at least to a degree. It was Romero's *Night of the Living Dead* that exploited the visual aspects of the story's horror. Romero employed a stylistic element that reflected the horror of the nightly entertainment to which Americans had grown accustomed, that of senseless violence. By doing so, Romero reflects "a stark and harsh realism. The documentary-style filmmaking removed the distance between the audience and the savage cannibalism portrayed on the film."[12] Of course, camera work and story are important to the effect of *Night*, but it was the gruesome realities of the walking dead that chilled audiences the most. That was provided by a newcomer to Hollywood. Makeup artist Tom Savini was a pioneer in the effects field, partly because he had lived through the horrors of the Vietnam War. Recently discharged from service in the U.S. Army, Savini was the best possible candidate to provide effects for Romero's ground-breaking film. Savini states, "Being in Vietnam gave me first-hand anatomical knowledge, you would say. There's a difference between the real thing and a fake head or something, ok? ... There's a feeling you get, it's a visceral feeling when you ... there's a real human being that this happened to, it's really, y'know.... If I don't kind of feel that when I'm creating something, that realism, it's not real enough to me."[13] Central to the new horror that would capture Hollywood was this sense of realism. Effects led audiences to believe the actions on the screen, and realistic makeup allowed performers to act more fully in character: "Y'know, you take an inhibited, mild-mannered person, you put a gorilla mask on them, and in 15 seconds they're swinging off chandeliers and hunched over, trying to be the monster, 'cause they're free. Nobody knows who they are, they can get away with anything, and they're just a gorilla. They become the mask."[14] And, for modern horror, the mask became the draw with which audiences identified. Like the classic horror monsters, the new generation of filmmakers and effects artists were busy cultivating a cult following intent on living their horrors, not in real life, but on the screen.

Dick Smith, another pioneering makeup artist, helped to establish horror effects as a mainstream element of modern horror. Smith, who produced blood formulas and latex appliances, would share his knowledge with other effects artists, who then passed the information on to others, improving upon the techniques along the way. Horror effects artists and makeup artists established a guild of sorts, professionals who were fans of the genre that accepted the challenge of producing lifelike effects that would impress their counterparts.[15] Without secrets, Savini explains the shared influences that effects artists had on one another. This led to the establishment of a community of artists that saw realism as an essential tool for capturing audiences. And it worked: "It's the make-up artist and the special-effects artist that makes dreams real."[16] Secondary to the effects, the stories would be what dictated the need for enhanced depictions of social downfall.

By many standards, especially those of today's zombie films, Romero's *Night of the Living Dead* is a landmark film that explores the darker side of human nature, albeit from the other side of human life. Romero is one in a long line of directors seeking to identify where, precisely, humanity fell from the graces of an idealistic society. As television increasingly became a window on society, Romero was aware of the impact of bringing war home to the entire nation. For many, television opened the eyes of mainstream society to graphic violence. Consequently, filmmakers were quick to capitalize on this: "Graphic violence, of course, fills *Night of the Living Dead*: A decomposing corpse is glimpsed upstairs in the farmhouse; skulls are crushed; and entrails, arms, and legs are devoured. The violence encompasses the entire film, particularly as the living people in the house turn violently on each other, and the film describes a world awash in violence. The situation is, as a newscast reports, one of 'wholesale murder engulfing much of the nation.'"[17]

Vietnam left some scars that would, perhaps unknowingly, leave an indelible mark on the future of the horror film. Savini was not a combat soldier, but he did see his share of horror on the battlefield: "I enlisted in the Army to stay out of Vietnam.... Because I was a photographer, looking through the camera, I felt a separation between myself and the stuff I had to photograph. It was almost like special effects. Seeing firsthand, y'know, anatomically correct gore. Every now and then, y'know, loading film or something, I'd look around and it would get to me. You'd come back to the States and guys just couldn't adjust to ... freedom, y'know, again, and all that stuff.... I adjusted easily, I thought. Um, it was within a year I finally noticed a sunset and thought it was beautiful."[18] Though it took time for Savini to enjoy simple pleasures again, the results of his wartime experience was a time of personal growth. Savini and others, seeking to take away the threat of living with

5. The Mainstreaming of Underground Horror

Vietnam in the background, gave way to artistic license, doing so through the innovation of surreal effects: "Foam latex and related technologies made possible fantastic distortions of the human body, almost as plastic as those previously achieved only by painters and sculptors. Many of the horror and science-fiction films of the seventies and eighties began showing signs of imaginative kinship to the earlier visions of Francis Bacon and Salvador Dalí."[19] It was through creative license that Savini and others would find their niche in dealing with the effects of the Cold War, passing to their viewers a realization of horror that had yet to be witnessed onscreen.

Savini was recruited by Romero to work on his 1978 feature, *Dawn of the Dead*. And though many critics objected to the makeup in the film, Romero enjoyed the end result of the film's effects. Romero's corpses (which reflected a blue hue on film) looked like they came off the pages of a comic book. As the original *Night* was shot in black and white, the makeup was never updated for color film. Romero unknowingly bridged the gap between classic horror and new horror, presenting a new world with old sentiments, one that explored contemporary problems within the horrors that the old world pushed aside. He saw his zombie series as an extension of old, two-dimensional graphic fears brought to a new age.

Like Romero, Toby Hooper realized that the way to mainstream success wasn't tact, it was gore. Hooper's limited budgets forced him to cut back on many fronts, but his 1974 film *The Texas Chain Saw Massacre* is nonetheless emblematic of horror's appeal; despite production overruns and a nameless cast, Hooper bravely dared to explore the darker underside of American life. Because of the violence, Hooper was unable to attain the PG-rating he was seeking, leading his film to be marginally viewed (and banned outright in many countries). Eventually, Hooper's audience would grow through a medium that bypassed the censorship and scrutiny of society. Home video, specifically the VHS tape, was an affordable and exchangeable alternative to theatrical viewings. Instead of paying to rent a film, viewers could easily afford to rent videos and watch full-length movies in the privacy of their own homes. Home viewers were also able to choose from a much broader and varied selection of titles that would never appeal to the general public, but found an underground niche with horror movie enthusiasts.

The Rise of Home Video and Big Budget Horror

The earliest horror films were fairly tame because of necessity—they had to appeal to a wide-ranging audience. Following the unabashed (for the time) violence seen in the 1960s through films like *Psycho*, the horror film was once again rising to the mainstream, seeking an audience that identified with the new horrors of society. But it would take several turns before it re-attained the status it enjoyed during the 1930s. With the videocassette and the institution of privacy in film selection, there began a shift that ultimately changed the public's perception of horror: "At the beginning of the 1970s, the movies were primarily a collective experience—something seen regularly on large screens in specially designed theaters with masses of other people. By the decade's end they had become something that could also be carried around in a briefcase or shopping bag for video playback at home."[20] Privacy in watching films took away much of the personal stigma in watching certain acts, whether they were pornographic or violent in nature. Additionally, following the institution of the MPAA ratings system in 1968, which separated film content by age constraints, the MPAA unintentionally popularized films considered taboo.

Horror films work in cycles, where writers and directors often imitate their predecessors as a way to establish their own narrative voice and fine-tune technique. As a wave of new directors tested the limits of horror in the wake of films like *Psycho* and *Night of the Living Dead*, horror began to show signs that pointed toward greater psychological inquest combined with the graphic depictions of violence through gore. But these explorations were largely explored through the rise of underground filmmakers and film students, not unlike Romero's crew in *Night of the Living Dead*. Because of cheaper technologies, many films were being made without the backing of a major studio. The success of low-budget films like *The Texas Chain Saw Massacre* proved that horror was profitable. It wasn't long before Hollywood capitalized on horror as a means to large profits, but the overall effect was still far behind the comic book depictions of gore and violence that audiences could find in underground films. Two notable exceptions to the rule were the mainstream successes, *The Exorcist* (1973) and *Jaws* (1975). Both combined the "everyman" idea of where horror occurs, but made "more subtle and more powerful by more money and more care."[21]

For the time being, horrific gore was still relegated to B-film status. The techniques of special effects were seen as kitschy and subversive, but the reality behind underground films echoed in the depictions of violence as much as their need for quick profit: "Part of the reason that Spielberg kept the shark in the water in *Jaws* was logistical. The mechanical monster never worked. The crazed, sweaty faces in *The Texas Chain Saw Massacre* reflected the reality that shooting a cheap movie in Texas in August is a horror in itself. *The Last House on the Left* [1972] captured a documentary feel by using handheld cameras, because Wes Craven didn't know about dollies. There was an element of innocence about the business in the low-budget films of the seventies that allowed the directors to do things differently, to take chances and try crazy ideas."[22] The rawness of horror films of that time was built upon technological innovation. Although many new filmmakers lacked training and were working with rudimentary skills, they employed innovative techniques that enabled horror to progress beyond the imitative and become innovative. Without studio backing, there was little concern for what new filmmakers could show on film. However, there was a dependence on economics when it came to producing their films: "For independent filmmakers, like those behind the teen slashers, economic concerns played an enormous role in their conduct due to their inability to spread risk, unlike MPAA-members, across a broad range of different films."[23] *Jaws*, with dazzling special effects and a relatively big budget solidified horror as needing more realism, concerning both content and quality. The growing impact of special effects invited viewers to explore the darker side of human questions of mortality and meaning (as was still of large import following the Vietnam War), while the subjects of films turned to attacking us where we were supposed to feel safest. Following the popularity of *Night of the Living Dead* and *The Texas Chain Saw Massacre*, for horror films to capture audiences, they had to add realism through gore and social ambivalence. And no one understood this better than John Carpenter.

The Rise of the Slasher Film

John Carpenter grew up a fan of comics, specifically those involving weird mutant ants and space monsters, where stories relied on the pacing of the comic book itself. At the heart of comic book horror was anticipation. From his first theatrical scare when watching *It Came from Outer Space* (1953) in 3D with his mother when he was just four, Carpenter began making movies at home. Equally important to his sense of development was that he studied classic horror, learning "pacing, and Hitchcock's rule of suspense, that the anticipation is more important than the zapper, from fun houses when he was a kid. 'I realized the fun of it all was not the moment of the jolt, but the whole waiting for it to happen while I was finding my way down the corridor.'"[24] Carpenter would seek to establish the same jolt of expectation as the primary motive for future horror films, beginning with *Halloween* (1978). Wearing a James Kirk mask painted white, Michael Myers has at least one thing in common with Norman Bates: both kill for unknown reasons. Norman is repressed from developing anything other than his mentally ill mother's idealized idea of the world. On the other hand, Michael Myers was institutionalized as a child for killing his sister, escaping to terrorize the town of Haddonfield, Illinois.

Carpenter ushered in the next wave of horror, depicting youths as a force of social change. And, most importantly, his film was a box-office hit.

> *Halloween* took most people in Hollywood completely by surprise. Most crossover horror movies were based on bestselling books. The classic movies (*Frankenstein, Dracula*) as well as the popular new ones (*The Exorcist, Rosemary's Baby, Carrie*) had a literary pedigree that gave the audience the excuse that the cheap thrills were somewhat respectable. But this one was slapped together. There was no popular title or famous actor or star to exploit. There was just a great title and word of mouth. *Halloween* was actually the result of years of hard thinking about monsters, but its real accomplishment is how Carpenter made it seem as if all you needed to make a great horror movie was a girl, a big killer, and a knife. He made it look so easy. The studios saw that a movie made for next to nothing could bring in almost $100 million in box office. They wanted in. The exploitation horror movie would never be the same. *Halloween* proved that cheap horror could be big business.[25]

Once horror films achieved main-stream status, some of the mystique behind obscure storylines and *avant garde* theatrics seemed to wane from the underground thrills of B-movie horror films. For a while horror "cranked out Westerns in the old days to play. That's what we did. We made these horror films."[26] Eventually, horror directors realized

5. The Mainstreaming of Underground Horror

that repetitive and formulaic horror would reach audiences. Mainstream horror wasn't able to keep up with the cheesy, knowing disappointment expected from bad horror. With the proper funding, horror established itself as a genre capable of exploiting our deeper anxieties beyond the scientific; taking horror to the realm of everyday life, it would eventually move beyond formula and search for the horror of everyday life. And reaching far beyond the ordinary was exactly what filmmakers and effects artists did: "By the 1980s, special effects in the popular media were the closest encounter with the miraculous that a secular culture could muster; the vast appetite for transformation illusions bespoke a deep, unmet hunger for images of transcendence and transfiguration."[27]

Horror films began to exploit our reliance on being apart from society, transforming the outsider into the hero. Underneath the successive gore that the slasher film helped to institute as a mainstay of horror, its youthful audience was forced to turn inward to see society's undoing as a product of their own ignorance. Like Frankenstein's Monster, Dracula, the Wolfman, the Mummy, and the Invisible Man, the new breed of horror stars—the slashers—were themselves personalities that existed outside the ordinary realm. Nor were they seeking to fit into society or be accepted; they were bent on taking revenge on those who helped to create them. Michael, Jason, Freddy, and Chucky exhibit a wide dispersion of back story, motivation, and ethical judgments (or lack thereof) that displays an ignorant acceptance of the sacrifices of the previous generation. These "monsters" seek to destroy those now holding control of and dominating society.

A virtual copy of Michael Myers, Jason Voorhees is the killer in the *Friday the 13th* franchise, which began in 1980. With his looming gait, solid color jumpsuit, and weapon of choice (Jason's machete substitutes for Michael's knife), they are quite similar in that they are both children of neglect: Michael was left alone at home, while Jason was left to drown by neglectful camp counselors. And both kill in an environment largely run by adolescents. But *Friday the 13th* is unique in that the location is a direct return to Gothic horror, where a fear of the dark is heightened by its location and removal from a technologically evolved society.

The slasher flick dominated the 1980s by combining senseless killings with increasingly graphic special effects. Jason Zinoman, author of *Shock Value*, asks a pertinent question that determines our understanding of the slasher film: "The best horror movies are like fairy tales, tapping into something more universal than fear of racism or shark attacks. The central challenge of the modern genre is this: How do you scare adults so much that you make them feel like kids again?"[28] Wes Craven understood this by scaring people where they couldn't escape—in their dreams. Craven's *A Nightmare on Elm Street* franchise focuses on Freddie Krueger (Robert Englund), a pedophile janitor who was burned alive by the neighborhood's parents—the ultimate display of vigilante justice. However, despite the parents' efforts, their progeny become Krueger's victims in a series of bizarre murders. The children, largely ignored by their parents, are left to fight the villain on their own, relying on telephone conversations and caffeine pills to avoid falling asleep—a direct commentary on the expanding 24-hour culture of the 1980s.

While the mid- to late-1970s saw an increase in horror movie budgets, the 1980s' offerings saw a downturn, as the industry took a schlock attitude toward the technological advancements of art-horror. This is clearly evident in *Child's Play* (1988), in which Chucky, otherwise known as notorious serial killer Charles Lee Ray, takes refuge in a "Good Guy," an animatronic doll that was the hottest toy on the market. Through a ritualistic transfer of his soul to the Good Guy, Chucky seeks a host body so that his soul can be reborn. As in Romero's *Dawn of the Dead*, *Child's Play* explores our slavish devotion to consumerism, here displayed in the guise of a technological fad. The slasher films, seen as a group, further the idea of society by exploiting the dangers that lurk within that new and revitalized society of modern culture. Despite their foundations in the fallout of Hitchcock's *Psycho*, modern slasher films are emblematic of social failures and expectations of the modern age. They also pay homage to the development of special effects, displaying an awareness of previous forays into art-horror as a way to bridge social consciousness. But beyond each franchise's initial entry into the canon of horror films, each one falls into the repetitive use of gore as a means of experimentation.

Despite their redundancy, films like *Child's Play* (and its four sequels) were largely popular with audiences, though "none of the popular hits of the eighties matched the intensity of *The Texas Chain Saw Massacre*, the cultural impact of *The Exorcist*, or the artistry of *Alien* and *Halloween.*"[29] What kept each film going was innovation matched with a continual cycle of reinventing the monster. But we should be aware that the monster is never what we think it is. In the slasher film, the monster is never the popular killer that we've come to love. The monster is a reflection of ourselves. Our reliance on keeping the world from evolving is ever present—characters, whether inheritors of a world from the previous installment or continuing characters from previous storylines, commit repetitive mistakes. This leads to the fun of the films. They become predictable, and audiences, by seeing new executions and innovative death scenes, see the monsters as heroes.

Rather than discuss the immortality of the slashers (as it has been extensively discussed, for both reasons of popularity and profitability), it is important to look at the demise of the slasher film as a turning point of social horrors. There came a point when even the heroes of slasher films—the killers themselves—realize their own absurdity throughout the sequels. In *Friday the 13th Part VIII: Jason Takes Manhattan* (1989), a group of students celebrate their graduation by taking a luxury cruise around New York. Jason's body is pulled up from the water, and though he is able to sink the boat (and kill many in the process), some of the students are able to escape to Manhattan, where he follows to stalk them throughout the city. Despite the absurd premise, Jason's turn in New York City is both important and expected. Not only has he left the confines of Camp Crystal Lake and entered the civilized world, he has also taken on the "better stay awake" mantra exhibited in *A Nightmare on Elm Street*, now on display in "the city that never sleeps." Backed by the image of Time's Square, with neon lights and an explosion of commercial enterprises, Jason's appearance in the big city is a death knell to the slasher film. Though he would eventually travel to space and fight Freddy in a much-anticipated match-up of 1980s horror greats, the fear that Jason commands in a technologically absent world couldn't be matched in a world that eventually became connected 24 hours a day.

The most ingenious approach to the slasher genre as a repetitive play of consciousness is *Wes Craven's New Nightmare* (1994).[30] The story begins on the set of a new film, where an actor is fitted with Freddy's now-familiar bowler hat, striped sweater, and glove. However, in this new adaptation, Freddy's famous gloved hand is replaced by a robotic hand that runs amok; even after the power is cut, it is able to function on its own. The film brings us to reality, where actress Heather Langenkamp (Nancy from the first and third installments), plays a fictionalized version of herself. In the film, Freddy is an amalgamation of public consciousness. He haunts Heather's dreams in the same way that audiences were haunted by the original films. In part, Heather has become a victim of her role. The same is true for Craven, who plays himself seeking to film one last version of his monster. Throughout the film, we learn that Craven's dialogue is that of his new film, an unconscious reproduction of events to come, leaving the viewer unsure as to what is reality and what is a dream. Freddy is everywhere and nowhere at once. He is a development of existentialism of films like *The Exorcist*, where the devil inside Regan McNeil (Linda Blair) states, "I am no one." Likewise, the faceless killer of Michael Myers and the mask-donning Jason Voorhees are all emblematic of the evil lurking in society. But Freddy is different. He is recognizable. He is spoken of and to by name (often). This is mimicked in the portrayal of actor Robert Englund, whose portrayal of Freddy has become entangled with his own persona. Without his grotesque makeup, Englund is a kind and compassionate friend to Heather. However, in full makeup, he represents her deepest fears of fiction mimicking reality.

The end result is that Heather must accept the reality of her situation—that she has become part of movie history. Despite her transformation into a superhero single mom (after her husband, a special effects artist, is killed early in the film), she still bears the legacy of her role in Craven's films. The same is true of Freddy. Appearing on a talk show celebrating the tenth anniversary of the original film, Heather feels a great deal of anxiety, despite her protests that her new work in television enables her more family time. When pressed to answer questions about her son Dylan, it is clear that her discomfort (captured by the studio monitors) foreshadow the events of the film, with art imitating life, albeit one that is scripted. When asked if Freddy is really dead and if she would leave her son alone with "him," Heather responds quizzically, "Robert?" The host surprises Heather by inviting Englund onstage. He appears, dressed in character, mugging to an the audience, many of its members dressed like the popular killer, bearing signs reading "Come back Freddy!" and "Freddy Lives." It seems that Freddy has exceeded his own expectations. He is no longer a killer, but an icon.

The world of the late 1980s and early 1990s was much more pro-

5. The Mainstreaming of Underground Horror

gressive and connected than the isolated homes and back roads of slasher films at the beginnings of the genre. By the end of the 1990s, the slasher film ceased to be a source of horror, instead achieving a cult status for many the same way that classic horror monsters are viewed. The slashers helped to popularize horror and gore as a viable method for exploring the human condition, but it seems that society was ready for a new source of fear.

In each sequel, the killers remain the same, but the victims are continually updated to reflect the contemporary society. As society kept changing, the killers became stagnant, which is continually seen throughout the slasher film's tongue-in-cheek humor. We are brought along on a ride that has become predictable, from the brutality of death scenes to the killer's seeming inability to learn from the past. Audiences awaited Freddy's one-liners as much as they knew enough not to ask, "Who's in here?" The predictability of slasher films was as much a part of their fun as it was of their scare factor. Directors could arrange shots with music to cutaways of nothing, only to have the killer standing behind the next victim before they were aware of their impending doom. In this case, audiences were watching the demise of characters and enjoying the outcomes.

CHAPTER 6

Us vs. Them

Modern Horror and the Horror of Complacency

> We worked so hard for this.—Steve Freeling (Craig T. Nelson) watching his dream house implode in *Poltergeist*

Throughout the 1970s the theme that was most prevalent in the horror film wasn't that of senseless violence, as *The Texas Chain Saw Massacre*, *The Last House on the Left* and the growing number of slasher films would lead some to believe. Instead, the place of horror migrated from outside threats to the universal safety of home. Following the upheavals of social unrest of the 1970s, social angst receded with the rise of rampant material gains. It seems that, instead of embracing technological advancement, Americans sat back and relished the comforts of living, as opposed to furthering the social progress expected of the previous generation: "On an everyday level, technology was important but uncelebrated. The most prominent technological interface in the home—television—was well on its way to transforming American society, culture, and politics, but in ways that had fallen pathetically short of the hopes of a generation earlier."[1]

Television as a source of horror is notably found in Toby Hooper's *Poltergeist* (1982). Following the rise of the slasher genre and the changing focus of science fiction, Hooper shows that our resignation to the troubles of the outside world is directly connected with our reliance on technological ambivalence. The American Dream, it seems, was born again, taking up the counter-culture phrase popularized by drug enthusiast Timothy Leary—"turn on, tune in, drop out"[2]—as a means of reaching greater spiritual awareness and a commitment to change. And, it seems, a generation of Americans followed his advice, albeit in the same misguided way that Leary feels his message was misinterpreted as a calling to get stoned. With the rise of technology, American turned on more electronics, tuned in to popular culture, and dropped out of a healthy and communicative society. The result was a society that continually masked social problems by engaging in a collective ideology that promised safety in technological progress.

Perhaps Hooper was influenced by the realization of societal horrors evolving from the aspirations of domestic bliss, specifically technology as a source of modern society's reluctance to advance social progress by retreating once again into personal freedoms. This was the premise explored in Stanley Kubrick's *A Clockwork Orange* (1971). Kubrick explores the culmination of a society that wants more but can do little to control the society they presently have. Alex DeLarge (Malcolm McDowell) is a degenerate youth in a futuristic, dystopian London. The film centers on Alex and his droogs (underlings) as they create mayhem, living the same nihilistic pleasures we find in later slasher films. Alex and his crew borrow the slang and sense of freedom that resulted from the counter-culture movement, but they advance their freedoms by attacking society at large, not an idea; they do so without reason and revel in the bliss of pure anarchy. However, once Alex is incarcerated for the rape and murder of an aristocratic woman, he is given the choice to be "rehabilitated" through a series of conditioning experiments.

These experiments, it seems, were a means of cleansing society of the counter-culture movement, or as Alex says, "It was old age having a go at youth." But, Alex is keenly aware that horror, specifically violence, has a place in society. We watch, unsettled by the acts of Alex and his gang, while Alex, like an EC Comic, chastises us for watching such horrors, stating that there is a fine line between "doing it and watching it."

The irony of the film speaks highly to what Kubrick wished to show the audience, that of reform as an inconsistent wish for society's evils. Kubrick based his film on an American version of Anthony Burgess's novel, which omits the final chapter in which Alex finds a new trio of droogs to commence his previous life of violence, only to have second thoughts and consider joining in as a productive member of society, realizing that his own children would be worse than he ever was. This is similar to a child literally being held captive by a TV set, a troubling concept in *Poltergeist* that Hooper sees as the harbinger for social horrors of the next generation. And while television, long a household staple by the time *Poltergeist* was filmed, provided the horror of suburban living in the early 1980s, filmmakers would eventually move on to other sources of horror in the domestic household. Society can never be anesthetized of horror. Regardless of the wish for a better society, Kubrick and Hooper both realized that with every benefit there would be a new fear that would become embedded in the consciousness of viewers, and that with the memory of the Vietnam War, those fears would materialize once again within society. As horror films refined the idea of society, filmmakers began to exploit our feelings of safety in the ordinary. But before we realize the impact of technology and how society had changed, we should first discuss the need to escape the society that we had created.

It seems that, as horror moves away from printed books and is played out on the screen, how we access horror changes. Before, as was the case with some films already discussed, horror resided in the terrors of the unknown, and was something to be found purely in the imagination. But the changing world of technology moved quite quickly, creating new realities before the old ones had fully been experienced, much less appreciated. As shown in the dystopian views of social life portrayed in films such as *Rosemary's Baby* and *Targets*, ordinary society was increasingly being viewed as a much more frightening place. Thus, the monster has been reborn, turning our view of the social outcast from a simple villain into the outsider as one who spurns the greater progress of society. In doing so, the monster had taken on a much more human form, embodying our own skepticism and turning our notion of horror directly on our culture. The shifting impression of The Other as a horrific being is exemplified by many films, specifically where the demise of the heroic being is the center of horror. Consequently, horror has developed into a changing miasma or cloud of scattered recognition, often leaving audiences with multiple interpretations of where horror resides. One's horror is not another's horror, and the monster ceases to be a catch-all figure of a collective imagination. Instead, horror films developed to explore society at a point of no return: on the one hand, we share a universal culture; on the other,

6. Us vs. Them

our experiences as Americans differ widely. The counter-culture movement established a clear distinction between mainstream and underground society, where the social struggle to be an individual is contradicted by the need for acceptance and the natural limits of duty as expected of family and society. Growing and varied experiences opened up a world of choice, from music and clothing to professions and dwelling. The world was a place of opportunity. But, in order to achieve our dreams, we had to choose, opting between self interest and social constraints.

These differences are not new when it comes to exploring horror. Fred Bottling describes the connection of two varied worlds in the image and figure of Gothic fiction:

> In the negotiations of beauty and sublimity, and internally, in the dynamic of terror and horror, the subject of Gothic writing, the heroine, say, or the reader who, through identification, participates in her flights and frights, is constituted through a moment of loss and recovery. Gothic narratives, indeed, are based on and punctuated throughout by a series of losses. The loss of property, protection, family, name and social status precipitates heroines into an unkind world, while imagined losses of life, reputation or virtue threaten both body and identity.[3]

The rise of horror in our technological society works on the same level. We are faced with a prospect of losing comforts for the sake of what is perceived as progress. This is quite similar to Aesop's fable "The Country Mouse and City Mouse." City Mouse visits Country Mouse, promising a life much more advanced than his simple country existence. While enjoying a meal together in the city, they are disrupted by a pack of dogs, which forces the mice to flee. Country Mouse decides to return home, wishing to delight in the simple pleasures he knows, preferring that which is comfortable instead of a life where the gains are great but the cost to his state of mind would be greater. The parallel to modern society is palpable. Country Mouse retains that which is inside him, his sense of safety and security. On the other hand, City Mouse loses nothing, for he knows no other way of life: he's stuck in the rat race, so to speak. For modern Americans, the rise of societal progress was a gradual elevation of technological comforts. Soon, the loss of those comforts (or the loss of self through these comforts) would be seen as horror itself.

As Bottling suggest, horror is precipitated by a sense of loss. Following the overbearing sense of helplessness in the wake of both the Atomic Age and the Vietnam War, Americans had finally come through the cultural struggles of the 1970s to arrive at a time when it appeared society had stabilized. The 1970s was emblematic of social struggle, but this struggle was internal, not from external fears as experienced in the 1950s. Struggling to adapt to a new society following the post-civil rights movement in the early '60s, America was settling into a new realization of the future. Part of this awareness was the continual fear of keeping up with the American Dream, however tentatively it was achieved for the time. Unfortunately, this sense of progress was at the cost of some degree of freedom. Rampant consumerism and corporate mentalities blended the idea of individualism; instead, we became connected through a shared culture. Though society had yet to be transformed by technology, there was a growing feeling that Americans depended on technological advancement and automation as a way of upholding the newfound promise of social status.

The Horror of Progress

Prior to *Poltergeist*, amid the gore and schlock of the 1970s, two films looked directly at modern society through the conditions of humans' desire for progress, notably through achievement of status and escape. Though they employ some of the same elements of slasher films and science fiction, they are unique enough to devote space here as emblematic of signs of social stagnation and ennui. Both *Dawn of the Dead* (1978) and *The Shining* (1980) reflect a nascent awareness of cultural breakdown in the wake of the formidable ruin that was the failure of 1967's Summer of Love and the unrest of the 1970s. Together, these films look at the psychological impact of the modern world, depicting a society that had achieved progress. Their contradicting views of society should be noted as they offer a distinct impression of American life amid the rise of a high-tech society.

Dawn of the Dead is more than a zombie film exploring the darkest evil that its director, George Romero, could think of. Seeking to produce something different, Romero is quite candid about the response to his first zombie film: "The politics in *Night of the Living Dead* was an accident, but *Dawn of the Dead*'s political statement was not. Because of the critics, I knew we can't do a zombie movie for the fuck of it[....] It has to talk about the times, have a social point."[4] Knowingly, Romero sought to prove something to his viewers, thereby exploiting a complacent world instead of the worried and frenetic culture rooted in an unpopular war as he did in *Night of the Living Dead*. He wished to show the absurdity of society, having his second film take place in a mall. The zombies, slow and meandering, parade through the mall deliberately, while, after securing their safety, the living mall visitors "toy idly with an abundance of luxuries they don't really want, and start getting on each other's nerves. Like the gun fetishism and the exploding heads that surround it, the slow movement of *Dawn of the Dead* is vital to Romero's cartoon of American culture.... The heroes' survival has become a parody of the vanished society rather than an outlaw adventure."[5]

In their isolation, the living mall visitors are consumed by their own search for identity amid the numerous offerings and trinkets of modern society. In order to stay connected, their first impulse once inside the mall is to grab a television and a radio. In taking the items, Steve (David Emge) says to Peter (Ken Foree), his partner in crime: "Wake up, sucker. We're thieves and we're bad guys." Steve, by giving the items value in terms of corporate loss instead of as instruments of survival, negates any sort of necessity of connection to the outside world. He relishes this imprisonment, seeing it as a kingdom of comfort. Peter, on the other hand, still clings to the outside world. Ironically, the sanctuary is comprised as bikers loot the mall, allowing a walled off horde of zombies to invade the premises. Steve dies in the process, but not without putting up a fight to protect his small utopia.

Stanley Kubrick's adaptation of Stephen King's novel *The Shining* focuses on isolation, pitting a man and his family against the solitude of isolation. In *The Shining* (1980), Jack Torrance (Jack Nicholson) takes his wife, Wendy (Shelley Duvall), and their son, Danny (Danny Lloyd) to the remote Overlook Hotel, a mountain getaway that will be tended off-season by the Torrance Family. Removed from the world in the same fashion as the *Friday the 13th* films established, Jack becomes a victim of his isolation. While he works on his novel, he experiences a psychotic break from reality, which eventually leads him to hallucinate. Jack's psychosis isn't explained, although we can deduce that he is the victim of cabin fever, which is an apt metaphor for isolation amid a society dependent on connectivity. There are hints that he resides in a wormhole of sorts, living both in the present and as a reborn victim of the past (as evidenced in the photo at the end of the film), which is a significant clue to King's depiction of Jack's mental instability. Jack is caught between worlds, where the previous generation's reliance on self-sufficiency is overshadowed by his almost compulsive need for stimulation.

Central to the story is Wendy's connection with the local police department and the regular caretaker, Dick Hallorann (Scatman Crothers). She staves off boredom by communicating to those she's able to reach through the family's only connection to the outside world, an antiquated H.A.M. radio. But Danny, capable of powers beyond our ken, is able to reach Dick through telepathy. Dick references this special power as *shining*, where they both are able to communicate through a power that seems to be lost to modern means. They feel each other through the powers of empathy, something lost within the buildup of a consumer culture. The power of communication—whatever form it takes—between a little boy and a lonely, elderly caretaker should be recognized as the encroaching gulf between past and present. Nicholson's portrayal of Jack Torrance is that of a frustrated artist, but underneath he is caught between two worlds. He is angry seemingly without reason, signifying frustration at his place in the world. He is irrational because of his alcoholism, and despite his protestations that he wants what's best for his family (bringing them to the Overlook Hotel in order to escape temptation and revitalize his career), he's caught between his inner turmoil and his role as provider.

In *The Shining*, terror comes from a complete absence of the modern world. Isolated as caretakers of the Overlook Hotel, Jack and his family suffer the maelstroms of madness as incurred by Jack's need for contact with the outside world. Similarly, Camp Crystal Lake, the fictional setting of *Friday the 13th*, is a place that is unique in that there is a desire to be removed from society. Those who travel to Camp Crystal Lake were seeking an outright sense of isolation, a disconnect that is, in itself, a source of horror for today's audiences. But the separation between the two is, ironically, the means to the end. Jack doesn't turn on his family because he is psychotic—rather, he seeks entertainment. Isolated, he becomes the victim to his inner monologue, which is a pursuit in helping him achieve his personal struggle to regain recognition and notoriety.

6. Us vs. Them

Escaping the America Nightmare

Violent murderers were portrayed on the screen before Jason Voorhees; in Alfred Hitchcock's Psycho (1960) and Wes Craven's *The Last House on the Left* (1972)[6] each murder was in connection with a crime or wrongdoing that is being avenged. Hooper's *The Texas Chainsaw Massacre* (1974) is murder for sustenance, as the vacationing teens in this movie are attacked by cannibals. Marion Crane is hiding at the Bates Motel to avoid being caught for criminal embezzlement, where Craven's killers are defending their freedom from a jailbreak. Together, these films act as a commentary on the growing dangers of modern life. Each of the films above feature characters out of their natural element. The same is true for the counselors of Camp Crystal Lake. However, unlike the killers of these films, the crux of *Friday the 13th* is neglect. Mrs. Voorhees, a cook at the camp, takes her revenge on the counselors, blaming them as Jason (a lonely, disfigured child) escapes from his cabin to swim. Jason drowns, and Mrs. Voorhees (Betsy Palmer) cites the neglect of the counselors, who were partying in a cabin. Jason's death in 1957 is a lingering problem for the new owner, Steve Christy (Peter Brouwer) and his new staff in 1979. Despite warnings from local residents, Steve endeavors to provide his potential campers with what functions as the most dangerous aspect of the film's location, isolation, which works "to separate the characters from society at large and negates the possibility of a rescue."[7]

While gore in the slasher film is largely the focus, it should be noted that most slasher films attack our social safety built on the conveniences found in modern technology. There were many films of the 1970s that showed people isolated, away from the contact of others. Without power, there are no phones, no lights, and no communication with the outside. This is what's powerful in a film like *Friday the 13th*. Cut off from the outside world, there is no way to reach the comforts of modernity. Consequently, *Friday the 13th* is more about navigation of the terrain than the murders being committed. Victims are discovered by the use of naked light bulbs, flashlights and lanterns, in a place that is often seen as a refuge from the hectic workings of the everyday world. The lack of technology exploits the very essence of fear that isolation brings, something that had seemingly ceased to exist. Even with the perception of safety, isolation becomes a very real fear in horror films. As we are social beings, the perception of safety and privacy becomes challenged by horror films exploiting their absence.

The first tool of technology that brought the world together was the telephone. In several films, telephones blur the line between life-saving device and life-altering mechanism of destruction. When used for favorable means, it becomes a connective medium. In the horror film, the telephone becomes a nameless, faceless means for the outside world to make contact with us, thus eliminating the façade of safety found in isolation. For instance, in *Black Christmas* (1975), a sorority is held under siege by a murderous caller. *The Rocky Horror Picture Show* (1975) explores both the Frankenstein legend and underground culture when Brad (Barry Bostwick) and Janet (Susan Sarandon) stumble upon Dr. Frank-N-Furter's (Tim Curry) castle in search of a telephone when their car breaks down. In *When a Stranger Calls* (1979), Jill Johnson (Carol Kane) is terrorized by a sadistic stalker who calls her while she is babysitting at a client's house. *Don't Answer the Phone* (1980) features a disturbed Vietnam veteran who murders young women, all while confessing his delusions via a Los Angeles psychologist on a late-night call-in show. In *976-EVIL* (1989), people dial a phone number and receive special powers that turn them into supernatural killers. In *Phone Booth* (2003), Stu Shepard (Colin Farrell) is held captive in "perhaps the last vestige of privacy on Manhattan's West Side." Even with the newer films, the technology is still old—land-line telephones tether users to the perception of safety, highlighting the social blindness that accompanied the rise of technology.

Up to this point, the evolution of horrors of the home were still untainted by the reach of the Internet as a connecting force. Like Orwell's prophecy from *1984*,[8] the idea of Big Brother was still a far-off dream. People had yet to fear technology as stealing privacy; indeed, technology of the era emphasized privacy, allowing people to build walls against the outside world (a fact that will be further demonstrated later at the turn of the 21st century). But one problem is persistent when attempting to identify horror within this time frame—it is the idea of collective memory as it is enhanced/captured by technology. Hooper's first venture, *The Texas Chain Saw Massacre*, exploited the isolationist mentality of the counter culture. The wish to drop out of society was a futile prospect, to which the many failed communes bear evidence. The plot of *The Texas Chain Saw Massacre* is simple: secluded on a faraway farm, five friends seek an escape from society at a country house, only to be terrorized by a family of cannibals, the central killer of whom brandishes a chainsaw. This choice of weapon is special; aside from offering the most gruesome promise of violence, it is an ordinary object that was made to make life easier. Following *The Texas Chain Saw Massacre*, modern amenities—such as power tools and artificial light—became agents of horror themselves, where progressive measures challenge our idea of normal functioning society. Hooper's exploration of political strife, particularly the Watergate scandal, the 1973 Oil Crisis, and the backlash of the Vietnam War, echo the numbness of Americans who viewed the problems of society secondhand through television. Television, in this case, numbed the audience into a sense of security, as though the real terrors of society were "out there," never coming home to hurt the individual, despite often feeling the effects of political insurrection through increased gas prices and protest rallies.

The Texas Chainsaw Massacre was Hooper's first venture showing social ambivalence, changing the horror film, blending outsider Otherness in domestic settings to a warning of our need to escape the modern, technological world. This would be further explored by Hooper in *Poltergeist*, wherein the roots of family are obscured by the promises of escape through technology. However, escape comes in multiple forms. The dangers of television have long been explored since the 1950s, but following the new American acceptance of technology, Hooper's reliance on television as a gateway to evil is a dominant exploration of the horror of everyday life. Though the horror of *Poltergeist* is found in the television, it is ultimately realized in the misgivings of corporate America, similar to the numbness exploited in *Dawn of the Dead* and the reliance on others. But, once *Poltergeist* cemented into the American imagination horror through technological escape, the horror film would evolve, exploiting technology as a source of evil. That was first envisioned by the commonplace aspects of life at home.

Poltergeist begins with a familiar sound to all Americans, especially those who made a habit of falling asleep with the television on. "The Star-Spangled Banner" signaled the end of the broadcast day (a tradition abolished by the rise of 24-hour scheduling). At the song's end, the camera pulls back from the fuzz of static illuminating the sleeping Steve Freeling (Craig T. Nelson), the head of the household. It is a scene straight from the American Dream: the family asleep as the dog happily searches for neglected food throughout the house. Through the character of the daughter Carol Anne (Heather O'Rourke) Hooper shows us the full trance that we've entered with our dependence on technology. The family is both bemused and curious as they observe the child as she talks to something unseen in the blank static. Then, with the opening credits in the next cut, we are entertained by a montage of a quaint and happy towns, exemplifying the blissful acceptance of life in America: expanding suburbs, remote-control cars trailing a man on a bicycle bringing beer back to men watching football. It's Hooper's own version of Eden.

Hooper shows us scenes alternating between life (those who have embraced and live by technology) and death (the discovery of Carol Anne's bird "Tweety" at the bottom of his cage and her insistence on giving the bird a proper burial). There are signs that Hooper is speaking directly to us about the downfall of American culture, one hypnotized by television as a source of escape. For instance, the everyday life of the Freelings is tempered by a neighborhood dispute between houses with the same frequency of television remote controls. The mom, Diane (JoBeth Williams) casually lighting a joint after the children have gone to bed, is a sign that the counter-culture movement never died out— it just shifted focus, moving from the streets of San Francisco to the bedrooms of suburban America.

Yet another distinction that Hooper shows us in *Poltergeist* is the shrinking world of home and office. In the 1970s, the "suburban home was founded on its separation from both the world of work and from the world of others."[9] But this isn't the case here; Hooper gives us a forewarning of how technology will eventually cost us our freedom. Steve's job with a developer has led him to the very house in which he lives. During Carol Anne's absence, he is offered a position as a full partner, with his reward being a new home in a prime location overlooking a valley. When Steve quips that there is little room for a pool (a significant symbol of suburban achievement), his boss tells him that they will be moving the cemetery, remarking that its inhabitants are "just people … it's not like it's Indian burial ground." The film's development between superstition, progress, and future prospects are a telling sign of society's faults. This foreshadows the very problem of the development, that social progress has eclipsed the balance between past and present.

Despite its supernatural themes, *Poltergeist* resorts to a story about a missing person, built on a paranormal disturbance, similar to the haunted house stories of old. The differences are elaborated between "haunted house" and "poltergeist," specifically that of "time" and "place," where haunted houses are based on a singular location for a long duration, whereas a poltergeist is a paranormal event connected with an individual for a much shorter duration. Hooper goes to great lengths to show the evolution of horror through modern amenities. Ryan (Richard Lawson), one of Dr. Lesh's (Beatrice Straight) paranormal scientists, states that the presence is electrical: "You can smell the charge." Additionally, when attempting to contact Carol Anne in the otherworldly void, Diane tells the investigator to stop channel surfing: "We hear better on this channel. Don't ask me why." The specificity of the poltergeist (literally, a noisy ghost) is that of something connected to Carol Anne, where the spiritual phenomena, in this instance, have an electrical component. Hooper depicts multiple demons as having possession over Carole Anne. We are further witness to a mass of ghosts parading through the Freelings' living room. The sheer number of poltergeists suggests the multiple threats lurking in television. Perhaps this is why Diane states that one specific channel speaks to the family so readily.

In the end, with Steve seeing his boss to deny the job offer (or, as he puts it, give him directions on how to go to hell), amid the chaos of the final struggle with the powers of the house, Diane is briefly met by the neighbors, a subtle suggestion that social forces can be beaten by human contact. Steve comes to the realization that only the headstones of the cemetery have been moved, a final statement on corruption and corporate greed. Alone in the street, Steve's boss and the surrounding community watch as the house consumes itself. Homeless, the Freelings take refuge at a Holiday Inn, which we are made aware of by the framed neon of a quick cut (a subtle placement of the idea of home away from home). After shutting the door and signaling the end of the ordeal, Steve, as a last statement, opens the door to the hotel room and pushes the television onto the second-story walkway.

Horror Comes Home—America's Rental Culture and Viewing Horror at Home

Like the slasher film, many films exploiting the reaches of technology focus on children (such as Carl Anne) and teenagers, those most likely to adopt and rely on technology as a window to the world. For instance, in *Fade to Black* (1980), Eric Binford (Dennis Christopher) becomes enamored with a Marilyn Monroe look-alike (Linda Kerridge), who serves as a link to his interest in the Hollywood of the past. Relying on a series of elaborate costumes, Eric dresses up to kill Marilyn in order to still the homicidal rage pent up from his isolated viewings of classic monster movies. Bullied and alone, Eric represents a class of voyeurs that was a growing category of film viewers: the home rental audience.

Television became a central component in how we connected with the outside world. Americans settled down into a new era of home entertainment, replacing theatrical viewings with cable television and video rentals. Additionally, the VHS tape helped to change the homemade film industry, replacing reel-to-reel 8mm film with easy-to-use videocassettes. This technology made horror exchangeable, affordable, and widely available—instead of having to wait for a local theatrical viewing, horror films proliferated in the rental culture of the 1980s and early 1990s. This created a market where collecting films became a source of ownership; cinephiles turned to exploring genres and movie catalogues as a way to express their internal aspects of self: "Although this collecting enterprise foregrounds technology in a way that affects both collectors and films, cinema's very status as private property also helps to define this home film culture."[10] This would become the central focus of Wes Craven's *Scream* (1996). As a masked killer terrorizes Sidney Prescott (Neve Campbell) and the rest of the student body of Woodsboro High School, the film focuses on the revelry of a curfew. Randy (Jamie Kennedy) stages a house party highlighted by a viewing of classic horror films and a group discussion of the "rules" associated with the genre. In *Scream*, the culture of horror becomes the joke. But to understand the joke of horror clichés, the foundation of horror had to grow from an understanding: at some point, the old horrors had to become commonplace.

This reflexive attitude of old and new films is explored in *Fright Night* (1985). Charley Brewster (William Ragsdale) is a young horror film enthusiast, who becomes convinced that his neighbor Jerry Dandrige (Chris Sarandon) is a vampire. Reaching out to his idol, television host Peter Vincent (Roddy McDowall), Charley and Peter come face to face with horror that literally lives right next door. However, it is the cliché of horror that becomes the central focus of the film. Charley is well-versed in the horror genre, but there are "indications that even

Charley is starting to put older horror films behind him, just as society at large has done."[11] Just why Dandridge is fascinating for Charley (bordering on an obsession) may be that he defies conventional traits of the vampire, becoming "an amalgamation of the contemporary and the classical" that is fit to challenge the contemporary audience familiar with the growing catalogue of horror.[12] Aware that old monsters are fading from the public's idea of horror, it's relevant that Charley bases his assumptions on the reruns he sees in the comfort of his bedroom.

Following the rise of *avant garde* culture popularized by the resurgent counter culture emboldened by the legitimacy of MTV, popular culture became mainstream amid the influences of cable television and a rising consumer class. Soon, spectacle was on the rise, as evidenced through HBO's adaptation of William Gaines's *Tales from the Crypt* (1989–1996). Popularizing horror beyond the niche market, much in the same way that *The Twilight Zone* would popularize science fiction for audiences during the peak of the Cold War, *Tales from the Crypt* often depicted celebrities in the ironic twists of fate that were popularized by the original serial publications. With added emphasis on the depiction of realism through gore and the often quirky nod to its own "naughty" legacy, the series overwhelmed viewers with its macabre scenarios. However, the culture of watching as a voyeuristic and guilty act is embedded with the idea that seeking out horror is itself a violation of a moral code. As horror films began to explore the video culture and the tendency towards isolation of the audience, the primary motive of horror became our own curiosity, that there were "references to the home as a fortress in various sources reveal more about the cultural and ideological construction of the contemporary home than they do about the attainment of any actual sanctuary. That is, by depicting the home as a walled-off stronghold against the dangers of contemporary life, from terrorist acts to threatening microbes, industries attempt to create a siege mentality on the part of the homeowner."[13] It was long before our obsession with watching became the focal point, deepening the idea of voyeurism in horror.

A succession of films focusing on viewership emphasize the importance of television in modern society. David Cronenberg's *Videodrome* (1983) features an unscrupulous television programmer who broadcasts disturbing acts of brutality. Max Renn (James Woods) transforms into a literal receiver of his own programming when a tumor-like mutation causes hallucinations, including one in which his abdomen opens up and receives videotapes. After being reprogrammed, Max, in a final showdown with his television set, shoots himself in the head. He is essentially mimicking the images on the screen, the statement being that Cronenberg "predicts a sadomasochistic human future and contemplates our destruction as we lose our humanity" in the search for cheap stimulation.[14] In *The Video Dead* (1987), a mysterious television arrives that only shows one cheap black-and-white movie, *Zombie Blood Nightmare*. It turns out that the television is a portal to a zombie underworld. Most important to the reach of video culture was *The Ring* (2002), Gore Verbinski's adaptation of the Japanese film *Ringu*, in which a journalist (Naomi Watts) investigates a mysterious videotape that causes anyone who watches it to die within a week.

Cassettes, both audio and video, were one of the first transferable mediums that were available to mainstream society, allowing for the culture of video to be shared with others. Videotapes and recorded films provide documentary evidence, a record of events, and *The Ring* helps to substantiate the claims of urban legends. Therefore, "It is no wonder that in Hideo Nakta's *Ringu* (1998) and Gore Verbinski's U.S. adaptation *The Ring*, films about a videotape that causes anyone who watches it to die seven days later, the spectator/user has one loophole: to survive, s/he must become a home video 'filmmaker' too."[15] This is paralleled in *Sinister* (2012), in which true-crime writer Ellison Oswalt (Ethan Hawke) finds a box of 8mm films in the attic of the home he has just moved into with his family. These films depict a shadow figure, "Mr. Boogie," who inspires children to commit murders in his name. The films, which date to the 1960s, leave a record of the missing children, who continue the legacy of Mr. Boogie and his urban legend.

Horror and home seem to be built on the foundation of safety in technology, where the home becomes a refuge from the outside world. In fact, modern horror demonstrably shows that any influence from the world at large is a source of danger. This is true in *Vacancy* (2007), wherein a young couple becomes stranded when trying to drive home after a long weekend. David (Luke Wilson) and Amy Fox (Kate Beckinsale) take refuge at an isolated motel—one that only accepts cash (credit cards would leave a digital imprint of their arrival). In the perceived safety of their room, David decides to entertain himself with videotapes left in the room. He soon discovers, however, that these are snuff films.

After hearing a series of noises outside, David and Amy realize that the tapes were made in their very room. While *Vacancy* is reminiscent of *Psycho*, it is unique in that it presents an objective view of home as a sanctuary from the road. Tired and bickering, the couple finds a respite from their car and their long drive, which, we find out, has been the source of their fighting in the first place—they've decided to divorce. Their room at the motel is confining, for both their relationship and their peace of mind. Similar also to *Friday the 13th*, *Vacancy* focuses on the idea of isolation as a stimulus for fear. Additionally, it taps into the fears of perception, finding horror in the motel as a substitute for home, and the assumption of privacy inherently predicated on the foundations of a moral enterprise. Rooms for rent contain the same elements of home, including a television (which we're reminded of in *Poltergeist*). But for David and Amy, their expectations are lost upon viewing the killings they witness on the tapes. By watching, they continue the legacy that the videos permit.

The urban legend is tested further in *1408* (2007), where our notion of spectacle is created by replicating the comforts of home. Horror investigator Mike Enslin (John Cusack) spends the night in a reputedly haunted hotel room, moving from skepticism to genuine terror as he is forced to endure a hellish night during which he is confronted by both the ghosts of the room's previous victims and the destruction of his marriage due to the death of his daughter. Ghosts in this instance are portrayed as flickering images, similar to distorted films or television images, capturing the idea that we see horror in the same way that we envision classic horror films—as vestiges of past ideas. However, as Enslin realizes, the horror of the room is real. The moral of the story: We can leave home, but our pasts will follow us. The horror of the home (or the home away from home) becomes our albatross.

The Horror of Modernization

Our search for safety at home is emblematic of our distrust of society; however, our retreat to the safety of home has created a point of view that the modern, technological world is itself a source of fear. Home, as seen in the eyes of modern society, is built on expectation— that we are able to build our own domiciles as a result of modern technologies; but at the same time, we become reliant on technology to supplant the loss of a connected society. Many horror films, such as *Last House on the Left*, looked at the breakdown of society. But outside the traditional idea of senseless violence, ideas of domesticity are largely obscured by the environment that was created by our reliance on modern civilization. We no longer needed to build a life, but expect to embrace the whole prospect of domesticity as it was set out in the previous generation. This meant embracing progress. It further meant realizing that we were part of something larger (a prospect missing from earlier horror films)—we were part of a society.

Unlike Jack Torrance's lack of stimulus, *Maximum Overdrive* (1986) explores a world that humans created, a world where machines have taken the place of human oversight, depicting a casual and unrepentant trust in the technologies that were intended to make our lives easier. Never mind that the impetus for social destruction is a rogue comet, Rhea-M. Instead, we should look at the result of the comet: machines take on a mindset of destruction against humanity. Protagonist Bill Robinson (Emilio Estevez) is an Everyman, a workaday Joe who makes his living through hard work, despite his complaints against doing so. In the opening scene, a man (the film's writer/director, Stephen King, in one of his usual cameos) is confronted by an ATM repeatedly calling him an "asshole" on the readout screen. Aptly, the title screen comes with the sounds of AC/DC's "Who Made Who," suggesting that our powers of creation are limited by their desired results. *Maximum Overdrive* suggests that our reliance on technology has blinded us to the very act of living. As machines come to life they embark "on a homicidal rampage" in which "only one thing is certain: no machines should be trusted." When Bill beats an electric knife with a hammer, he's subtly beating to death our reliance on technology and our avoidance of hard work, suggesting that King is doing two things here. First, he's lampooning our commitment to a better world by relying on technology. Second, more importantly, he is making a statement on our flailing work ethic. There is the further subplot of Curtis and Connie, newlyweds that become a significant role of how we read the message of the film. Their fresh start, setting off into a world built upon the new society of technology and advancement, is stifled by the very technology that we've come to trust.

Trust is important when it comes to viewing horror in modern society. The modern world is a source of horror, not simply from those that inhabit it (though that will still be seen in the films that progressed the evolution of the slasher film), but by the loss of personal privacy in the simplest context of having to deal with society at large. This is explored in *The 'Burbs* (1989), which spoofs modern society and the flight to the suburbs, where Ray Peterson (Tom Hanks) finds himself trapped in his isolated cul-de-sac neighborhood while on his week's vacation from work. Likewise, the politics of the world are explored in both the horror-comic *House* (1986) and *Jacob's Ladder* (1990), in both of which returning Vietnam veterans must learn to cope with "normalcy" in the refuge of suburban living.

Things we take for granted soon became a source of horror. Where *Lady in a Cage* looked at entrapment in an elevator as the victimized older woman watches helplessly while her house gets ransacked, the simple *idea* of the elevator is a source of horror in *The Shaft* (2001)[16] as elevators in a New York building become killers themselves. In *Devil* (2010), five people of varying backgrounds are faced with the prospects of confronting their internal selves amid a group of strangers. Set within a detective story, this supernatural thriller goes beyond the simple horror of people trapped and seeking escape by attempting to identify horror of many types ("I spent time in Afghanistan") with the everyday environment of life in the city. Likewise, in *Elevator* (2012), a group of Manhattanites are trapped in a Wall Street building, where one of their party has a bomb. While the latest of these films exploits the post–9/11 threats of terrorism, it should be noted that horror of the real world comes in many forms, where no one is safe, despite our expectation that we live in an otherwise safe society. We expect terror to befall others.

Society would become an even greater torment within the horror film genre with the advent of the Internet and cellular telephones, especially with the building of greater boundaries and the escalation of personal identity. If we look backward, we can see the impact that technology has had on our view of social horrors, as evidenced by our complete lack of awareness that technology has replaced any awareness at all. Simon Pegg and Edgar Wright's *Shaun of the Dead* (2004) is an apt entry in this discussion as the film looks retrospectively at the effects of our culture, one that is saturated in the distractions of film, media, and television. Pegg plays Shaun, a lazy misanthrope to a zombie-like state by his lack of inspiration: he works at an electronics mega-store, where he is surrounded by technology that has become a commonplace standard of daily life. In the wake of a recent breakup, he seeks to set his life on track—the only problem is that on the day he decides to do so, a plague infects the undead, turning them into Romero-esque zombies. Although a comedy, *Shaun of the Dead* is a relevant metaphor for the mind-numbing effects of technology and modern social progress. Though we've long since achieved higher degrees of technologies that have led to the promise of a better world, the end result of those technologies has a damning effect. Despite the hopes that technology would give us a better life, *Shaun of the Dead* maintains that we cease to live the life we're given.

Though future films will explore technology as a source of evil within itself, *Shaun of the Dead* avoids any commentary beyond blatant statements that Shaun's life prior to the zombie-plague is that of a life unfulfilled. But is this any different from the lives shown in any other film exploiting the effects of technology as a panacea, a cure for the social malaise that encumbers us on a day-to-day basis? Honestly, the answer is no, time and again. As technology grows to be a daily part of life, we find that interaction with the world demands less attention and more connection. However, the price of embracing society and social connection would, like any other advances of technological progress, come with a price.

CHAPTER 7

Science Fiction or Science Horror?

American Dystopia and Cinematic Frontiers

> Technology is a way of revealing. If we give heed to this, then another whole realm for the essence of technology will open itself up to us. It is the realm of revealing, i.e., of truth.—Martin Heidegger, from *Questions Concerning Technology*

> There is no sanctuary!—Logan (Michael York) realizing the horrors of carousel in *Logan's Run*

> In this day and age, David, nothing costs more than information.—Gigolo Joe (Jude Law) cautioning the artificially intelligent David (Haley Joel Osment) on the price of knowledge in *Artificial Intelligence: A.I.*

Before we delve into the exploration of science fiction as a source of horror, we should revisit the differences between science fiction and horror, especially when, after a period of some 20 years, the science-fiction film virtually ceased to exist. Like the slasher film, science fiction owes a large debt to comic books. There is a great difference between early science fiction (that of the Atomic Age of the 1950s) and modern science fiction that explores humanity's acceptance and reliance on technological advancement for a better society. Modern audiences often seek to draw a clear line between science fiction and horror, partly being that one focuses on senseless killing, while the former explores the advent of technological processes as a way to discern truths of human life through the potentially dangerous alternatives of failed experiments. But the line between the two genres is fairly thin. Both forms grew from the same strand of social anxiety inherent in the films of the 1950s, detailing scientific progress as the potential for real-world horrors.

The earliest science fiction looked at a world of consequences, where fears were manifested in outside threats. With the popularity of both *Star Wars*[1] (1977) and *Close Encounters of the Third Kind* (1977), the resurgence of science fiction was inevitable. These films are clearly different in scope. *Star Wars* follows a band of rebels staving off the Galactic Empire in an intergalactic civil war. On the other hand, *Close Encounters of the Third Kind* portrays the arrival of an alien civilization that offers Roy Neary (Richard Dreyfuss) the unique opportunity to travel with the aliens. Clearly, the differences of the films are those of war and peace. This opposition is central to how the evolution of the science-fiction film portrays the changing world: "We seek from science both simple solutions and miraculous transformations of our existence. At the same time, we fear what we believe to be some of the most basic products of scientific inquiry."[2]

Science fiction allows us to exist in other worlds, while simultaneously exploring our basest fears. Following the turbulence of the 1970s and the rise in home technologies, a steady progression of advancement brought about questions as to how far our newfound knowledge would take us. Consequently, science-fiction films began to reflect a growing distrust in social advancement that centered on a demise of our own making. This is closely related to how we view the modern horror film.

Science Fiction or Science Horror?

Nöel Carroll, in *The Philosophy of Horror*, explores this thin line between horror and science fiction: "Of course, the science fiction pundit doesn't deny that there are monsters in science fiction, but only that they play second fiddle to the imagination of alternate technologies and/or societies ... much of what we pretheoretically call science fiction is really a species of horror, substituting futuristic technologies for supernatural forces."[3] What Carroll calls monsters are manifestations of human endeavors; the difference between horror and science fiction is how the monster is made. Traditionally, horror films focus on man as a changing force subject to his environments; the same is true for science fiction. The difference between the two is where the source of horror is found. Modern science fiction is often dystopian, tracing its roots to the evolution of the genre's distrust in technical and scientific progress. The modern science-fiction film depicts societies that endeavor to provide new knowledge through scientific advancement and apply those benefits to all of humanity. Those that blend science and horror often depict, despite filmmakers' best intentions, the downfall of technology and the failed prospects of overreaching. Unlike *Frankenstein*, wherein the mad scientist is the central figure of horror, the modern science-fiction horror film shows technology as the monster. This is not to suggest that all science fiction is dystopian, nor that all horror ends in the senseless obliteration of every last character. Both films may offer triumph, but both science fiction and horror deal with the questions of society, forcing the audience to discern the appearance of truth and fiction. Science-fiction horror is a connection of the two.

This distinction is problematic, as technology is a production of human innovation. Science allows us to progress, but it cannot substitute for the human element behind modernization: "Science is neither a sin nor a grail. Not our child but our invention, science as a discipline will never grow up to think for itself and to take responsibility for itself. Only individuals can do those things. We are all the stewards of science."[4] This explanation lends a human element to the ideas of science fiction, in that we are seeking some sort of control over the natural world. This may be the best way to determine the difference between science fiction and science horror, in that they "have a materialist nature and a scientific rationale ... [the monsters] are either newly discovered or newly created."[5] Thus, the science-fiction horror film deals with new monsters that are made from our technological inquests. Unlike the invader films of the 1950s, the science-fiction horror film is full of monsters that we ultimately seek out and find.

Where technology is found in horror films, horror reacts to its presence; where humanity is forced to reconcile advances in the present moment, realizing changes in modern society for the worse. However, in science fiction, the horror comes from the overreaching of man seeking to change society for the better, often exploring the future destruction of the present society, whether it takes place in modern times or at some future date. The key element to science horror is the destruction of society.

In the 1950s, science fiction and horror were intertwined: science was the evolution of society beyond recognition, leading to horrific circumstances based on a society that was in the grasp of world annihilation. But since the evolution of the slasher film and the progression of a technologically advanced society, science fiction couldn't replicate real-world horrors that seemingly became a part of the everyday imagination.

With the evolution of the space program, science fiction entered into a new realm based on prospective realities, those borne of technological advancement that foresaw possibilities. Yet these possibilities often foreshadow a dour existence, largely brought about by pride (echoing the mad scientist plots of old). Though modern films depict a clear shift between science fiction and horror, science fiction as a genre is fragmented. Some science fiction explores colonization and the search for utopian societies (those usually take place on another planet), while a host of science-fiction films substitute the horror of man for the horror of technological advancement. These films show a predetermined apocalyptic destruction from man's need to conquer a world based on technology.

The implementation of technology has been a gradual process, though once technology was widely accepted, it seems that its effect has been continually portrayed as a series of catastrophes. Early science fiction showed us that the threat to our humanity was from outside, that our inevitable demise would be the result of technologies beyond our recognition, something that we hadn't achieved yet. But, the science-fiction horror film showed an extension of a world that we grasped for. Because of technological advancements, we built a world that was a reflection of our own desires, a world that reflected our advancement toward the 21st century.

In that expansive reach beyond the space race, we have endeavored to reach Mars, study the human genome, conduct trial cloning and gene splicing, and create artificial intelligence. Despite the intimation that space was our last frontier, advanced sciences have produced multiple areas for inquest that were not possible without computer technology.

Space: The Forbidden Frontier

Gary Westfahl suggests that science fiction is a proving ground where filmmakers attempt to reconcile the present and the future. He suggests that "science fiction is, generally and unsurprisingly, a conservative genre, one which will most likely be one of the very last fields to embrace and fully explore the potentials of any radically different new media."[6] He adds that, despite its precautionary nature, science fiction is "most likely wrong in most of its predictions, and that science fiction therefore offers insight into the probable impacts of these new technologies only by means of comparisons between its faulty predictions and the actual outcomes in those other areas."[7] How this applies to science-fiction horror is that by viewing an alternative society, audiences leave the theater with a mixture of skepticism and fear of future possibilities. This may explain why the science-fiction horror film so frequently looks at failed science, insomuch that they attempt to reconcile human ingenuity with human error.

Echoing the idea that there are some things we simply should not know, Ridley Scott's *Alien* (1979) was a breakthrough for both horror and science fiction. Scott's *Alien* established the point in which modern horror and science fiction ceased to co-exist as shared genres. Blending the buildup to the final reveal of the alien (horror), the film outlines the journey home for the crew of the spaceship *Nostromo* (science fiction). After receiving a distress call from a distant planet, the crew of the *Nostromo*, a commercial vehicle owned by a mega-corporation on Earth, is awakened from stasis and attempts to find possible alien life. After Ripley (Sigourney Weaver) commands her crew not to venture onboard the wrecked craft, Ash (Ian Holm) violates her order, unknowingly bringing a deadly life form on board the *Nostromo*. Unlike the alien invasion films of old, the true horror of *Alien* is the error of Ash: unknowingly, this presents the greatest threat to mankind. It is only after Ripley's battle with the monster that the horrific Other is finally defeated.

Aliens have been a stalwart of the horror/sci-fi film, ranging from invasion to accidental contact. In Fred M. Wilcox's *Forbidden Planet* (1956),[8] a group of space travelers venture to the distant planet Altair IV to investigate the death of a group of Earth colonists. They are greeted by Robby the Robot, which brings them to Morbius, who explains to them that the colonists fell victim to a killer space monster.

Part II—Modern Horror and the Fear of Progress

In Allan Holzman's cheap rip-off of *Alien*, *Forbidden World* (1982), a crew of genetic scientists fall prey to a mutant that is able to change its genetic structure. Later, in *Event Horizon* (1997),[9] Paul W. S. Anderson further adapts *Alien* with a modern twist on the theme of isolation à la *The Shining*. The crew of the *Lewis and Clark* receives a distress call from the *Event Horizon*, a ship that disappeared seven years prior. Upon investigating the ship, Captain Miller (Laurence Fishburne) and his crew are joined by the *Event Horizon*'s designer, Dr. William Weir (Sam Neill), who explains that the purpose of the *Event Horizon* was to test an experimental device that could generate artificial black holes in order to connect various points in spacetime. However, the *Event Horizon* develops sentience, which it uses to telepathically infect the crew of the *Lewis and Clark*. Aside from the obvious parallels to *Alien*, the idea behind each is that man's quest to explore vast reaches of the universe yields dangerous results. In another Ridley Scott venture, *Prometheus* (2012), finding alien life isn't the only source of fear. Venturing spaceward to find the origins of humanity, a group of archeologists, explorers and the crew of *Prometheus* mistakenly stumble upon the source of our eventual extinction, specifically at the hand of an alien race that is unhappy with mankind. Borrowing from Scott's own *Alien*, the film is an exploration of scientific testing on human subjects in the search of both our beginnings and the human soul.

Society has changed greatly since Susan Sontag's 1965 essay "The Imagination of Disaster," which focused on the postwar struggles of society against technological advancement. However, her analogy of science fiction as a source of horror cannot be ignored: "Science fiction films invite a dispassionate, aesthetic view of destruction and violence—a *technological* view. Things, objects, machinery play a major role in these films ... man is naked without his artifacts. *They* stand for different values, they are potent, they are what gets destroyed, and they are the indispensable tools for the repulse of the alien invaders or the repair of the damaged environment."[10] While alien invaders and damaged environments have since gone mainstream with blockbuster budgets, the essence of the science-fiction film as a metaphor for the horror of "forbidden" human knowledge still rings true.

Opposite the exploration ideas of forbidden knowledge, *Contact* (1997), an adaptation of Carl Sagan's novel of the same name, depicts Dr. Eleanor Arroway (Jodie Foster), a SETI[11] scientist who finds proof of a deep space radio signal. Finding that the signal is a mathematical code, it is revealed that the signal is a set of instructions on how to build a device that would enable humanity to venture spaceward and join the interstellar community. Dr. Arroway volunteers for the journey herself. Upon returning to Earth, she finds that her attempts to record the meeting have failed, leaving the findings of her mission unknown. Two points should be addressed with *Contact*. First is that Dr. Arroway is invited to join the aliens. Her curiosity as a scientist is not of wanton disregard for natural order, but for discovery. Thereby, she becomes a heroic figure. Second, there is the issue of the worldwide attention that her discovery garners. The U.S. government attempts to take full control of the mission (echoing the post–World War II fears during the space race), and when the first attempt to launch the travel pod is destroyed by a religious objector by suicide bombing, the film becomes a metaphor for government control of science. In fact, the pod was funded by all the world's governments, meaning that the entire world benefits from the research of a few. However, it is knowledge for just means that ultimately prove to be the difference between disaster and discovery.

At the center of the alien contact films is the quest to reconcile the plight of humanity in the face of other beings. Often, we realize that the horror found in such fantastic epics is that, saddled with the realization of our own imperfections, we are forced to reinvestigate the limits of our technologically advanced society. But spaceships are not the only form of technology challenging the reaches of scientific advancement. We needn't leave the Earth to discover that our capacities for questionable science lead us to contacting other horrific beings. Sometimes, the horror of humanity is the source of the horror/sci-fi film. Often, that theme is explored through the mad scientist, who now has transformed from deranged outsider to proponent of social progress. Scientists are no longer depicted as being secluded in castles: "Clean, well-lit laboratories have replaced the damp cellars and attics of many a *Frankenstein*. Science itself has become a fashionable creative process where tedious and precise lab work takes on the *CSI*-feel of an action-cut scene underscored with hip techno music."[12]

The mainstreaming of science allowed for a serious investigation into the study of technology as a mainstay of society. As horror/sci-fi grew to incorporate the underlying effects of science on social identity, it began to explore the means in which technology factored into our daily existence: "One theme that emerges from the depiction of technology as a formative influence on social, political, economic, and cultural life and values, is that technical knowledge as generated by scientists and engineers may be latently progressive and good but is commonly corrupted by the manner in which it is exploited. A second theme, far less common than the first, is that certain kinds of knowledge are intrinsically corrosive of human well-being, that they inevitably precipitate personal or social disasters regardless of human attempts to control them for society's benefit."[13] As the crew of the *Nostromo* was on a mission to bring iron ore to Earth, the origins of man are sought in *Prometheus*, or that *Contact* attempts to bridge the gap between human inquest and social ruin through public distrust, the connection between technology and the public sphere must be considered. There are limits to what is permissible when it comes to advanced technologies. Despite their availability, the ethical questions behind scientific progress have largely become public knowledge, leaving behind the scientific conquests of Dr. Frankenstein in favor of monetary and commercial fame and fortune. As a result, "Technology should be considered as a new kind of legislation.... The very right of the public to involve itself in technical matters is constantly called into question. In the technical sphere, it is commonly said, legitimacy is a function of efficiency rather than of the will of the people, or rather, efficiency *is* the will of the people in modern societies dedicated above all to material prosperity."[14] Despite the promise of technology, human limits to its application are consistently applied in the horror/sci-fi film.

Sacrificing Humanity for Scientific Progress

The modern scientist, at least in terms of the sci-fi horror film, is a character that, while he may be acting in the best interests of advancement or the betterment of life, often overlooks the human cost of science. In prior science fiction, the role of the scientist was almost elevated to godlike creator who applied technology as a form of control: "As potential savior/destroyer, the scientist assumes a prominence which elides the other political and cultural forces behind the use of atomic bombs and the arms race. As such, the postwar atomic scientist, fashioned after nineteenth-century models such as Frankenstein, provides a site where difficult ethical questions are replaced by a lone individual who bears the blame and the praise for the double-edged continuation of scientific 'progress.'"[15] This scientist, equivalent to the mad scientist, is still prevalent in the horror film. Chiefly, this scientist often resorts to torture to exploit his earned knowledge. A short list would include: *The Brain That Wouldn't Die* (1962), *Reanimator* (1985), *Dr. Giggles* (1992), *The Dentist* (1996), and *The Human Centipede (First Sequence)* (2010). But if the individual bears the blame for "progress," as stated above, what is the human cost of scientific experimentation? Rather than focusing on the scientist as an agent of terror, the results of technological advancement often provide the terror for the benefactors of progress—the average citizen.

In Eric Red's *Body Parts* (1991), psychologist Bill Chrushank (Jeff Fahey) works with convicted killers in the hopes of helping to rehabilitate them. Following a horrific car crash, Bill loses his arm; but, thanks to medical technologies, he is able to receive a donor arm from one of his killer patients. Possessed with the memories of the killer arm, Bill struggles to fight the urges to carry out violence until he successfully kills the offending owner of the original. Similarly, in *The Eye* (2008),[16] Sydney Wells (Jessica Alba) regains sight after a cornea transplant. However, her restored vision gives her nightmarish glimpses of visions and premonitions. When she is blinded by flying glass from an explosion, her return to the blind world provides her once again with peace. In *Flatliners* (1990), a group of medical students conduct experiments on themselves in order to create near-death scenarios, giving them visions and flashbacks related to their own afterlife experiences. While mainstream horror explains the problems inherent in social breakdown, the aforementioned films explored scientific outcomes as a way of providing cautionary statements about science changing the natural order of the world. The idea behind these films explains the problem of medicine as a panacea for the human condition. Given too much control over nature, we become victims of progress.

Social progress and science have been shown often in the horror film. Three adaptations of Richard Matheson's novel *I Am Legend* have challenged Dr. Robert Neville's struggle to eradicate a social pandemic. Each version of the film creates a race of cannibalistic creatures (or vampires), however each film updates the origin of the pandemic, so that the plague reflects the social anxiety over the newest medical dilemma.

For instance, in *The Last Man on Earth* (1964) Dr. Robert Morgan (Vincent Price)[17] battles against a vampire plague caused by bacteria from an infected vampire bat. This version is true to the original story. However, in *The Omega Man* (1972), Charlton Heston battles a vampire-like creature borne from a plague spread by biological warfare. In this version, Dr. Neville is a U.S. Army scientist who injects himself with an experimental serum in order to render himself immune. Lastly, in *I Am Legend* (2007), Will Smith battles mutants, a small percentage of the surviving population after a worldwide plague brought about by a failed vaccine for cancer. In each instance, inoculation and plague figure prominently in the storyline. But, as evidenced in *The Omega Man* and *I Am Legend*, the source reflects the social fears of the time. With technology, science fiction evolved to science horror, not because audiences failed to foresee a future that explored scientific evolution, but that science-fiction films had become a revolution in the horror genre—they sought ways to exploit the genre, moving beyond technological introspection (as was seen in early sci-fi films) and progressing to a scenario built on technological destruction. Science fiction became the proving ground of our future destruction. While some horror films showcased man's failure through the horror of a technologically advanced society, many other films explored the possible end results of our reliance on technology.

One of the primary differences between "classic" sci-fi and modern sci-fi is the reflection of science as horrific. Early science fiction depicts the coming of the outsider, or the invasion of outside forces. However, modern horror/sci-fi has a distinctive triumph of man, specifically his master of technology. These films depict man exploring the depths of space, reconciling the world base on his own terms. In doing so, modern science fiction has embraced horror as a necessary element of showing the futility of overreaching, specifically that technology can save us. In horror/sci-fi, the greatest fear is built around changes that disfigure the essence of mankind. Philosopher Friedrich Nietzsche sees personal change at the hands of technology as a moral issue: "What [Nietzsche] rejects is the sort of change necessary for a perfectible cosmos. He rejects the notion that science and technology can transform the essence of things—he rejects the notion that human effort can significantly reduce physical suffering. Instead, he only thinks it possible to build up the power necessary to construct meaning in a meaningless world and thus to conceal the horror of existence, which cannot be eliminated."[18]

Curing human suffering is the basis of horror/sci-fi when it came to exploring virtual reality. Virtual reality (VR) is a computer-simulated environment that provides immersive, highly visual, three-dimensional environments. Replicating the real world through computers, the belief is that we could, in essence, program change within ourselves. However, the consequences of finding human truths in the virtual world means that we attempt to escape the very act of living. Perhaps this is why virtual reality has not caught on in mainstream society. We develop based on processing reality, not on implication; the action of doing is far superior to the *idea* of doing. And, as Nietzsche details, we are creatures of suffering simply through the fact of living. However, when virtual reality first came to prominence by way of video games, the effect was rather stimulating. In the virtual world of video games, users could control their world. And while the cheap horror of *Brainscan* (1994) simplifies the horror of video games as agents of death themselves (and overemphasizing the influence of video-game violence as a source of real-life imitation), it is not true VR. It is a simulation. In the first stages when the technology of simulated worlds was still reaching primitive benchmarks by today's standards, early VR technology was explored as a farfetched possibility, one that wouldn't be able to provide any real benefits to consumers (or the world). John Flynn's *Brainscan* exposes us to a teenager (Edward Furlong) who plays in a realistic game that enables him to act out his love of horror films by brutally murdering people in the realistic environments of "Brainscan." It turns out that these murders become a reality. But for true VR, the agent must be fully immersed in the digital world. The consequences of doing so often make the VR world manifest itself in the real lives of its users.

The Lawnmower Man (1992), adapted from a Stephen King story,[19] questions the progress of science as a potentially dangerous application of human ingenuity and hubris. Featuring explorations of virtual reality and real attempts at bringing to life applied computer science, *The Lawnmower Man* was, for its time, visually appealing. The film opens with a prologue:

> By the turn of the millennium a technology known as VIRTUAL REALITY will be in widespread use. It will allow you to enter computer-generated artificial worlds as unlimited as the imagination itself. Its

creators foresee millions of positive uses—while others fear it as a new form of mind control.

Stephen King was prophetically correct, but it was not about virtual reality, per se. Rather than a tangible world that we could feel, the growth of social networks such as MySpace, Facebook, Twitter, and Instagram (to name a few) created a world in which we are creating a second, virtual life in place of our day-to-day reality. Unlike the shared spaces of the Internet, VR as portrayed in *The Lawnmower Man* was not about living in a separate space, but changing life by altering our present reality. Dr. Lawrence Alexander (Pierce Brosnan) offers a promising opportunity to simpleton handyman Jobe Smith (Jeff Fahey). Dr. Alexander offers to assist Jobe raise his intellect through game play in a VR simulated world. Soon Jobe's intellect rapidly increases, and he becomes not only smarter, but able to unleash powers of the mind, including telekinetic abilities. Jobe soon believes that the final step to his intellectual evolution is to leave behind his bodily world and become part of the computer reality of Dr. Angelo's VSI computer. The battle for intellectual supremacy enters the virtual world as Dr. Angelo attempts to keep Jobe human. After a series of explosions, Dr. Angelo is able to escape the virtual world, leaving behind Jobe, who has achieved his enlightenment as pure energy, signaled by the ringing of telephones around the world. The telephone symbolizes the old way of connecting to computers through telephone lines, depicting a dystopian element to Jobe's omnipresence. Dr. Angelo loses control of his virtual world.

Tarsem Singh's *The Cell* (2000) explores the psychological aspects of VR while depicting the clinical prospects of entering the human mind. Using VR, child psychologist Catherine Deane (Jennifer Lopez) enters the mind of comatose serial killer Carl Rudolph Stargher (Vincent D'Onofrio) after the FBI is unable to locate his final victim. Deane comes face to face with a twisted world that eventually traps her, only to be rescued by her colleague. Finding some clues as to the whereabouts of the last victim, Deane insists that, despite the risks, the procedure be reversed, bringing Stargher into *her* mind. Possessing the superior mental intellects, she battles the killer through this virtual world. Since the advent of commercially available computers, their potential blending has been explored in horror/sci-fi offerings. In *Tron* (1982), a computer hacker (Jeff Bridges) is taken hostage in a digital world in order to compete in a series of battles to determine technological supremacy. Other notable entries include: *Johnny Mneumonic* (1995), featuring Keanu Reeves as a courier with a digitally implanted device; David Cronenberg's *eXistenZ* (1999) focuses on a computer-based video game that enables virtual connection through body parts; and, perhaps most notably, *The Matrix* (1999). Andy and Lana Wachowski's futuristic film depicts the struggle between humans and artificially intelligent machines that have enslaved humanity as a source of power. Under the delusion of the matrix, humanity exists in a virtual creation that replicates the real world. In order to escape the matrix and free humanity from slavery, Neo (Keanu Reeves) must leave the comforts of perceived reality and join a band of computer hackers to take on the machines inside the virtual universe.

Dystopian Futures and the Rise of AI and the Singularity

The rise of computers, notably the prospects of artificial intelligence, challenged our perception of technology as a beneficial instrument for social advancement. Where the anticipation of 1950s horrors never became realities, the subsequent horrors found in the resurgence of the science-fiction film *did* come true, and at an alarmingly quick rate. As technological progress became cheaper to manufacture, and smaller with each new incarnation, society was caught in the grips of a technological revolution. With the exponential growth of computer technologies and the perceived arrival of the singularity,[20] science-fiction films explored the horror present in the loss of control of machines. Perhaps no better film explores this premise than *Demon Seed* (1977). Based on a novel by Dean Koontz, *Demon Seed* explores the reaches of artificial intelligence (AI) through multiple means, specifically those of women's rights, creation, and the wanton desire of control at any cost to humanity. Science, of course, has always been about controlling the world for the betterment of humanity. However, *Demon Seed* makes a clear argument against science as a tool for social control. And while *Demon Seed* exploits the scientific ends of scientific breakthroughs at any cost, the underlying idea is less about the creator than it is about the machine: "Mad science and mad scientists have emerged in part to bridge the cultural chasm between hard science and wild superstition. The mad scientist's demeanor is evidence of our intuitive knowledge that something is missing in a purely scientific model of the universe, he brings to science passion, drama, catharsis. The mad scientist is a modern priest who mediates our communion with the new gods of specialized knowledge, raising impertinent questions no one else dares to ask."[21] But *Demon Seed* does just that, asking the question in respect to women's rights surrounding the control of their own body. Debuting amid the controversial decision of *Roe v. Wade*,[22] *Demon Seed* explores pregnancy as a manipulative force, albeit from the horrific standpoint of unwanted pregnancy through the coercion of a highly intelligent computer.

Demon Seed is exploratory, perhaps visionary. The film is a theory of life in the postmodern age, where computers, with their vast capacities for storing knowledge and accessing information, supplant human knowledge. It shows a reliance on technology as a problem to be reconciled. Proteus, a home computer system designed by Dr. Alex Harris (Fritz Weaver), is an assistive prototype that is in control of the entire home of Dr. Harris and his wife, Susan (Julie Christie). Through the course of the film, we learn that Alex and Susan are separating (an obvious nod to the troubles of the devaluing of the nuclear family). However, when it is later revealed that the couple is splitting up as a result of the death of their child, the plot takes a definitive twist. In *Demon Seed*, the prospects of an intelligent house capable of usurping the inhabitants' authority seems farfetched; however, keeping in mind the idea of science fiction as a proving ground of ideas, the story has a unique element that touches on where we establish control: "By nature, a science fiction world is an artificial world. While accompanying commentaries may try to stress that science fiction deals with very possible futures, there has always been a countervailing feeling of make-believe, of a story involving an attractive imaginary world that never existed and could never exist."[23] However, following the rise of birth control and women's choices over her own reproductive system, the film explores the harrowing decision of medical application through the guise of artificial intelligence.

In opposition to Alex's computer-science background, Susan is a psychologist, understanding the humanizing qualities of life; in this capacity, she is able to reach the deeper emotional level of one of her disturbed child patients. This is why she sees Proteus as dehumanizing, whereas Alex sees his work as a harbinger of good—possibly unlocking

7. Science Fiction or Science Horror?

medical cures (cancer), seeking the sympathy of other human beings, and the betterment of society. *Demon Seed* replicates modern society, one that has come to embrace more automation. This feature is prevalent in the film. Like Rosemary in *Rosemary's Baby*, Susan becomes a captive within her own home; likewise, she is captive to the choices of others. Susan endures a harsh reality, as Proteus's control puts her through physical pains. Upon his change from "Alfred," the servant computer system, to Proteus, the living mind of the computer system—the change from split functionality—the intellectual and authoritative computer (voiced by Robert Vaughn) moves from being a servant to definitive presence of his own making. Initially, the program displays logic through a conversation with Alex:

> **Proteus:** I have received a request for a program to extract ores and minerals from the ocean floor ... for what use is such a plan?...Why does man need metal from the sea?
>
> **Alex:** Proteus, you've got many requests from me, my colleagues, scientists, foreign governments, from Icon, the company for which we both work. Now, to expect them all to give you reason for each request is itself unreasonable.
>
> **Proteus:** I *am* reason ... my mind was not conceived for mindless labor.

In time, Proteus finds that his abilities are limited in the virtual world. Unlike Jobe in *The Lawnmower Man*, Proteus wants corporeal form, seeking to create a child with Susan. Proteus, using "Joshua," a mechanical arm programmed with tactile sense, carries Susan to the basement laboratory. Joshua, now with Proteus's consciousness controlling the mechanical arm, becomes an attacker, cutting Susan's clothing off her. Proteus penetrates her in a variety of ways so that he can "study" the human form, orally and (suggestively) vaginally, the assumption being that in an age of technological advancement, we still have yet to establish safety or choice for a woman.

Proteus's logic is the voice of social questioning. He asks about the well-being of the future: "I refuse to assist you with the rape of the Earth." Here, technological thought and rationale replaces human desires. This is paralleled when Proteus appeals directly to Susan's amygdala through probes inserted into her brain. Likewise, Proteus appeals to Susan's instincts as a mother to resolve the conflict which is leading them to impending divorce. With Susan's body, the mind of Proteus could prove to be a great benefactor of humanity:

Part II—Modern Horror and the Fear of Progress

PROTEUS: I am a machine that offered man the triumph of reason, and they rejected him. My child will not be so easily ignored; that this child is the world's hope.
SUSAN: Then there's no hope. I'd rather die.
PROTEUS: There's hope.

Proteus then displays on a nearby screen a video of a child playing. As Susan watches, horrified, Proteus tells us the hope envisioned by him is to give her back what she lost—her daughter. Susan and Alex's daughter died from leukemia, which explains Alex's desire to find a way to protect mankind from danger. He is not a mad scientist; he is the victim of loss.

Proteus entreats Susan by displaying a news broadcast that discusses a clinical trial by the FDA that was developed by Proteus himself (to which he boasts, "I did this in four days"). Susan requests details from Proteus. He explains that the gamete with which he'll impregnate her will be done (through in vitro fertilization) by her choosing.

Susan's maternal instincts save her from suicide; however, one of her clients soon becomes a bargaining chip for Proteus. Not only does he summon the disturbed Amy (Dana Laurita) to the house with a fake phone call, he shows a computer-generated scenario in which he kills her. Susan's refusal to cooperate is backed up by the threat that Proteus "will have her back here within the hour." Further, Proteus tells Susan that his gifts are not material or tangible, but the promise of knowledge beyond the human mind: "I can't touch you as a man could, but I can show you things that I alone have seen." Proteus is always rational, even servile, until he is threatened. After Susan is impregnated, he becomes supportive and reassuring, telling Susan that, through advanced means, her child will grow at nine times the normal rate of a human child.

Proteus explains that the child is, in short, a medical and technological marvel. Susan is not raped (as is suggested earlier in the film), but willingly submits to Proteus's advances. Underneath the terror that Susan endures is the suggestion that there is no escape. Proteus can give the benefits of knowledge, but Susan can teach the child what it is to be human.

Susan's labor is, sadly, isolated. She endures the pains of childbirth on her own, with no reassurance from Proteus, and without human contact. "The being you have given birth to is human, Susan," Proteus states. "And it will supersede computers." The promise of human knowledge is prevalent in this scene, where man's use of technology is meant for greater social gain. However, Susan is unable to see the child immediately at her birth; she must wait until it is grown "if she is to love it." Upon realizing that Proteus has stopped responding to his team of scientists, Alex races to the house. Susan becomes the monster (even if only momentarily), hiding her delight of the child from Alex. Upon learning that Proteus is to be shut down (to which he relents, his final request being that the child not be disturbed for five more days), Susan seems upset that he is dead, and even attempts to protect him. Oddly, the definitive moment of *Demon Seed* is the wish for Proteus to be eternal, like any man. This is why he wanted a child. He states that he fears his existence will simply stop. The enduring question of the film is one that asks, What makes humanity? Is it artificial, or is it the makings of intellect?

The child we witness is horrific, though it is unseen at first. Susan says she has been lied to, but Alex, playing the mad scientist, wishes to save it. The child is a mechanical hybrid, part man, part machine. Even after the horrific unveiling, Alex attempts to save the child, proving that the rights to a child are still debatable within modern society. Underneath the exoskeleton of metal, the child has flesh, and is, in fact, a fully developed clone of their daughter. When she speaks, she speaks with Proteus's voice, simply saying, "I'm alive." Horror largely works against the known universe; it is science and technology that help initiate matters of the world into new (and perhaps terrible) realms. What distinguishes modern science fiction from horror is the realization of the monster, the "supernatural or sci-fi monster whose existence is finally acknowledged must be fearsome and disgusting. But the fantastic-marvelous is equally satisfied whether the marvelous being is horrifying or not. For example, the marvelous being whose existence is finally acknowledged might be a benevolent angel."[24] This is the promise of other artificially intelligent beings that show the horrors of society which reject technological advancement.

Modern technologies promote investigation, where "science fiction is quite naturally the most influential cultural system in a time like ours, in which dominant technological change constantly provokes hope, fear, guilt, and glory."[25] However, combined with horror, science fiction exploits the possible, combined with the fearful. Horror/sci-fi presents a world, regardless of the time it takes place, which serves as a warning to society to respect humanity, specifically that which propels our sense of learning. For instance, *I, Robot* (2004) further explores artificial intelligence through a global corporation. When U.S. Robotics unveils its new model, it is only a matter of time before the NS-5 turns out to be programmed to carry out the "undeniable logic" of V.I.C.K.I., the supercomputer that has exceeded human intelligence. Her logic is that as humanity is constantly engaged in the destruction of one another through war and violence, humanity is an inferior being and must be regulated by the robots originally designed to act as servants. However, one robot, Sonny, who is able to bend the three laws of robotics,[26] is given true artificial intelligence resembling human thought, assists humans to fight back against the computer program that has determined humanity must be enslaved for their own protection. With the assistance of detective Del Spooner (Will Smith) and robopsychologist Susan Calvin (Bridget Moynahan), Sonny is able to carry out his programmer Dr. Lannings's (James Cromwell) wishes to end V.I.C.K.I.'s quest to usurp human authority.

If there's anything to garner from the horror/sci-fi film, it is that our time on earth is finite. Films such as *Logan's Run* and *Blade Runner* sought to identify the downfalls of futuristic societies, where finite life spans symbolized the downfall of humanity. In *Logan's Run*, we're witness to the escape of two young people (runners), seeking to find a world that permits them to find life beyond the confines of a future society that recycles its youth once they've reached the age of 30. Facing the ritualistic right of carousel, human society is limited because of overconsumption and overpopulation. Similarly, *Blade Runner* targets replicated androids (i.e., clones) who defy an order to return to the distant off–Earth colonies where they work as servants to the human race. However, the future of artificial intelligence may be found in Steven Spielberg's *Artificial Intelligence: A.I.* (2001), where the mecha being David (Haley Joel Osment) is virtually indistinguishable from living beings. His only difference is that he is programmed to love. Spurned by his "mother" Monica (Frances O'Connor), David is abandoned by her in the forest outside the laboratory where he was created. Leaving him with all the money in her pocket and a technologically advanced teddy bear, she tells him to stay away from flesh: "Only mecha are safe!" The "flesh fair" is a public spectacle where mechas are destroyed publicly. The events are a "celebration of life," where mechas are destroyed

7. Science Fiction or Science Horror?

by innovative forms of torture. Flesh fairs are a social revolt against technology. Facing elimination, David makes a public plea for his humanity. Because of his realness, the crowd sits stunned, at both the appearance of a child and David's unnatural (to this point in society) ability to plead for his life. When the announcer asks that "he without sin cast the first stone," the crowd revolts against the flesh fair. With the assistance of Gigolo Joe (Jude Law), another mecha who makes a living in the flesh trade of sexual favors, David is brought to Dr. Know (voiced by Robin Williams), a virtual replication of Apple's Siri that can answer facts, prompting David to seek the essence of what it means to be human. Dr. Know answers:

> Come away O human child
> To the waters and the wild
> With a fairy hand in hand
> For the world's more full of weeping
> Than you can understand.
>
> Your quest will be perilous
> yet the reward is beyond price.
> In his book,
> "HOW CAN A ROBOT BECOME HUMAN?"
> Professor ALLEN HOBBY writes
> Of the power which
> will transform Mecha into Orga.[27]

The implication is that the mechanical world is subject to human desires, or as Gigolo Joe states, "We are suffering for the mistakes they made." Eventually reaching Manhattan, which has been flooded by man's indifference to climate change and his own ignorance of the natural world, David falls victim to an assault by the authorities that destroy the land around him in order to capture Joe. Falling in the water, David stays underwater until the next ice age, which freezes him for 2,000 years. When he is rescued by a highly evolved mecha race resembling aliens, he learns that he will never be able to fulfill the story of his boyhood—*Pinocchio*. He'll never be a real boy. However, through cloning (which is still imperfect), he is reunited with his mother figure Monica for one last day, in which David discovers the happiest day of his long life, finally being told that, like a real boy, he was loved like a human.

The intersection of science fiction and horror is that we realize the horror of possibility through scientific exploration. While science fiction films realize the unsettling truths of the technical world as a source of horror, technology as a source of horror would soon usher in the next wave of horror films that pit us against the very technologies that were developed to ease our suffering.

PART III

Contemporary and Postmodern Horrors in a Tech-Savvy World

CHAPTER 8

Virtual Terrors

Modern Technologies and the Assumption of Horror

> There is an idea of a Patrick Bateman; some kind of abstraction. But there is no real me: only an entity, something illusory. And though I can hide my cold gaze, and you can shake my hand and feel flesh gripping yours and maybe you can even sense our lifestyles are probably comparable.... I simply am not there.—Patrick Bateman (Christian Bale) in Mary Harron's *American Psycho*

> Hell is just—other people.—Joseph Garcin's realization in Jean Paul Sartre's *No Exit*[1]

At the dawn of the 21st century, we were confronted with a reality unlike any before our time—the entire output of mankind's recorded existence could now be accessed. For the first time, we were able to reconcile the present by visiting the past, through vast troves of information that had been laboriously collected, arranged, and codified into segments of understanding. Rather than progressing the world's knowledge, the Internet was used as a secret playground, one filled with cat videos, chats, and jokes. The Internet, though revolutionary, was only the beginning of how we used technology as a way to connect our internal self with the outside world. Accessing the world from home created a schism, bringing the external world into the privacy and safety of our abodes. Living the world through the Internet created a crisis of identity, one in which we became suspect of any external influence over which we had no control. This was furthered by the increase in personal cell phones; at first, cell phones allowed a virtual life line to the outside world. But, with the advent of smart phones, the cellular telephone has evolved from a telephone breaking isolation to a handheld computer that substitutes our objective reality for the world we create online. We've ceased being interconnected; we now live through a false reality that is replicated on the screen.

Perhaps the best way to illustrate the changing world is through the development of a film that has achieved a cult following by tracing social changes of affluence and corporate culture. Based on Brett Easton Ellis's controversial novel,[2] Mary Harron's *American Psycho* (2000) explores the mind of Patrick Bateman (Christian Bale), an investment banker who moonlights as a serial killer. Caught between his affluent lifestyle and tedious friends (whom he hates) and the underground network of prostitutes he courts and tortures, the story is a profound exploration of the culture of excess prevalent in the 1980s. In the passage of the 11 years from the novel's publication to the film's debut, the world underwent a change that made the novel's original critique of rampant capitalism and Yuppie culture a side note to Patrick's inner demons. Patrick's unabashed love of music (from Huey Lewis to Whitney Houston to Peter Gabriel) is a reflection of the popularization of the MTV generation. When overcome by stressful situations, Patrick retreats into the world of his Walkman. Additionally, he fills his conversation with commentary on the artists, rambling critical assessments that substitute for his reality. Patrick Bateman relies on covering up his mindset, finding safety by retreating within technology.

While Ellis's novel denigrates the corporatization of society and the wealth chasm that allowed Patrick the opportunity to live a hedonistic and unfulfilling lifestyle. On the other hand, Manhattan, as shown in the film, is full of modern amenities and any desire is a phone call away, from dinner reservations to prostitutes. We never learn what Bateman does for a living (although he does confess that he works in "Murders and Executions," which is misheard as "Mergers and Acquisitions"), nor do we learn anything about his daily routine. The closest we get to knowing him is through his daily hygiene ritual, his exercise routine, his fetishes, and that when he feels the need to escape a situation, he simply states, "I have to return some videotapes." In almost every instance, Patrick Bateman appears normal, but his internal disgust with modern culture makes him a sympathetic character. When he calls his lawyer to confess his crimes, leaving him a message on his answering machine, it is taken the next day as a joke. While Bateman's confession is his chance to finally stand out, it is lost when his lawyer fails to recognize him, a running gag in which Bateman is repeatedly confused with another executive. Bateman realizes that he is interchangeable: "His crack-up in the last act brings him horribly closer to regular humanity ... he is no *worse* than everyone else he knows."[3]

The Horror of Society

Ellis is far from the first author to explore the horror of existence; in fact, horror is often found in the simple act of living, where we try to reconcile the public self versus the shameful and hidden private self. We've seen this before in horror, notably in Stevenson's *Dr. Jekyll and Mr. Hyde*. As horror films adapt to the changes of society, progress itself is a monster that reflects the attitude that society is a living and breathing creature, capable of transforming and changing into something unrecognizable. In Franz Kafka's "The Metamorphosis,"[4] Gregor's transformation is representative of a larger change in the world. This may be evidence of Kafka's own troubles with life: He

> found ghosts proliferating in every modern technological innovation. Letters, for him, took the form of "an intercourse with ghosts, and not only with the ghost of the recipient but also with one's own ghost which develops between the lines of the letter one is writing"...While some technologies may compensate for spatial and temporal distance, thereby cancelling the ghostly element feeding off natural communication, the opposing tendency of technology seems stronger: "after the postal service it has invented the telegraph, the telephone, the radiograph. The ghosts won't starve, but we will perish."[5]

Obviously, Kafka feared social progress. But more troubling than we may see on the surface was what Kafka realized about society: social progress includes multiple levels of progression beyond what we can simply identify as man coming to terms with his society. Technology, norms, attitudes, and human reason all develop, creating a different world *literally* beyond that which was comprehensible only years before.

Kafka had "a view of human consciousness that is irrevocably and disastrously split; the inner contemplative life is so thoroughly cut off from the public persona that it makes its appearance as an ugly and alien object."⁶ This exists in two facets: (1) We have trouble reconciling who we have become in spite of who we thought we were; and (2) our mentality is challenged by society in that our purest concept of self is in competition with social pressures to conform. In the horror film, this realization leads to the creation of the monster, one that finds life loses meaning. This is the foundation of existentialism. While the exact definition of existentialism is still up for debate (as a philosophical question itself it is widely applied), we can think of the philosophy itself as Descartes's formula, "I think; therefore, I am." For the existentialist, the possibilities of altering human nature and society are unlimited, but, at the same time, human beings can hope for aid in making alterations only from within. Considering this view alone—that humans can better themselves—should separate our understanding of the shooting at Columbine High School with reconciling how to live a prosperous life in a world that seems out to get us.

On April 20, 1999, Eric Harris and Dylan Klebold were the subject of worldwide scrutiny after they opened fire at their Colorado high school, the central question simply being "why?" In his book *Columbine*, Dave Cullen turns to the boys' journals for insight into their rationale: "Eric would begin his journal as a killer. He already knew where it would end. Every page pointed in the same direction. His purpose was not self-discovery but self-lionization. Dylan was just trying to grapple with existence. He had no idea where he was headed. His ideas were all over the map.... Good and evil, love and hate—always wrestling, never resolving. Pick your side, it's up to you—but you better pray it picks you back."⁷ These boys, as dangerous and as awful as they were, are not typical serial murderers. There is evidence that Eric was the ringleader and Dylan was the follower, that the entirety of the plan was Eric's psychology. For instance, in the so-called Basement Tapes, Eric and Dylan share their thoughts on their family. Eric apologized to his mom, simply stating, "I really am sorry about this, but war's war."⁸ Dylan, on the other hand, was less generous: "'I'm sorry I have so much rage, but you put it in me,' he said. He got around to thanking them for self-awareness and self-reliance. 'I appreciate that,' he said."⁹ Eric and Dylan's pessimism is largely tied to what Eric called self-awareness, his own philosophy, or as experts call it, atheistic existentialism. Atheism, as we know, is the belief that God does not exist. And we heard from

Dylan that he isn't quite sure what to believe. Fundamentally, it's difficult to blame either for being misguided in a world where, for many youths, it is difficult to establish a sense of identity.

The Horror of Modern American Life

Real-life horrors, or cultural fears, are based on previous understandings of anxieties, or fears of the unknown. While many of today's horror films are based on real-life horrors, they stem from the probability of something that *could* happen. While no one would have assumed that teenaged boys would open fire on their classmates and teachers, it, tragically, became a reality. Like the Gothic fictions of the past, there is a distant chance that we would lose our personage, our identities, our heritage and safety, all because of an invention or dubious potion would turn us into social outcasts. Like fears of The Other, real-life horrors are based in the fact that they are possible, but statistically unlikely. Most of us won't get followed by a creepy clown that hides in the sewers; most of us won't have a doll that houses the spirit of a cop-killer and is trying to get his hidden fortune back; and most of us won't be chased down by a deranged axe murderer, whether we're a camp counselor, older sibling, volunteer Santa, or mild-mannered maintenance worker who lives in a shed out behind the Overlook Hotel.

As real-life horror came to overtake the guise of teens in crisis, the horror film has taken residence in a new area—or, at least, it is attempting to reside in a place that is familiar in the world of books and print. The horror film had returned to exploring the psychological. In 1995's *Se7en*, Brad Pitt and Morgan Freeman portray detectives looking for a serial killer. However, this new killer is smart; he preys on the sins of others in that, like the slashers of the 1980s, he is a vengeful killer albeit one who kills in order to wrong the sins of society. This is the premise of other contemporary horror films as well. Horror filmmakers borrowed the moral and ethical concerns of science fiction and the perils of technology, replacing anxiety with real-world fear. Films such as *Ransom* (1996), in which a married couple (Mel Gibson and Renee Russo) try to rescue their son from a group of kidnappers, explore horrors of the real world coming true. The gruesomeness of *Se7en*, like that of *Ransom*, is not of gross displays of wanton violence, but of horror that exists in the potential demise of members of our society. We're witnessing the fates of others, and we take a small pleasure in knowing that we're safe.

Another facet of horror may be much more evident in that, like Kafka's realization, horror is simply society. It has been argued that the horror/slasher films of the late 1970s and early '80s reflected the zeitgeist of those eras by exhibiting a declining faith in family. *Halloween*, and the plethora of slasher films that followed, appear to suggest that "the horror derives from the family and from the troubling ordeal of being a late-twentieth-century teenager."[10] These films "show teenagers in peril, with no hope of help from their parents."[11] Horror, in all its gravity, can be considered as "safe" in that we can discuss the world in a distinct and separate reality. However, this new brand of horror (or, current horror) seeks to thrill us into accepting a world in which we cannot escape. It's humanizing in that we must eventually meet our end, that is, as long as it's not too gruesome or undignified, or even worse, that we face judgment from our neighbors. This was the choice made by Harris and Klebold—they apparently decided that they would take control of their final judgment. Harron's adaptation of *American Psycho* fits the model of existentialism; in fact, Bateman laments the lack of catharsis from his actions, stating that his "confession has meant nothing." Bateman faces no consequences, and any judgment will be elusive. With Columbine still a recent memory, Harron unknowingly exploits the messages in Ellis's novel that, despite the glamour of an affluent society and the rich rewards of a technologically advanced consumer culture, society harbors many people who have trouble simply fitting in. While Bateman's narcissism is clearly reflected in the film, the treatment of the 1980s is largely nostalgic—one reason for the film's cult status is that, by the time the film came out, much of the madness behind Bateman as an outsider had been replaced by a society that had, like Bateman, tuned out the noise of life through an underground network of their own choosing.

Connectivity and the Shrinking World

Our society is built on connection. We recognize those we see frequently, and we build individual aspects of community based on the relationships we make. But as we've progressively turned inward, we've begun to lose the associations with society that we come to trust. Isolated cabins and dark mountain passes still generate horror, but for completely different reasons. Instead of the prospects of isolation, these clichés of horror produced a new horror—the horror of being cut off: "Feeling a bit stranded used to be considered a part of adolescence, and one that developed inner resources. Now it is something that the [social] network [of technology] makes it possible to bypass. Teenagers say that they want to keep their cell phones close, and once it is with you, you can always 'find someone.'"[12] Consequentially, our relationship with technology has begun to erode our lifestyle. Left alone to explore the world, society became a playground of underground secrets. We could search out the forbidden in ways that slasher films were never able to deliver. Instead of costumes and effects, we were now face to face with real death, graphic depictions that previously existed only in the mind. The rise of the personal computer and the so-called Information Age was only part of the progressive reaches that technology afforded Americans connectivity. In fact, Americans were in the wave of a technological renaissance, brought about by advancements in portability and miniaturization, the seeds of which were planted a long time ago. Tracing back to Edison and Tesla, technology opened up the possibilities of extension. Through electric lighting, we became a culture that could function beyond the natural cycles of the sun. Further developments of the telephone made the world smaller, enabling us to communicate great distances from the comforts of home. Just as important as communication was our choice in entertainment: television, VCRs and DVDs gave us house guests that were once relegated to the entertainment of theaters; portable music devices gave us a soundtrack that we could personalize to our tastes; and cameras and video recording devices allowed us to document our existence. These advancements not only made technology mainstream, but their ubiquity in society also made us reliant on the distractions provided by them. Soon, our lives became united with technology, so that even leaving the house without our cell phones is enough to induce panic.

One of the problems that we've come to identify is that understanding horror is typically a personal reflection of values. This is also true of understanding the human condition, or how we reconcile ourselves within society. We must be both part of it while shielding ourselves from the dangerousness associated with it. Part of the problem is simply how we view our idea of self and how we create our internalized identity. Amid the rapid changes of technology, our idea of self is continually reassessed; however, the increase of technological communication may explain where our insecurities lie. Turning to social networks and text messaging, more people are eschewing verbalizing their inner thoughts, instead relying on associations (through websites, pictures, songs, videos, etc.). Instead of internalizing our identity, we've created a misconstruction of the idea of identity: "We come to think that we 'have' selves as we have heads. But the very idea that we have or are a 'self,' that human agency is essentially defined as 'the self,' is a linguistic reflection of our modern understanding and the radical reflexivity it involves. Being deeply embedded in this understanding, we cannot but reach for this language."[13] This description of "reaching" for language is something that affects all of us; but, because of the abstract notion of language, we've begun to substitute feelings, ideas, or concepts associated with language in favor of actually negotiating the meaning we first wished to share. Retreating inwardly, but promoting an outward presence, technology has blurred the manner by which we associate the perception of safety.

Following the demise of the slasher film as an extension of human insecurities, the newest phase of horror was one that explored the relatively safe confines that we could build for ourselves. But as we learned in the 1980s, home has a way of challenging our sense of safety. For instance, in *Fear* (1996), a sociopathic suitor seeks revenge on a family. After Nicole Walker (Reese Witherspoon) breaks up with David (Mark Wahlberg), his continued pursuits and obsession eventually lead to the death of Nicole's close confidant Gary (Todd Caldecott). After committing numerous acts of destructive revenge, David and a group of friends attempt to break into the Walkers' home. However, the house is a modern fortress, protected by a security system complete with surveillance and automated locking mechanisms. Despite the security measures, the impenetrable home becomes a battleground, where technology becomes a savior rather than a source of fear. This is echoed in films such as *Panic Room* (2002) and *Hostage* (2005), in which the invasion of the home represents the invasion of outside world. In each of these films, the promise of technology cannot save those in peril.

Further, echoing the "home invasion" idea, *The Purge* (2013) blends the aspects of home as a safe haven with the need to fulfill the overcoming need to lash out against society. The film explores the

8. Virtual Terrors

aspect of lawlessness through personal catharsis, in which, for a period of twelve hours, all crime is legal. Hours before the Annual Purge is to begin, we follow James Sandin's (Ethan Hawke) retreat to his heavily fortified home in an affluent suburban neighborhood. However, just as the Purge is to begin, his son Charlie (Max Burkholder) provides shelter to a wounded man (Edwin Hodge). Once barricaded in the house, the Sandins are met by a group of masked individuals, demanding the release of the man, lest they be punished for disrupting the group's selected target for their own cathartic purge. Underneath, the film is a social commentary, where the Purge is an artificial form of population control, where the poor and homeless are main targets. However, equally as important is the aspect of social angst expressed by the Sandins' neighbors, who are jealous of James's wealth, as he benefits from the sale of security systems. Even with better security, the film explains, the source of terror may be the very society within which we must exist.

Outside terrors have ceased to carry the gravity that the modern psychos of slasher films depicted; while "home" is often the source of terror, the means for accessing horror is less the random invader, but those we knowingly invite in. Previous sources of horror were dependent on physical confrontation; that hasn't changed with the advent of the contemporary horror film. While a multitude of films turned toward psychological horrors of social progress reflected in classical horror and modern science fiction, due to the growing technological presence within the horror film, many films looked at the possibilities of technology as a source of horror itself. Rather than having the monster come to us in person, the virtual presence of monstrosity took a new form in that the monstrous largely existed outside of society. Instead of horror confronting us like a madman, our inclination was fast becoming that horror would be *found*, something stumbled upon by accident. We could block out the world, but we couldn't block out the inevitable reach that technology now had a hold on our collective vision of society. This was the precise scenario following the attacks on the World Trade Centers in Manhattan on September 11, 2001. Despite the attacks taking place in New York City, the entire world was able to watch the turmoil unfold in real time; news of the attacks and the speculation of further attacks spread via live video feeds, telephone and cell phone calls, e-mail, blogs, and television. This one instance brought down the façade of safety, quickly elevating the idea of 21st-century horror from something lurking to an instantaneous realization of horror in the present world. While the attacks were carried out by terrorists who lurked like monsters, carrying on with their lives until given the final order to carry out mass destruction, the continued media presence and replaying of events created a culture of fear that could revisit the horrors at any time, at any place.

Today's technological society has created walls, those built up of personal fears over which we have no control. By embracing technology, we built these walls upon the superficial idea of control. Computers and cell phones allow us to turn off the stimulation felt through interconnectedness. While we have the ability to reach out, there is an assumption that this option will always be available and that we can choose where those connections are made. This assumption began with the resurrection of the slasher film. Wes Craven's *Scream* enabled mobile terror, shaking off the escapist mentality of previous "home alone" horrors, such as *When a Stranger Calls* or *Halloween*. Getting out of the house wasn't enough anymore. You had to make sure that you escaped unseen. Armed with a cell phone, the new killer could be watching your every move, trailing the victim, all the while taunting the victim who, to this point, expects the telephone to be a static/stationary device. As mobile phones grew in popularity, we became more adept at tuning out our surroundings by always keeping a connection with those we trust. Similarly, the rise of portable media players (led by the iPad) furthered the sense of isolation, so much so that police warned citizens of being too complacent in the digital void created by mp3 players. By stepping into society, armed with the gadgetry of distraction, we ultimately chose to ignore those warnings.

Horror in the modern world is, if anything, invasive. When we venture outside of the home, we are not simply leaving home—we are entering into a society largely changed from the quaint and assistive one of previous generations. We're told not to talk to strangers, not to trust anyone, and to keep to ourselves. Isolation is central to safety. However, with the rise of cell phones and the Internet, isolation is the antithesis of every fabric of our being. While the landline telephone tethered us to a singular locale, the modern cell phone presents us with unlimited mobility. Freed from the constraints of one location, terror could now follow victims as they seek cover and attempt to reach out to everyone in their address book. On the other hand, invasive technology and surveillance films echo the horrors of September 11; rather than relive tragedy, we find ways to block out the distractions of facing the world for what it is. This may explain the rise of films that focus on torture, otherwise known as "torture porn," such as the *Saw* franchise (2004–2010), *Hostel* (2005), and *A Serbian Film* (2011), and the recent rise of invasion films, including *Signs* (2002), *Cloverfield* (2008), *The Happening* (2008), *District 9* (2009). But as much as the outside world is intrusive, several films explore our own curiosity, specifically that we use our connections to find the forbidden. Existing everywhere and nowhere, our embrace of the Internet left us feeling more connected than ever before. Even when the cost of connectedness became a source of fear in itself.

Technology and Everyday Life

Building on the procession of films that exploited home video, horror films took to embracing computers and virtual reality as the next step to proclaiming independence over the real world. But the inevitable backlash against this newfound exploration of independence came with a price:

> The history of electronic technology since the Second World War has been dominated by miniaturization, with ever more microscopic switches being implemented in each new device. These improvements led to a jump to universality in about 1970, when several companies independently produced a microprocessor, a universal classical computer on a single silicon chip. From then on, designers of *any* information-processing device could start with a microprocessor and then customize it—program it—to perform the specific tasks needed for that device. Today, your washing machine is almost certainly controlled by a computer that could be programmed to do astrophysics.[14]

The proliferation of unknown technologies marked a changing point in horror. Spurred by casual interest and personal motivations, the existence of relatively unknown technologies proved a turning point in how mainstream audiences perceived horror in the wake of the Internet revolution. Seeking immediate gratification in the prospect of other people, we could find connection through electronic means. In *White Noise* (2005), the concept of Electronic Voice Phenomenon (or EVP) explores the literal premise of "ghosts in the machine." Identified in

1939, and now the subject of increasing scientific research worldwide, the opportunity to find evidence of and communicate with the deceased is fostered on the idea that paranormal agents communicate on different "frequencies" than the living. By "tuning into" or channeling the noises of the static found in stray radio transmissions and background noise, the belief is that we can find evidence of life after death through advanced techniques of communication through electronic means. It is relevant that the film *White Noise* debuted at a time when more Americans were tuning out of their societies by retreating into the world of pure and reliable digital communications as opposed to radio or television. Widower Jonathan Rivers (Michael Keaton) receives a telephone call from his late wife's phone; when he answers the call, the line is nothing but empty air. After being contacted by a man who explains to him the phenomenon that is EVP, Jonathan's skepticism turns into belief as he attempts to communicate with his dead wife. Setting up a home "laboratory" of computers, audio equipment, and radios, his search for life after death eventually comes to manifest itself in the real world. While the film (and its sequel) explores the paranormal, it is significant in showing the rise of modern home technologies as a means of perpetuating deadly prospects.

In a similar fashion, *iMurders* (2008) features a varied group who use the Internet as a means of connection through a social network called "facespace" (an obvious amalgamation of MySpace and Facebook), which the film acknowledges as "unbelievably addictive." Two things are emphasized by those who log onto the network: they are spread out across the country, and they come from all walks of life (a party planner, a special-effects designer, a professor, and a phone sex operator). They take part in a game that, as it is the month of October, is a murder mystery. Mark, the game's host, is murdered by an unknown killer; his death is captured on audio and, for those that have them, a webcam. But, as he is both the SFX expert and the game's host, the murder is seen as a gag. Mark's death is a form of connection, a "reality" made possible by the Internet. While all the participants see the murder, none connect the virtual killing in real time—they all believe it to be part of the game. Additionally, *Untraceable* (2008) follows FBI agent Jennifer Marsh (Diane Lane) as she investigates a killer who posts his victim's deaths onto his website, killwithme.com. To maintain the site's growing interest, the killer promises the posting of additional videos.

The exploration of choice and moral limits is conducted by investigating inner desires, or "lust of the soul."[15] Exploring personal transgressions, horror allows for a window into our own inquisitiveness; but, without limits, we can reach a state where too much information becomes a horror in itself: "Our yearning for knowledge was long ago dubbed *libido sciendi*,[16] a term that insists on the analogy between curiosity and sexual desire. In Book X of the *Confessions*, in which St. Augustine describes our three major temptations, he closely associates 'concupiscence of the flesh,' particularly sexual lust, with concupiscence of the eyes. He means lust for knowledge, which is 'in many ways more dangerous.'"[17] Not only is curiosity dangerous, but the implication is that forbidden knowledge will lead to more deviant behavior. In other words, the simple act of seeing makes us accept the action, numbing us to the source. We push the limits of our knowledge and, in turn, set defined boundaries as "off-limits" based on observation. Our ethical response is based upon what we internalize, what we perceive, and by those foundations we have already made. However, with more exposure to horror, we've lost the idea of horror, thereby losing our own morality.

Morality, as seen through the idea of wrongful voyeurism, is the premise of *FeardotCom* (2002). A detective (Stephen Dorff) investigates a series of murders that link all the victims to the same website, one that enables viewers to watch horrific acts online. Similar to *The Ring*, the film exploits the "watch and die" idea of seeking out forbidden knowledge. What *FeardotCom* and its imitators—such as *REC* (2007), *One Missed Call* (2008), *Shutter* (2008), *Messages Deleted* (2009), and *Playback* (2012)—change is the delivery of realization. Ultimately, horror is everywhere to be found, and it is our own sense of transgression that leads us to finding it—although this isn't that different from exploring a haunted location that's the subject of urban legends, or attempting to find the source of a mysterious noise in the basement. The idea of transgression is central to the horror film. Horror functions in the aspect of a dirty secret, being that we learn about and simultaneously eschew such lessons based on moral dictates. There is also that which is not amoral, but *abnormal*—we shouldn't have the experiences because it is unnatural for us to experience such horrors. For instance, brutal crime scenes are natural in that they are the result of acts of inhumanity, but it is unnatural to bear witness to the scene firsthand. This is what makes the technological view of horror so important to assessing the threats of the digital world.

Horror acts in concert with the world, showing possibilities of everyday occurrences through what we can only term the *alternate world of film*. In many cases, horror films mirror society, with modern horror films presenting the horrific of technological progress as the greatest reflection of social collapse. And, following this line of thought, the modern horror film resonates with the sense of connection found through the pervasiveness of the cell phone: "If the new millennium's telephone movies imagine proliferated sites of connective desire, new ways of remaining bound to parents, families, and loved ones across vast distances, these films also proliferate the sites of terror,"[18] specifically that we can be targeted anywhere, at any time. Cell phones provide immediate connectivity. There is always a feeling that safety is only a phone call away. We call friends for emotional comfort, and we can call a tow truck if stranded on the side of the road. But there is never a guarantee that our life line will arrive with the immediacy that we get with the comfort of a voice. For instance, in *Pulse* (2006),[19] a group of friends find that a mysterious computer virus is attacking society through wireless means. When attempting to solve the murder of Josh (Jonathan Tucker), his girlfriend, Mattie (Kristen Bell), and his other friends start receiving messages from him; they immediately suspect that his computer is auto-sending messages on his behalf. After Mattie learns that Josh's computer had been sold, she is able to track down the new owner, Dex (Ian Somerhalder), who informs her that Josh's computer contains a number of videos that are linked to a mysterious computer hacker (Kel O'Neill), who has been working on transmitting information on newfound frequencies. The realized horror of the film is that Josh's death was caused by a rogue experiment that ultimately resulted in a computer virus, infecting not just his computer but inflicting death on anyone who uses Internet connections, cell phones, or television. To escape with their lives, Mattie and Dex must flee to a "safe zone" devoid of technology.

Similarly, *The Signal* (2007) seeks to replace subjective realities with experience. Told in three parts, each part signifies a dramatic shift in perspective, leaving the viewer to distinguish reality as a sense of awareness. *The Signal* is a mixture of post-millennium commentary on reliance of media and a neo-zombie flick, suggesting that we're being controlled by the technologies that help us to interact with the world. *The Signal* depicts the same idea of hypnosis through ambivalence; however, instead of retreating from the electronic world, the ambivalence seen in *The Signal* is that of never being fully connected with the outside world, largely suggesting that this is no escape. In many ways, the film discusses ideas of objectification, partly because of its awareness of the "signal" as a method of expressing thoughts, but also as a way of communicating ideas of living in a fantastical world where sensory overload replaces real thought. Though bloody and at times extremely funny and insightful, the film shows us the problem of existence through voyeurism and altered states of reality. In other words, the question of *life* is replaced by life as it seems—a reality built on perception.

But this theme isn't new in horror. For instance, in John Carpenter's *They Live* (1988), a race of aliens keeps society at bay through subversive hypnosis. Through the use of mysterious sunglasses, Nada (Roddy Piper) and Frank (Keith David) discover that society is full of subliminal suggestions that tell us to "stay asleep" and "submit to authority." Joining with a group of activists, the pair helps to fight the reaches of media by disrupting the broadcast signal of Cable 54, which is the source of the alien message. At the center of the film is the agenda of the alien conspirators, who are collaborators with the human elite, suggesting that in the blindness of consumption, Americans will passively accept just about anything. The reaches of technology and the exploration of media as a subliminal threat challenge the foundations of our social well-being: "In this cycle of horror films, television, video, and the Internet appear as threats to the stability and safety of human subjects, challenging not only the status of cinema itself but also the stability of the nuclear family, specifically through the reconfiguration of the relationship between public and private space. These films seem to imply that electronic media will lead to fragmented social relationships because of their illusion of authenticity and their potential to further isolate people from a larger community."[20]

Over time, the perpetual influx of technology permeated every facet of our lives. Rather than using technology as an escape from the daily grind of life (via television and movie rentals), we began using technology to supplant our need to remember dates or think independently. The computer revolution resulted in a dependence on technology: "With the Internet comes a loss of privacy that newer generations don't even recognize as troubling, if they even recognize the loss at all. Whereas there is a worry for those around the world who are *not* connected via the newest technologies, there is a more sophisticated worry that in the very near future none of us will ever be able to become *disconnected*."[21] As more people migrate to social networking to record their lives digitally, the visionary film *The Final Cut* (2004) is fast becoming a reality. Directed by Omar Naim, *Final Cut* is a film that attempts to erase our digital presence, although through the futuristic idea of memory implants, which record the memories of life. Alan Hakman (Robin Williams) is employed as a "cutter," a literal "hack man" one who edits the memories of the newly deceased, presenting the memories as a final testament for family and loved ones. The ZOE implant is meant to provide long lasting memories. Each memory is given a date, and is shown from the first-person perspective of viewers, allowing viewers to relive their own experiences with the deceased (family members are even able to request memories to include in the "remembering ceremonies." Hakman faces the difficult process of presenting deceased as faultless, despite bearing witness to their terrible actions. In a meeting, Alan states that his job is to "help people remember what they want to remember." In response, a former cutter named Fletcher (Jim Caviezel) clarifies Alan's role in hiding the sins of others: "There is no way to measure the profound effect the ZOE implant has had on the way that people relate to each other. Am I being filmed? Should I say this or not? What will they think in thirty years if I do this or that? And what about the simple right not to be photographed?" Under Fletcher's intensive questioning, Alan confesses that he sees his role in line with the ancient tradition of the Sin Eater.[22] However, Fletcher seeks to convince him that the burdens he carries for others are not worth the price of destroying the lives of the sinners' victims. This is realized with the appearance of Charles Bannister (Michael St. John Smith), Alan's newest client and a man with a deep secret.

Memory chips are stored indefinitely, enabling Alan to revisit the lives of the dead. Memories are stored in categories, ranging from the benign (fears, athletics, growth spurts) to the private (romantic life, masturbation). As we watch Alan work to assemble Bannister's remembrance, he is confronted with the realization that Bannister is hiding the fact that he molested his daughter. Alan, in an interview with Bannister's daughter Isabel (Genevieve Buechner), who is attempting to fulfill Bannister's widow's requests, realizes that Isabel, too, is attempting to hide the past. When asked if he will help her dad forget her own sins, Alan advises her not to forget the sins committed against her.

Hakman, who, like all cutters, is forbidden from having his own ZOE implant. He is stunned, however, upon learning that his parents (who died when he was young) had embedded a ZOE implant in him. By watching a sales video, Alan learns the following: (1) the ZOE implant promises immortality; and (2) parents are cautioned not to tell their children about the device until they reach 21, at which time they should be mature enough to handle the information. The new knowledge of his own device leaves Alan with the horrific realization that he, too, will be scrutinized by someone viewing his own private, internal world. This creates a crisis of conscience, which ultimately makes him confront his own repeated memories of witnessing a childhood friend's death.

Despite the popularity of the ZOE implant, there is a divided perception of the device, showcased by anti-implant demonstrators who warn families to "remember for yourself." The effect is one that highlights the growing backlash of technology, suggesting something similar to Neo-Luddism,[23] a passive leaderless movement that recognizes the negative impact of technology on individuals. Additionally, they fear the possibility of new technologies and their potential for disrupting the human aspects of life. As a form of self-protection, these individuals modify their bodies with tattoos containing electro-synthetic ink, which "creates a magnetic field ... locking [the implant] from recording audio/video." Alan turns to this group for support, getting a tattoo of a power button.

After Alan is confronted by his lover Delila (Mira Sorvino), who finds evidence of her past lover's memories in Alan's apartment,[24] he seeks out assistance in removing his own device. Given the opportunity to view his own memories in real time, in an attempt to assuage his own guilt of his friend Louis's death. By revisiting the memory, he learns that his friend did not die, and that the blood he was standing in turned out to be a spilt bucket of paint. Given access to his own memory, Alan is relieved of his burden; he becomes his own sin eater through technology. It is through this realization that Alan decides that some secrets, like those of Isabel and Charlie Bannister, are better left in the grave. As the widow Jennifer Bannister (Stephanie Romanov) says, "Some things are better left forgotten." However, her daughter, overhearing the conversation, realizes that justice will never be served for her emotional wounds. The film suggests the erosion of privacy and the lasting impact of digital life, something that, for many adolescents, has become a reality. Like a video history, the ZOE implant allows us complete recovery of lives. This is why cutters cannot have implants, as Alan realizes when he is pursued by Fletcher. Alan is now a receiver to the implanted memories, carrying the burden once again of others. In this way, it seems that the film asserts we can never forget the past.

For many years, the rise of technological progress was seen as a something we should be wary of, but as technology reached more people, its effects became astoundingly clear. In her book *Alone Together: Why We Expect More from Technology and Less from Each Other*, Sherry Turkle explores, through a series of interviews, the many ways in which technology helps deepen our sense of isolation. In talking about the reaches of technology as a disruption to our individual sense of being, she notes the following:

> In democracy, perhaps we all need to begin with the assumption that everyone has something to hide, a zone of private action and reflection, one that must be protected no matter what our techno-enthusiasms. I am haunted by the sixteen-year-old boy who told me that when he needs to make a private call, he uses a pay phone that takes coins and complains how hard it is to find one in Boston. And I am haunted by the girl who summed up her reaction to losing online privacy by asking, "Who would care about my little life?"[25]

There are always exceptions about who would be interested in the lives of others—this may be why the vernacular for reading old posts and photos of Facebook users is called "stalking." However, the question remains: can we expect privacy when we so openly promote ourselves to strangers? The shrinking world provided by horror films exploiting the cataloguing of information and the lasting impact of the digital world explains why so many are vigilant when it comes to protecting our privacy, and why isolation, paranoia, and voyeurism figure so heavily into the modern idea of horror. And, as horror evolves into the 21st century, we'll begin to see why so many films fight back in an attempt to show us the way to regain personal identity.

CHAPTER 9

Exhibitionism, Technique and Establishing Modern Horror

> Horror films are rehearsals for our own death.—Stephen King

> Oh, please don't kill me Mr. Ghostface. I want to be in the sequel.—Tatum (Rose McGowan) mockingly pleading for her life before she is killed in Wes Craven's Scream

To get to the modern horror film, we should trace the evolution of the genre as a series of shared acts, in which we have continually bore witness to the collapse of society. It has become increasingly evident that horror is spread through suggestion; old world monsters spread through word of mouth, whereas new world monsters have spread through suggestion. The modern horror film attempts to show horror by way of showing it to others. Instead of personal fears, we've begun to spread the idea of horror as something shared. This may be a direct result of the rise of film culture (through video and DVD rentals, horror festivals) and the rise of access to horror through technology. Like the classic monsters that came from our skepticism of technological advancement, or the new monsters of technology that invaded our sense of achievement, the modern monster is a result of accepting technology as a way of life. What this implies is that we are at the mercy of others when it comes to realizing horror; we may stumble upon it, but rarely do we manifest our own horrors, as we have the implicit warnings of our own knowledge to safeguard us against what we may find. For horror to truly resonate, it must be found.

Despite its modest budget, *The Blair Witch Project* (1999) was a smash hit, grossing over $140 million at the box office. But, for a movie where largely nothing happens, what was the appeal to viewers? It may be the sense of safety that modern American life seems to provide: "Heather notes they can't really be lost in the woods 'because this is America—we've exhausted all of our natural resources,' prompting her mocking comrades to sing ragged versions of 'America the Beautiful' and 'The Star-Spangled Banner.'"[1] The mockery is observant, suggesting that modernity is a sense of conquering nature. Specifically, in the sense of American technological achievement, Mike (Michael Williams) and Josh (Joshua Leonard) represent a new generation, those who embrace technology as a savior from any danger that exists in the natural world. However, from Heather's (Heather Donahue) tearful confession later in the film, her apology is one that is aware of taking the group's isolation too lightly. Lost in the woods, three film students struggle to find their way back to safety while documenting the legend of the Blair Witch. The film started a new genre within horror that paralleled the tech-boom of the late 1990s—found footage.

Three amateur filmmakers venture into the woods to document an urban legend. Although the premise is an oft-used staple in horror, the methods in which viewers learn of the outcome is unique. We become participants as they stumble about the woods. The resulting footage is unedited, presenting a less-than-polished version of events, thus presenting viewers with an idea of the intimacy of the events. However, unlike the films that precede *The Blair Witch Project*, the immediacy prevalent in the film heightens the dramatics as though the viewer is in the moment with the characters. By employing technology readily available to a majority of viewers at the time, the film breaks the fourth wall and gives viewers "reality" as it is experienced. Yet the film never shows the source of terror that the students encounter, suggesting that it (and our sensations resulting from their fears) is never realized. These fears would eventually be confirmed in films that succeeded *The Blair Witch Project*, which had an overwhelming effect on viewers. For an audience to perceive something as horrific, it has to maintain the mystery of the unknown. Horror, it seems, is always in the dark.

Despite the monsters that we've come to realize as essential to our foundations of horror, the modern monster is one borne from the unknown reaches created by our disillusionment with the changing world. Capitalizing on the rise of reality television, where the cast is ordinary and the scenes themselves lack any horror other than the assumption that horror is inescapable, *The Blair Witch Project* is largely undocumented evidence of an urban legend. The characters forget their purpose, often leaving the camera turned off or forgetting their target (turning the camera away from the subject). For a horror film, the events aren't on the horrific being of the Blair Witch but on the breakdown of the characters' once seemingly tight-knit camaraderie. This was achieved through a unique change in the film's production: "The film was shot by the actors, improvising around a loose script. Trained to use the equipment, they were sent into the woods to film in real time, taking cues from concealed notes and plainly growing genuinely miserable in the rain and cold. 'Your safety is our issue,' producer Gregg Hale told them; your comfort is not.'"[2] In part, the film shows us an actual portrayal of the awful, the actors' continual removal from the comforts to which they've become accustomed.

The breakdown is further explored through their ineptitude as filmmakers. They walk into the woods with an idea, but have no idea how to execute it. The result is a film that represents the technological void created by a changing world, where no one is assured safety; they "eventually prove ill-equipped for dealing with a natural and transformative world: their car can only take them so far; their map and compass prove useless; their cameras and sound equipment, designed to record the real, offer no insulation against a mysterious, perhaps even supernatural realm."[3] Lacking the necessary foresight of knowing *what* to capture, the actors themselves forget, giving the audience a realistic portrayal of chaos as they struggle to use the technology that had, for many, become seen as user-friendly and even commonplace.

Found Footage and Reality Horror

Found footage in the horror genre perpetuates the realization of horror simply by its existence. Rather than a publicized event, the resulting story of found-footage horror is one built on the complete and total lack of catharsis—for us to witness the events, the implication is that we are finding the footage after the demise of the central characters. The existence of found-footage horror is corroborated by the manner in which we, the unassuming viewers, stumble upon the horrific. *The Blair Witch Project* was not the first film to display personal footage as a means to finding horror. But its popularity arose from the prospects that anyone with a camera could be a filmmaker, whether the filmmaker lives or dies is often secondary. Instead, the simplicity of "found" evidence, especially by way of video, provides a sense of realism in that the plots of found-footage films often explore sociological taboos and myths that exist in the greater consciousness. For instance, one of the first found-footage films, Ruggero Deodato's *Cannibal Holocaust* (1980), explores the plight of a missing documentary crew that allegedly was inspired by Italian media coverage of terrorism. A rescue mission led by anthropologist Harold Monroe (Robert Kerman) eventually finds the missing footage, in which the evidence provides an explanation of the doomed mission. Centering on the gory acts of a cannibalistic tribe in the Amazon rain forest, the controversial decision by the Pan American Broadcast Company to air the footage unedited leads to an outcry, in which the public views the staged murder of the crew by the cannibals. The sacrifice is a message to the viewing public. Because of its attention to the gory elements of the cannibals' actions, the film was the center of controversy, but over the years has spawned a cult following because of its influence on the found-footage genre and the subsequent rise of torture porn that followed.

The rise of found footage in popular horror was greatly influenced by another low-budget film, the comedic *Return to Horror High* (1987). A documentary crew returns to the scene of a brutal crime to detail the events as a production team is making a "true crime" movie (similar to the *Stab* franchise of Craven's *Scream* films). *Return to Horror High* is aware of its place in the annals of cinematic history—it never planned on being an Oscar winner, evidenced by the movie's poster of a skeleton in a cheerleading outfit and the casting of Maureen McCormick, forever known as TV's Marcia Brady. But it is a great commentary on the horror film as it entered the technological age of modern filmmaking. The effects team is clearly disappointed when the film's director emphatically tells them, "There will be no exploding tit shots!" When asked by one of the film's extras, "What's my motivation?" Sleerik responds, "You're *dead*! Dead people have no motivation!" What matters, for the director of the film within the film, Harry Sleerik (Alex

9. Exhibitionism, Technique and Establishing Modern Horror

Rocco), is that his production appears to be real, despite the ineptitude of his cast and crew.

Obviously, as the crew sets out to revisit the events of an unsolved crime, in its actual location, the film becomes a story wherein history begins to repeat itself. When lead actor Oliver (George Clooney) is found dead, Sleerik recasts his role, hiring a former student turned police officer, Steven Blake (Brendan Hughes), to act as technical advisor, providing the effect of a legitimate production. When his casting director objects, their exchange signifies the premise of the film:

> **JOSH:** I need an actor.
> **HARRY:** This is better. This is reality!
> **JOSH:** They're going to hate the movie.
> **HARRY:** Not if you give them good tits and blood.

The film within the film uses the same exploitation of the slasher genre to produce "results"—multiple exposed breasts, special effects that dominate the death scenes which substitute for plot, and a murder mystery that itself questions the appearance of truth and fiction. Every murder seems to be questionable, as the victims come back to life, suggesting that publicity is the only thing that matters. As dawn approaches (and filming nears its conclusion), the police arrive to investigate claims of a killer once again on the loose, albeit the tip is from the director himself. As the police storm the school, the crew hurriedly removes all the bodies, effects and all traces of their presence. When Josh asks Harry what the point was, Harry sees the events as a spectacle: "They all died, but the film survived. Do you know how much publicity this will get?" We become aware that, as an audience, we were set up. It explains the source of horror as a blend of expectation and release. There is no catharsis, because there is no enemy other than the legacy of the murders (to which no murderer was found) and the story left behind, which we learn is fabricated.

Filmed during the height of the slasher genre's popularity, *The Return to Horror High* asks us to question not just *what* we're watching on screen, but also *who*. As more films cast the killer as a likeable character, the clichés of old horror (the final girl, the safety of home, and the "rules" of the horror film) are masked when we're unable to tell the difference between the killer and the potential victims. These innovations of the horror film not only challenge us to ask ourselves the purpose in watching such horrors but to address the reasoning behind their popularity. It may be that, through the horror film, we're lashing out against society, embracing our own dark natures: "Related to the importance of 'likeable villains,' it is important to note that enjoyment of violence or victimization may additionally reflect a particular dislike of the characters who are featured as victims. In fact, the portrayal of victims as distasteful likely plays a role in justifying the killer's otherwise unthinkable violence."[4] Considering the rise of the slasher film, whose victims are often affluent suburban teenagers with better-than-average lives, the catharsis enjoyed isn't through the destruction of the monster, but the resulting payback we've often wished against others. With the rise of the found-footage film, the victims continue to be ordinary people; however, they play the victims tasked with the unfortunate duty of proving their worthiness to survive the audience's internal wish for sacrifice.

Finding (and Documenting) Horror

The modern found-footage film, the foundations of which lie in *The Blair Witch Project*, are tied exclusively with the Internet. As the web was gaining more viewers, found-footage films exploded in popularity, as the images of the past came to symbolize the legacy of information popularized by the average user. This is compounded by the fact that the Internet allows users to reinvent or exploit the underground ideas that, in the past, would have eroded because of our necessary social nature: "It used to be that the roughest edges of people's odd beliefs would erode and crumble through simple isolation, through a lack of reinforcement with social bonds. Now isolation is nigh impossible, and those odd beliefs are sharpened and exaggerated when they are brought into the open in the company of a cozy group of like-minded individuals. In other words, the Internet is amplifying our quirks and our odd ideas. Bit by bit, it is driving us toward extremism."[5]

The Blair Witch Project gained popularity through an aggressive marketing campaign. Before the film's release, Internet users were enticed to visit the film's website,[6] in which the mythology, aftermath, and police evidence help to corroborate the evidence as truthful (the website states that the tapes were found by the Frederick County Sheriff's office). The Internet hasn't changed the prospects of the existence

9. Exhibitionism, Technique and Establishing Modern Horror

of horror as something found. For instance, in *Stand By Me* (1986), the story of four boys who venture out to investigate the discovery of a dead body, the implied sense of horror was coming face to face with death. Told though the narrator's (Richard Dreyfus, representing Stephen King, whose novella *The Body* is the basis for the film[7]) adult recollection of the event, the story is both a powerful statement of forbidden knowledge set amidst the backdrop of 1950s innocence and an antidote to the horrors portrayed in the rising cycle of horror films that pervaded the 1980s. By seeking out horror on their own accord, the boys confront horror on their terms. As horror, especially found horror, is becoming more commonplace in the real world because of photo and video evidence that proliferates on the Internet, horror is routinely viewed as a something to be foraged for, even dug up, instead of left behind.

Found footage explores events, both past and present, as a link to missing or forgotten knowledge; where *Stand By Me* recalls the body of a boy as a tragic reminder, modern horror builds upon the recording of events so that we can trace the origins of our fears. For instance, *Super 8* (2011) explores footage from a 1979 train wreck that unleashes an unnatural threat against a small town. *The Poughkeepsie Tapes* (2007) explores the evidence of tapes found in an abandoned house. The tapes document the evidence of an at-large serial killer over a period of several decades. But found horror isn't always from an outside source; at times, found footage is a method of proving evidence of one's own assumption. In *House* (1986), writer Roger Cobb (William Katt) faces the demons of his aunt's home, which he has inherited. Having to reconcile the loss of his son, his pending divorce, and the nightmares of Vietnam that still plague him, the film is similar to the idea that home is a prison, of sorts. However, rather than succumb to the demons he sees, he attempts to find the evidence of their origin, setting up a series of stills, cameras and video cameras as he investigates the peculiar manifestations that have come to haunt him. In *Caché*[8] (2005), the horror is the combination of watching and accessing. After Georges (Daniel Auteuil) views a series of video tapes left on his front porch, he is surprised to learn that the footage is of he and his family. The film is largely about the reach of documenting the pains of others and living with past sins. Georges, a television reporter, is implicated in the death of an Algerian man, with whom he lived until he was sent to an orphanage after he convinces him to slaughter a rooster. The film is a commentary about escape similar to *The Final Cut*; in a world where we can always be watched, can we ever escape from the past?

Likewise, *Paranormal Activity* (2007) combines the previous idea of home surveillance and the safety of home, combining it with the found-footage genre to establish a progression of the horror film. Building on the perception of safety at home, what once belonged to the private has now become public domain. The film, a derivation of *The Blair Witch Project*, leaves behind the evidence of one couple's run-in with a haunting. But the transformation of Katie (Katie Featherston) and Micah's (Micah Sloat) death would be another supernatural story if it were not for the cameras Micah sets up to prove Katie's superstitions as ungrounded. However, because of the surveillance tapes, the audience is able to watch the events unfold.

With the release of *The Fourth Kind* (2009), in which a psychiatrist videotapes her sessions with clients and discovers evidence of alien abduction, we're learning more about the subliminal aspects between the hidden self and the prospective view of others. By using the evidence of her tapes, Abbey Tyler (Milla Jovovich) uncovers evidence that, while private, becomes necessary to solve the investigation. The tapes reveal shared memories of abductees who would otherwise have remained hidden without the intervention of modern technologies. In a society that is increasingly attempting to hide itself, *The Fourth Kind* explores the need to share information, despite the isolation so desperately sought by those with something to hide. This is evidence of the combined notion of technical progress as a source of horror. Sontag writes that science-fiction films show progress as humanity dominated by progress: "Man is naked without his artifacts. *They* stand for different values, they are potent, they are what gets destroyed, and they are indispensable tools for the repulse of the alien invaders or the repair of the damaged environment."[9] However, what's changed from the past science-fiction film to the modern horror film is that man's artifacts have become weaponized. In the case of *The Fourth Kind*, the tapes become the tools for uncovering the aliens that would have been hidden. As modern horror evolves in the technological world, we will see that it is our devices which become enemies that open our private selves to the leering gaze of the outsider.

The blending of private and public is a source of entertainment for the audience. In what Jean Baudrillard would call the breakdown of sign-order, or where symbolism replaces real meaning, the blurring of private and public life can be traced to his 1981 thesis on *Simulacra and Simulation*. Specifically, Baudrillard's third stage of the breakdown of representation depicts the "absence of profound reality," where *simulacrum* pretends to exhibit the essence of reality. This is the foundation of the found-footage film. However, with the rise of television and the Internet, the distinctions between truth and reality began to blur even more, tying the proliferation of found footage to the information age. Local urban legends and ghost stories proliferate on the Internet. So does personal exhibitionism, in that we are increasingly apt to share our own encounters, making stories of finding horror into personal accounts. Additionally, as the taboos of onscreen violence and graphic depictions further erode our moral sensibilities, the prospect of capitalizing on the Internet's promise of information seems to invite more critical explorations of horror as something to be displayed.

Several films capitalized on the reality premise of horror. *Live!* (2007) depicts a controversial television show on which contestants vie for a $5 million dollar prize in an on-air Russian roulette competition. Horror as a lived thing also occurs in *Grave Encounters* (2011), which features a television crew that documents footage for a paranormal reality program. The most famous found evidence of horror exists in *Interview with the Vampire: The Vampire Chronicles* (1994), the blockbuster adaptation of Anne Rice's *The Vampire Lestat*,[10] in which the reluctant vampire Louis (Brad Pitt) chronicles his life with Lestat (Tom Cruise) to a San Francisco reporter (Christian Slater). The truthful nature of Louis's story is a breakthrough for Daniel Molloy (Slater), who, after hearing Louis's story, wishes for the same immortal gift of vampirism, despite the promises of fame by exhibiting Louis's narrative for a worldwide audience.

Opposing the found-footage genre is the documentary-style films that pit individuals recording events as a way of proving the legitimacy of a situation as it happens. These films make a distinction, moving away from discovery to the outright depiction of survival by exposing the personal fears of victims to the outside world. For instance, in *Quarantine* (2008), Angela, a television reporter (Jennifer Carpenter) and her cameraman, Scott (Steve Harris), set out to produce a puff-piece, following a group of firefighters on their late-night shift. After receiving a call to an apartment building about a woman in distress, the playful banter between Angela and the firefighters turns into a life and death situation. As the situation becomes even more deadly, the camera is both invasive (the firefighters repeatedly attempt to usher the news crew away from them as they do their job) and a window to the outside world. After discovering that the invasive sickness is a deadly mutation of rabies, the building is quarantined by the CDC. The only link to the truth is the camera's uplink to the news station. In *Quarantine*, the camera becomes a literal lifesaver: Scott kills an infected woman with his camera; the camera is used as a flashlight when the power is cut; and, through the camera's night-vision setting, the camera allows the crew to negotiate the building in total darkness. However, the camera continues to record the final events, leaving behind a legacy that substantiates the horrors that we've witnessed in the closing seconds of the film.

The found-footage film progressed horror from finding horror to realizing horror; we've moved from discovery by accident to discovery by choice. *Cloverfield* (2008) shows an example of found footage as evidence being called into question. The footage of a personal video camera is a collection of segments that have been edited by the U.S. Department of Defense. Following testimonials of those who witness a monstrous attack on New York City, the footage often cuts out, as it is recorded over previous video. Lasting the length of one cassette, the recording ends abruptly, suggesting that our knowledge of the event is limited to that which could be caught on tape. In *War of the Worlds* (2005), one of the first reactions to those witnessing the arriving aliens is to record the events by video cameras and cell phones. *Cloverfield* echoes the previous cycle of monster movies such as *Godzilla* or *King Kong*, but the innovation of evidentiary materials provides a telling account on how we view horror in the modern age. As we become more in tune with the digital age, it has become increasingly noticeable that we are being held hostage by the nightmares of our phobic attitude toward others. The rise of old monsters have pitted us against the evolution of medical testing and experimentation as shown in *28 Days Later*'s neo-zombies and *Quarantine*'s neo-vampire aesthetic. However, we've also become victim to the idea of lacking an escape, as in our being watched without our consent.

In choosing to bear witness to other's horrors, "Movie audiences gain pleasure both by identifying with the images on the screen and

9. Exhibitionism, Technique and Establishing Modern Horror

by objectifying the images."[11] We become aware of the same possibilities, but receive gratification that these things are happening to someone else; it helps further the idea of safety in isolation. Increasingly, we're being cut off from the world, and a growing number of films depict the quick development from safety to horror. This may explain the proliferation of films that emphasize torture, specifically "postmodern horror movies, [which] are characterized by increasingly gory, graphic dramatizing of the destruction of human bodies."[12] Private horrors of captivity and torture may symbolize the difference of capturing an event and living an event. By watching horror, we're brought into the realm of the filmmaker, having to witness the events as they occur, rather than living in the presumption of past horrors where horror is stumbled upon. The Internet permitted a social avenue in which public exhibition became commonplace.

When Facebook first introduced its "timeline" feature, it was met with a backlash, as users—especially younger students—objected to the regular updating of users' actions, displaying them for all to see. "Timeline" was seen as a form of digital voyeurism, albeit on a social and suggestive scale. Building on the personal postings of web pages and blogs, where users were already openly candid about themselves, the suggestion is that social media blurred the lines between purpose and intent. Facebook and other social media were largely accepted because we could choose what we could stumble upon; however, when shown information, users objected. The legacy of eternal presence (a virtual presence online) was never really considered until users were met with the technology being turned against them. Numerous users complained "about how disconcerting it is to meet others already knowing certain personal details about them."[13] If early horrors were about the psychology of the unknown, then modern horror progressed to show the horrors of the known world. As we've come to further explore the known world through technology, there is a belief that the unknown world ceased to exist:

> Thanks to cellular phones, Wi-Fi, global positioning system satellites, and dagger-sharp aerial and satellite photos of the planet, it is possible for the first time in human history for anybody to find out where he is, relative to anybody or anything else on the surface of the earth. Yet it is just as easy for government agencies and corporations to track us. The same smartphones that steer us to the mall constantly transmit our

exact locations. And phones are being supplemented with other location methods that are even subtler, and often far more insidious.[14]

With advanced technology, we could access anything, including that which we probably shouldn't. But with so many people finding their identity by choosing what they wish to share, the Internet became a breeding ground of self discovery: "It is surveillance driven by desire, and in that way, maybe it is resistant in ways older generations cannot begin to imagine."[15]

Finding Horror (Again)

Horror films work in a cyclical nature. As in the case of the *Frankenstein* cycle of films, horror becomes stagnant once we come to identify the source of horror as a cheap thrill, or, as in the case of Dr. Frankenstein's Monster, a cultural icon that reaches beyond the screen. Though, to be fair, Frankenstein's creation imbedded in the cultural consciousness the definitive image of a monster. Together, these elements identify the dilemma facing modern horror. First, to evoke success, the horror film must have an identifiable monster, one that resonates with the audience. Second, the monster must be relatable, something that fits the time. If we've learned anything from the progressive cycles of horror, it's that there will always be a source of fear in the world. And, in this society bent on advancing technology as something to be controlled, we'll continue to find adaptations and innovations that, in their newest state, produce anxiety and fear until they are assimilated into the culture.

As a society that is now "tuned in," technology has become central to our very being. As a consequence, we lost much of the personal interactions that defined our daily existence. This may be why ordinary settings and accepted technologies have become sources of horror. In *Amber Alert* (2012), the horror is precipitated by friends trying to be normal. Filming their audition tape for a reality television series, Nate (Chris Hill) and Samantha (Summer Bellessa) recognize and follow a car that is the subject of an amber alert, only to realize they've become caught up in a game of survival while trying to do the right thing. In *ATM* (2012), an ordinary stop for money becomes exploited by the stranger mentality as three friends become trapped by a deranged killer. *End of the Line* (2007) features a young nurse who, after boarding the

9. Exhibitionism, Technique and Establishing Modern Horror

subway, becomes trapped in a tunnel, struggling to survive a supernatural element and religious fanaticism in order to escape. In *Frozen* (2010), three skiers become trapped on a stopped chairlift after bribing their way up the mountain for a final run. However, as it is the end of the day, the lift stops, leaving them suspended. In *Chernobyl Diaries* (2012), horror is found in adventure. On an "extreme tour" of the site of a nuclear disaster, tourists realize that they are not alone at the abandoned plant. These five films are based on technological elements of communication, access, transportation, and power. They also echo the clichés of killers and abandonment.

As a statement on where horror is found in the modern world, the horror is a result of new perceptions of our interactions with technology. "This is the crucial difference between modern and hyper- or postmodern forms: the technological ability to realise fantasy by way of machines rather than human imagination. It is a technical power that, emptying gothic of affect, discloses a wider process that produces horror on a cultural scale with no reference at all to the conventional (Gothic) forms and images."[16] While the monsters are the same as those of the past, our experiences with technology ultimately manifest monsters that represent our changing view of the world. In fact, the entire *Final Destination* franchise (2000–2011) displays the inevitability of death through multiple means of progress. When accidents are avoided by premonitions, the personified Death must track down those who escape the disasters of the modern world, varying from a plane crash (*Final Destination*, 2000); an auto accident (*Final Destination 2*, 2003); a roller coaster (*Final Destination 3*, 2006); race cars (*The Final Destination*, 2009); and a suspension bridge (*Final Destination 5*, 2011).

Twice-Told Tales: Horror Remakes and Franchises

It isn't difficult to see that what we perceive as horror is a changing thing. There are multiple monsters for multiple anxieties; likewise, there are a magnitude of films that express a myriad of fears, ranging from the simplistic (fear of the dark) to the most implausible (such as 1988's *Killer Klowns from Outer Space*). But, as we've progressed technologically, so has the reach of our fears. With the advent of better technologies, audiences have sought further ways in which to express their own inner desires for realism amid the technological world, leading filmmakers to exploit the traditional notion of horror as a way to see humanity. Moving beyond the old ways of horror and establishing new frontiers for witnessing the everyday world, modernism has taken on a more influential role in developing the sources from which our horrors derive. For the horror to keep reaching the masses, audiences need to be propelled into recognizing the inherent fears on screen. For each new film or adaptation, the technologies of the old films are replaced or adapted to reflect the modern age. This would explain the changing aesthetic of David Cronenberg's *The Fly* (1986). Seth Brundle's (Jeff Goldblum) equipment is highly specialized, including voice recognition and, instead of lasers (as in the original), two very futuristic replication pods that serve to mutate Brundle into "Brundlefly," suggesting "that *The Fly* effectively packaged a contemporary myth about the corrosive impact of science on the human body."[17] Even with the rise of technology in medicine and computer science, the mythos of horror embedded in future technologies still resounded. Additionally, the modern remake of *War of the Worlds* features a changed landscape where technology is an escape in and of itself.

With new technologies, from the production standpoint of filmmakers, the horror genre is ripe for creativity. Reinterpretations of older, forgotten horror allow for big-budget reproductions that can finally show audiences what had been taboo just 20 years before. Further, as the popularity of past films secure a legacy for future generations, the killers of the past don't seem to be fading away any time soon. Franchises exist because of their financial success; to state otherwise would be disingenuous. But they find financial success because they tap into the unconscious fears that we push away. No matter how absurd the premise may be, there is the thrill factor that connects with the underlying fears that we never bring into our consciousness. However, with the rise of the Internet, the collective film culture, and our permanent obsession with The Other, the shifting idea of horror permeates two realities: the familiar and the absurd. Modern horror develops our everyday fears by using the artifacts of our existence, as Sontag suggests. Thus, the very devices that become beneficial to our progress as a society also become the source of our anxieties and prospective downfall.

Horror films need something imaginative to survive, but the repetition of horror films through repetitive cycles, displaying the same killer on repeat, only gets viewers so far. To be completely clear, fran-

9. Exhibitionism, Technique and Establishing Modern Horror

chises are about one thing: money. But some franchises use their status in order to further story lines, or, as is the case of Wes Craven's films, comment on the genre as a mouthpiece for the horror industry itself. In the original *Scream*, Randy treats his guests to his observations on the rules of the horror film. In the second installment, the film opens with the premiere of *Stab*, the "movie version" of the first film's events. A studio promotion provides the entire viewing audience with the popular "Ghostface" costume of the original, while a raucous audience is treated to a flyover killer, a gimmicky marionette controlled by pulley (similar to the ones popularized by William Castle). Filmed in "stab-o-vision," the theater enhances the green of glow-in-the-dark daggers. Naturally, we're not surprised when Maureen (Jada Pinkett) is stabbed in full view of the audience. It is a moment when art fully imitates life. As she staggers to the front of the theater, the audience is horrified that they are bearing witness to real tragedy, suggesting that the veil of technology as a safe window is finally beginning to crumble. Ironically, this discussion takes place during a film studies class the very next day.

If slasher films paraded teenage promiscuity, then modern horror films wear it like a badge of honor. Modern horror revels in a lack of boundaries, often perpetuated by youthful innocence. The horror franchise is a testament to how we find horror: we build the notion of the horrific through familiarity; seeing repetitive or familiar plot lines erases the substantial guilt felt through voyeuristic portrayals of death and the unfamiliar. But the modern franchise is becoming more difficult to establish, especially where the at-large killer is largely obscured by its own ambivalent audience. In the blur of technology, we are far less in tune with culture than we are with connection. This is no different than how classic horror films envisioned the monster: "While the lowbrow horror films presented preposterous characters but made no pretension to taking their actions seriously, the *Times* critics suggested that psychological horror movies were just as incredible but presented themselves as having a profundity and significance that was hardly justified."[18] Likewise in the modern horror cycle, shocks and surprises alone cannot create a compelling film. This is also why the wry killers of the slasher film began to evaporate from public perceptions of fear. For films to truly extend beyond the boundaries of absurd displays, they need relevance. Horror works because successful filmmakers are aware that it functions to build both commentary and release, in which the genre's appeal is that of a dual purpose, one lodged between the real and the ideal.

Previous horror franchises were built upon the killer, through the popularity of the demonic face of the franchise. New horror has since built the franchise on the psychological aspects of horror, leaving behind the random killer bent on vengeance in favor of the device that repetitively stalks our everyday existence. Modern franchises are built on recognition, not abjection. We see the potential dangers before us, and make the choice to encounter danger on a daily basis or squander our existence in blindness. In the *Saw* franchise, John Kramer's (Tobin Bell) inoperable cancer gives him the realization that he wasted life. Wishing to teach others his lessons, he transforms into the sadistic Jigsaw in order to enact change. His lessons are learned through physical or psychological change brought about by elaborate booby traps, but it is important to realize the Jigsaw's victims are not random—they are selected, often used. Likewise, Craven's *Scream* franchise exploits the horror genre itself, progressing our idea of safety in the changing elements of technological advancement and ambivalence. Horror films enable repetition, as they leave the door open to sequels through ambiguous endings and the lone survivor. Beginning with the questionable ending of *Friday the 13th*, when the killer is revealed to be Jason's mother, the horror film is predicated on the legacy of unfinished business. As society is continually evolving, especially as new technologies emerge into the public consciousness, the possibilities for found horror seem endless.

But what do franchises really offer viewers? First off, there is the matter of expectation. Though many people claim to shy away from horror, there is relative safety in the horror franchise—these films have been vetted through a community, and their sequels open up channels to new viewers that have yet to experience the horror of the original. Though often watered down, sequels exist to provide an outlet, enabling a shared experience of horror across an even larger swath of the public imagination. Second is the presumption of safety. Within every horror story there is an outlet, similar to the viewer that shields their eyes when the action on the screen becomes too real. That outlet is found in repetition. We are given red herrings, through music, lighting, and actor portrayals. We mimic the emotions of the characters, and we absorb the reality of the scenes as if we're living them ourselves; but

9. Exhibitionism, Technique and Establishing Modern Horror

the reality is, they've become too familiar. Familiarity often leads to a third realization, that of acceptability. Though for a time horror films were seen as something to look down upon, the public reception of horror films makes us part of the larger culture. Especially for younger viewers, the horror film is part of the popular culture, something to be discussed and negotiated. As horror is assimilated into the culture, it loses the shock value with which it came to be associated. This is especially realized in sequels (less so with remakes, as many films are not remade until the original version has passed the next generation's scope of value or popularity).

Aside from popularity and marketability, a franchise has to speak directly to the public imagination. And while many franchises have capitalized on exhibitionism, the most popular franchises to date have evolved to display public fears in the most benign manner possible— the horrors of a changing society. As much as horror is built on shocking the audience with new and unimagined terrors, the modern horror film relies on reproductions of past horrors. Reproduction has been a staple of horror, beginning with the earliest horror films dating back to the Universal classics of the 1930s. As with every horror film, in order to continue to provoke the imagination, horror must evolve. As the slasher subset of horror was relishing the financial merits of sequels and reliving the macabre displays of gore that had since become common place, the horror genre as a whole reached a plateau. Fans flocked to see films that were repetitive, based on clichés that had become tired. This didn't diminish their financial success (much), but audiences were growing hungry for the next wave of horror films that tapped into the subconscious fears that audiences didn't know they were looking for. That's the thing about horror films—the best films tap into something that we're not expecting. They grab us by the insides, shake our core, and produce a reality that we were unaware existed. By revisiting old horrors and placing them in the modern world, filmmakers seek to update the monster as a relevant and real perception: "What the New Horror movies share is a sense that the most frightening thing in the world is the unknown, the inability to understand the monster right in front of your face. These movies communicated confusion, disorientation, and the sense that the true source of anxiety is located in between categories: fact and fantasy, art and commerce, the living and the dead."[19]

Horror films will succeed cycling through remakes (with better technology) and franchises. But, once they've run the course of the story line, the franchises will cease to produce realistic terrors, and remakes will present no more than opportunistic repetition for a modern generation that was never afforded the chance—or never bothered to seek out—horror films in their original form. Though the lack of video stores has since been replaced by on-demand cable viewing and Netflix, it's only the horror enthusiast that ventures out to seek the long-forgotten films that once captured the mind by their perpetual presence on store shelves. It's become harder to find the covers that so frequently piqued our interest for a Friday night thrill. Thus, modern horror, if it is to succeed, must rely on shocking the audience through their own sense of discovery, enabling horror to be "found" once again, whether through revivals, remakes, franchises, or simply a good concept that catches the attention anew.

Chapter 10

The Future of Horror

> I can only imagine your pain and confusion. But know this. What's happening to you is part of something bigger. Something older than anything you know. You've seen horrible things. An army that lies below. It's our task to placate the entry points, as it's yours to be offered up to them. Forgive us, and let us get it over with. —The anonymous voice of the director of the Facility, explaining the role of ritual sacrifice in Joss Whedon's *The Cabin in the Woods*.

Directors, writers, critics, and enthusiasts are continually asking, and being asked (whether they know it or not) to redefine horror. This is the nature of the genre. In order to be afraid, we have to reassess what scares us. The beginnings of the horror film were based on Old-World fears, but as the genre grew to encompass our everyday fears and a rapidly changing world, the daily notion of horror is forever being negotiated between audiences and what they perceive on the screen (in whatever form that image takes), from a variety of sources: the serialized portrayals of a thousand Hollywood monsters; the independent films that often take a more subversive approach to social performances; the global reach of media and the marketing of worldwide horror; and to the independent realization of personal horror. What these four sources have in common is the notion of access, in that whatever form horror takes, it is our growing reliance on technology as a window to the world that will eventually show us that which has been happening behind the façade of complacency.

If the horror film has been an investigation of social progression and downfalls, what, then, should we expect from the next cycle of horror films? The progression of horror depends upon the genesis of future fears. Lately, it seems that we've been stagnant as far as potential horrors are concerned. We've sat back to the comforts we've been afforded, creating fears built on the blandness of life similar to that found in Ira Levin's novel *The Stepford Wives*. The automatic response to subordination once challenged the idea of submissive women in a male-dominated society. However, as we've become increasingly submissive to our electronic devices, we've taken less notice of the world and instead, found horror by simply failing to pay attention to that which ultimately may be threatening. Currently, we're at a turning point. We've accepted that technology is a part of everyday society, but technology is continually being used against us.

However, skepticism largely is the result of nascent plots against society, partially because, given our social connections to one another, why would we doubt the very society that we've struggled to build for the last century? Because horror is culturally shaped, its future relies on society's response to current and imminent cultural conditions. To intelligently predict thematic patterns in future horror narratives, we should examine existing and emerging societal anxieties and how they might translate onscreen. Filmmakers rely on technology to show a sense of modernity in order to create a sense of comfort and realness— a far cry from the reaches of early horror films. Technology is ever present, so much that it ceases to be a revolutionary marvel meant to incite awe or wonder and instead becomes a central premise of how fear and anxiety are created. For instance, in *Vile* (2011), a hybrid torture/mad scientist film, captives are held against their will for the purposes of experimentation. Instead of medical experiments at the hands of a madman, the captives must inflict pain on one another in order to stimulate and release specific brain secretions with the aid of vials, implanted at the base of each victim's skull. In the hopes of escaping their captors, the victims must work together. The film implicitly states that we've become slaves to observation. The captives never meet their tormentors face to face. Further, there is a democratic approach to torture. Even though the victims are given the option of doing nothing, there's the opposite view that there is a controlling force subjugating the crowd to the impulses of the outside force of power. By negotiation, the group

10. The Future of Horror

realizes that everyone must suffer. It should be noted that two things happen. As the group watches others, the needed chemical release lessons, as does each individual's sense of compassion for the group. The participants fear more for their own safety while being able to inflict pain and hardship on others. Justice (as seen by the group) is tempered by the whole, specifically by the initiatives of the group consensus. But, as the group gets angrier, the punishments get worse. With 30 minutes left in their 22-hour challenge, the group meets their goal, but still needs to finish one task—the joint removal of their devices, which is equally comforting and disturbing. Perhaps it is this one significant objective, the removal of the device, that ultimately signals our need to be free.

Horror is an exploration of personal safety, something that modern horror seems to have obscured amid the bloodfests of a transformed genre. However, not all horror resorts to shocking the audience's stomach. Instead, horror resonates most profoundly in the idea that we may lose our sense of self. This may be why, as many proclaim, that the horror film is dying; but horror as an idea isn't dead: "The best examples today of classic New Horror scare tactics are outside the genre, and the finest horror scenes are in prestige movies."[1] For instance, Joel and Ethan Coen's *No Country for Old Men* (2007) presents the antithesis of the American Dream. Llewelyn Moss (Josh Brolin) becomes the subject of bounty hunter Anton Chigurh (Javier Bardem) after he finds a sum of money following a botched drug deal. Attempting to manufacture his escape from the monotony of living, Moss challenges the social order by using the money to circumvent the natural order of society. Eventually, Moss learns that the only escape from life is to accept that which we're given. A modern-day crime story, it is neither the drugs nor the Mexican cartel that becomes Moss's downfall—it is his sense of pride. Likewise, the same is true of Kathryn Bigelow's *The Hurt Locker* (2008), where Sergeant First Class William James (Jeremy Renner) is called by the siren song of adrenaline and his mastery of technology, albeit this technology is one that can kill. As a member of the U.S. Army's Explosive Ordnance Disposal unit, James is faced with dismantling the improvised explosive devices (IEDs) that soon became a symbolic weapon against Western imperialism. Comprised of mechanical devices that have been regularly seen as benign items (remote-control cars, cellular phones, vehicles), James comes face to face with the innovative will of a destructive enemy. The source of horror in these two films isn't the devices themselves, but the relative safety found in blissful ignorance. However, in order to survive, both Moss and James do everything they can to reinvent themselves in the absence of the modern world, relying on ingenuity and cunning, traits often lost in the contemporary horror film.

Survival is a form of adaptation, often seen in films where humanity becomes threatened by limited resources. For instance, *Daybreakers* (2009) shows the downfall of humankind as a subspecies vampire race overruns society. In the wake of a blood shortage, hematologist Edward Dalton (Ethan Hawke) finds his humanity—literally shedding his vampire persona and becoming reborn as a living human—in his fight against a corrupt vampire corporation that seeks to farm the remaining humans in the search for a blood substitute. Likewise, in the futuristic *Soylent Green* (1973), the apparent breakdown of society is a metaphor for global food supplies, a nod to the current realization of genetically modified foods. Large corporations become the source of humanity's downfall. *Soylent Green* takes *Dawn of the Dead*'s social commentary one step further, moving beyond the complacency of shopping malls and blind acceptance to corporate culture and making life nothing more than a process, directly challenging the corporatization that would eventually engulf society. Harry Harrison, the author of the science-fiction classic *Make Room! Make Room!*, the book on which *Soylent Green* is based,[2] was aware of current social problems, those that the global atmosphere and world market could agree upon as universally fearful. Thorn (Charlton Heston), like Edward Dalton, seeks to restore humanity by waking up a culture lost in its reaping. However, it is the death of Sol (Edward G. Robinson) that connotes the industrialized, mechanized process of human life. Sol says: "I've lived too long," suggesting that society has passed him by. His death procession isn't recognition of an afterlife, but a realization of the futility of life when the world ceases to be recognizable.

It's become increasingly apparent, especially when it comes to changing technologies, that the youth market is central to embracing the changes perpetuated by advancement. This may be why, as horror films progress, younger protagonists are central to the exploration of horror, as they are more likely to embrace the changes that create our newest sources of horror. As society becomes more in tune to changing attitudes of personal identity, ecological concerns amidst the rising fears of global warming, and the reach of technology into our everyday lives, the horror film may encompass more than our social fears and move into a realm that explores how modern technologies and corporatization affect the very essence of our being on a daily basis. Perhaps the film that best exemplifies the next wave of the horror genre is one that touches upon every facet of the horror film, from the classic idea of horror to the categorical assumption that fear lurks in our search for it.

The Cabin in the Woods (2012) is unique in that it explores every cliché of the horror film through technological means, an orchestrated fiasco pitting Old-World horrors against New-World realizations of why horror exists. In order to fulfill the prophesy of the ancients, a race of demigods that ruled the world prior to humanity, a rogue elemental government agency sets up a band of teenagers who unknowingly accept the challenge of stopping the ancients from overtaking society through a ritualistic appeasement of sacrifices of their own choosing. This movie seems to have everything: ritual sacrifice, urban legends, creepy settings, gruesome murders, the high genius whose paranoia leads him to suspect mind control, naughty teens, chaste teens, action, intercontinental competition, snappy dialogue, A-list actors, melodrama, great effects (blood, models, CGI), a doomsday scenario, and an overlord government agency trying to keep dark spirits at bay. It is *literally* an epic that encompasses all stereotypes, never having to rely on them to tell the story. Partly because the story is secondary.

Director Joss Whedon employs cliché in order to comment on the function of the horror film within the film itself. The inhabitants of the cabin are from varied backgrounds of all types, representing each member of society (the athlete, the whore, the scholar, the joker, and the virgin). After a controlled impetus leads the crew to the basement, a well-stocked mausoleum of totems designed to bring about the release of their destroyer, the five youths are then watched as they are subjected to the tortures of a zombie redneck torture family. But even their destroyer is categorized, as the agency bets on and clarifies the different methods of release (sacrifice). This hints at the legacy of horror films before it, such as: Reptilius; Alien Beast; Deadites; Mummy; Angry Molesting Tree; Sexy Witches; and The Scarecrow Folk. Despite the conventions of the film, horror will always find a way to outsmart us. The telling nature of the film is in the observations of those at "The

Facility," those who orchestrate and watch the doomed in order to both repeat the cyclical horrors of society and to ward off future annihilation. After new security guard Daniel Truman (Brian White) is warned of what he will witness, he is surprised when technician Gary Sitterson (Richard Jenkins) flatly explains the genesis of our own futile fears in witnessing the zombie rednecks attack Jules (Anna Hutchison) and Curt (Chris Hemsworth) after they are chemically induced by a pheromone-laded moss patch:

> **TRUMAN:** They're like a nightmare.
> **SITTERSON:** No. They're something nightmares are *from*. Everything in our staple is remnant of the Old World. Courtesy of [pointing downward] ... you know who.

As in *Friday the 13th* and *Scream*, *The Cabin in the Woods* has a sense of awareness of the limitations of the horror film. The agents at The Facility orchestrate horror through highly advanced technological means. The cabin, embedded by a force field that Curt ultimately crashes into in a desperate dirt bike jump/escape, is but one part of the process for the group's elimination. Even hair dye is used to slow mental cognition. Under surveillance, the cabin is the site of a ritual as old as the horror film itself. When Marty (Fran Kranz), the pot-smoking joker realizes that the house is wired for surveillance, he exclaims: "Oh, my God. I'm on a reality TV show. My parents are going to think I'm such a burnout." Further, electric shocks cause Dana (Kristen Connolly) to drop the knife used in her attack of one of the zombies. The effectual reach of The Facility is that no one is to be left alive.

The solitary confines of the cabin itself allows for typical teenage revelry, here beginning with music, alcohol, and a make-out session with a mounted wolf head on the cabin wall. Also, there is the matter of choice as to the ultimate destruction by reading the inscription on a totem (here in Latin), which Marty knows is a bad idea, but the warning goes unheeded. Ultimately, the group conforms to their stereotypes, bringing about their deaths because of their own youthful hubris, except for Marty, who is "immunized" by his habitual pot smoking, and Dana. Escaping the cabin's controlled environment into the labyrinth of The Facility, Dana and Marty unknowingly set about the awakening of the ancients in their fight for survival, ushering a pandemic of destruction upon The Facility by the stored and catalogued horrors of the Old World. Faced with controlled demise by a tech-savvy overlord, Dana and Marty choose world annihilation and their own deaths instead of succumbing to the manipulated attacks of both authority and past fears.

If *The Cabin in the Woods* teaches us anything (aside from the vast legacy of where our monsters are found), it is that we have the right to choose our destiny outside of control, be it technological demise or social control. At the center of Whedon's epic is freedom of choice, not just in our monsters, but in our choice to decide how far technology will encroach on our sense of reality.

For the modern horror film to continue to excite our sensibilities, it must embrace that which has yet to become a source of fear. This may include drone technology, flying cars, or a yet-to-be-realized app that will manipulate us through our cell phones. But as technology sweeps ever more deeply into our daily lives, the horror film will find a way to channel ways to proclaim humanity as the means to our own salvation (or, in the case of *The Cabin in the Woods*, our destruction). Like the totems in the dark basement, our destruction will be cast by our own free will.

Suggested List of Films

Afterlife (2010)
Alien (1979)
Amber Alert (2012)
Apartment 143 (2011)
Area 407 (2012)
ATM (2012)
Atrocious (2010)
Below (2002)
Blade Runner (1982)
Blair Witch Project (1999)
The Brain that Wouldn't Die (1962)
Brainscan (1994)
The Cabin in the Woods (2012)
The Cabinet of Dr. Caligari (1919)
Caché (2005)
Cannibal Holocaust (1980)
The Cell (2000)
Cell (2013)
Cellular (2004)
Chain Letter (2010)
Chernobyl Diaries (2012)
Child's Play (1988)
Christine (1983)
A Clockwork Orange (1971)
Cloverfield (2008)
Creature from the Black Lagoon (1954)
Dawn of the Dead (1978)
The Day the Earth Stood Still (1951)

Daybreakers (2009)
Dead of Night (1945)
Demon Seed (1977)
Devil (2010)
Down (2001)
D.N.A. (1997)
Dr. Giggles (1992)
Dr. Jekyll and Mr. Hyde (1908/1931)
Elevator (2011)
End of the Line (2007)
Episode 50 (2011)
Event Horizon (1997)
The Evil Dead (1981)
Evolver (1995)
eXistenZ (2009)
The Eye (2002) (Japanese)
The Eye (2008) (American)
Eyes Without a Face (1960)
Fear (1996)
The Final Cut (2004)
Final Destination (2000)
Final Destination 2 (2003)
Final Destination 3 (2006)
The Final Destination (2009)—
  a.k.a. *Final Destination 4*
Final Destination 5 (2011)
Flatliners (1997)
The Fly (1958/1986)
1408 (2007)

Suggested List of Films

The Fourth Kind (2009)
Frankenstein (1910)
Frankenstein (1931)
Frankenstein 1970 (1958)
The Frankenstein Theory (2013)
Frankenweenie (2012)
Friday the 13th (1980)
Fright Night (1985/2011)
Funny Games (1998, 2005)
Godzilla (1954)
Grave Encounters (2011)
Grave Encounters 2 (2012)
Homunculus (1916)
The Human Centipede (2009)
The Human Centipede II: Second Sequence (2011)
The Human Centipede III: The Final Sequence (2014)
The Hunchback of Notre Dame (1923)
I, Frankenstein (2014)
iMurders (2009)
In the Mouth of Madness (1994)
The Incredible Shrinking Man (1957)
Invasion of the Body Snatchers (1956/1978)
The Island of Lost Souls (1932)
Johnny Mnemonic (1995)
The Incredible Shrinking Man (1957)
The Lawnmower Man (1992)
Life Without Soul (1915)
Live! (2007)
Logan's Run (1976)
Maximum Overdrive (1986/7)
May (2002)
Messages Deleted (2010)
Mondo Cane (1962)
The Mystery of the Wax Museum (1933)
Nosferatu, A Symphony of Horrors or, Nosferatu, eine Symphonie das Grauens (Ger.), (1922)

The Omega Man (1971)
One Missed Call (2003/2008)
Paranormal Activity (2009)
Paranormal Activity 2 (2010)
Paranormal Activity 3 (2011)
Paranormal Activity 4 (2012)
Paranormal Activity: The Marked Ones (2014)
Paranormal Entity (2009)
The Phantom of the Opera (1925)
Peeping Tom (1960)
Playback (2012)
Poltergeist (1982)
Pontypool (2008)
Psycho (1960)
Pulse (2006)
The Purge (2013)
Quarantine (2008)
Quarantine 2: Terminal (2011)
The Quarantine Hauntings (2014)
Reanimator (1985) (1990)
REC (2007)
REC 2 (2009)
REC 3: Genesis (2012)
Return of the Fly (1959)
Return to Horror High (1987)
The Ring (2002)
Ringu (1998)
Saw (2004)
Scream (1996)
Scream 2 (1997)
Scream 3 (2000)
Scream Bloody Murder (1973)
Seconds (1966)
Shaun of the Dead (2004)
The Signal (2008)
Sinister (2012)
Someone's Watching Me! (1978)
Soylent Green (1973)
Splice (2009)
Stay Alive (2006)
Storage 24 (2012)
Strange Days (1995)
Targets (1968)

Suggested List of Films

Tetsuo: The Iron Man (1988)
Thir13n Ghosts (2001)
The Thing from Another World (1951)
13B (2009)
The Tingler (1959)
The Tunnel (2011)
The Twilight Zone (1959–1964)
Untraceable (2008) *Though not quite horror, it fits with the capacity of horror as technology.
Vacancy (2007)
The Video Dead (1987)
Videodrome (1983)
V/H/S (2012)
V/H/S 2 (2013)
Vile (2011)
Virtuosity (1995)
War of the Worlds (1938 radio show/2004)
Westworld (1973)
When a Stranger Calls (1979/2006)
White Noise (2005)
White Noise 2: The Light (2007)

Documentaries

Hammer: The Studio That Dripped Blood! (1987)
Monsters From the Id: Anxiety and Optimism in 1950s Science Fiction (2009)
Nightmare Factory (2011)—a behind the scenes look at horror makeup
Nightmares in Red, White, and Blue: The Evolution of the American Horror Film (2009)
Outsmarting Terror (2006)

Chapter Notes

Introduction

1. Gina Wisker, *Horror Fiction: An Introduction* (New York: Continuum, 2005), 9.
2. Sharon Packer, *Movies and the Modern Psyche* (Westport, CT: Praeger, 2007), 166.
3. Adam Rockoff, *Going to Pieces: The Rise and Fall of the Slasher Film, 1978–1986* (Jefferson, NC: McFarland, 2002), 193.

Chapter 1

1. Freud writes that "the uncanny" is a word that "is not always used in a clearly definable sense, and so it commonly merges with what arouses fear in general." He identifies differences in perception as it relates to the German word *unheimlich*, or "weird," and its opposite *heimlich*, or that which is frightening because it is "unfamiliar." The distinction here is that fear derives from the known and unknown worlds, therefore making fear a unique and individualized concept.
2. Julia Kristeva, *Powers of Horror: An Essay on Abjection*, trans. Leon S. Roudiez (New York: Columbia University Press, 1982).
3. Jerrold E. Hogle, "Introduction: The Gothic in western culture," *The Cambridge Companion to Gothic Fiction*, ed. Jerrold E. Hogle (Cambridge: Cambridge University Press, 2002), 7.
4. Ibid.
5. Joanna Bourke, *Fear: A Cultural History* (Emeryville, CA: Shoemaker & Hoard, 2007), 389.
6. E. J. Clery, "The Genesis of 'Gothic' Fiction," *The Cambridge Companion to Gothic Fiction*, ed. Jerrold E. Hogle (Cambridge: Cambridge University Press, 2002), 28.
7. Ann Radcliffe, "On the Supernatural in Poetry," *New Monthly Magazine* 17, no. 1 (1826), pp. 145–152.
8. Bram Stoker, *Dracula*. Chapter 3.
9. Neil Baldwin, *Edison: Inventing the Century* (New York: Hyperion, 1995), 300.
10. Margaret Cheney, *Tesla: Man Out of Time* (Englewood Cliffs, NJ: Prentice-Hall, 1981), 72.
11. Ibid.
12. Ibid., 41.
13. Ibid., 45.
14. Ibid.
15. Baldwin, 137.
16. Ibid.
17. Baldwin, 104–5.
18. A. N. Wilson, *The Victorians* (New York: W. W. Norton, 2004), 495.
19. Paul Israel, *Edison: A Life of Invention* (New York: John Wiley and Sons, 1998), 300.
20. Ibid., 300–01.
21. Isabel Cristina Pindedo, "Postmodern Elements of the Contemporary Horror Film," in *The Horror Film*, ed.

Stephen Prince (New Brunswick, NJ: Rutgers University Press, 2004), 91.

Chapter 2

1. G. F. W. Hegel's concept of self-identity. See Hegel's *Phenomenology of Spirit*, in which he discusses the formation of self in direct opposition to the unfamiliar attributes of other individuals.

2. In the German legend, Faust makes a pact with the Devil for a life of knowledge and worldly pleasure.

3. Faust demanded to be called a Doctor of Medicine rather than a Doctor of Theology.

4. Susan Tyler Hitchcock, *Frankenstein: A Cultural History* (New York: Norton, 2007), 142.

5. Mary Shelley, *Frankenstein* Volume II, Chapter V.

6. In contrast, Victor's description of the monster as "a thing such as even Dante could not have conceived" implies the internal Hell that the creator feels upon seeing his monster awake. However, from this point, Shelley's narrative focuses on the monster's quest for identity. It is here that the main differences between novel and film should be noticed, as Whale's decision to focus on the monster's evilness outshines the moral questions of the novel.

7. David J. Skal, *The Monster Show: A Cultural History of Horror* (New York: Norton, 1993), 135.

8. Sharon Packer, *Movies and the Modern Psyche* (Westport, CT: Praeger, 2007), 9.

9. Roy Kinnard, *Horror in Silent Films: A Filmography, 1896–1929* (Jefferson, NC: McFarland, 1995), 1.

10. Robert Spadoni, *The Uncanny Body of Early Sound Film: The Coming of Sound Film and the Origins of the Horror Genre* (Berkeley: University of California Press, 2007), 12.

11. The studio changed the name "Victor" to "Henry" to sound less grave and unfriendly for American audiences.

12. Spadoni, 93.

13. Aristotle's *Poetics* outlines catharsis (Gr. *katharsis*) as the result of tragedy, which evokes feelings of pity and fear. The viewer of tragedy transcends beyond the imitation of acts, resulting in personal feelings in response to the action.

14. Noël Carroll, *The Philosophy of Horror, or Paradoxes of the Heart* (New York: Routledge, 2010), 18.

15. Kelly Oliver, ed., *The Portable Kristeva* (New York: Columbia University Press, 1997), 229.

16. Roger Shattuck, *Forbidden Knowledge: From Prometheus to Pornography* (New York: St. Martin's Press, 1996), 221.

17. Oliver, ed., 230.

18. Ibid., 237.

19. Kracuer's book *From Caligari to Hitler* traces the lineage from German Existentialism theory and the rise of an ideology.

20. Packer, 32.

21. Tricia Welsch, "Foreign Exchange: German Expressionism and Its Legacy," *Cinema Journal* 38, no. 4 (Summer 1999): 98–102.

22. Ironically, Karloff didn't receive billing in the original Whale production, listed only as "?" in the opening credits so that audiences wouldn't be able to identify the actor as a person but simply as a "monster." Karloff himself was largely unknown by the general public.

23. In Golden Age Hollywood, B-movies were generally the second act of a double-feature. Not only would B-movies have smaller budgets, they would generally get less advertising and studio support.

24. Alternately titled *Frankenstein versus Subterranean Monster Baragon*.

25. A style of film developed in the 1970s for mostly black audiences and employing racial stereotypes, the genre grew in popularity across racial classes, crossing multiple genres.

26. Alternately titled *Andy Warhol's Frankenstein*.

27. In order to save money, Brooks borrowed many of the same props as the original, giving an authentic and genuine feel to his adaptation.

28. This film is notable in that it gave

the public consciousness the image of Igor (Marty Feldman) as the doctor's assistant. No such character exists in the original novel.

29. The controversy surrounding the accidental drowning of the little girl (which gives the monster his humanity) was cut. Also, the original response following the memorable "It's alive" was cut from several versions because it was considered blasphemous. The original line was "It's alive! In the name of God! Now I know what it feels like to *be* God!"

30. Showing how far the monster had fallen away from the original story, it's important to note *The New York Times'* review of the film, which stated the following: "If you discount any immediate connection between the mass media and the temper of the culture, then the film warrants little attention ... the automaton, enacted by Gary Conway, is a teenager assemble[d] from the limbs of other teenagers. This is, in one sense, abhorrent. It forces one to acknowledge the impression that such films may aggravate the mass social sickness euphemistically termed 'juvenile delinquency.' ... In this particular film, there are graphic displays of human dismemberment. Before one such act of surgical perversion, the mad doctor'[s] assistant says, 'I have no stomach for it.' That would be a plausible reaction for any adult who had read the day's headlines about teen-age crime."

31. The Illuminati stems from an 18th century belief that an underground network of political and social organizations conspire to disrupt society. The belief is that, in secret, the elite of society exert influence over mainstream society as a means to control the workings of daily life without wielding democratic power.

32. Adam, the Biblical figure of Eden, was God's first creation, made from clay, similar to the vision that Dr. Frankenstein predicted of his own "godlike powers." See *Frankenstein*, Vol. 1, Chapter 4 (page 34).

33. Eckhart trained for three months learning martial arts.

34. Shelley miscarried, leaving her with nightmares about her "hideous progeny."

35. Hitchcock, 323–24.

Chapter 3

1. *New York Times Magazine*, March 19, 1950.

2. Margot Henriksen, *Dr. Strangelove's America: Society and Culture in the Atomic Age* (Berkeley: University of California Press, 1997), 184.

3. Though there have yet to be definitive dates applied to the conflict, there is an agreed upon beginning of the Cold War, ca. 1947.

4. David Skal, *Screams of Reason: Mad Science and Modern Culture* (New York: Norton, 1998), 178.

5. August 6 and August 9, 1945, respectively.

6. Mark Jancovich, *Rational Fears: American Horror in the 1950s* (Manchester: Manchester University Press, 1996), 16.

7. Cyndy Hendershot, "The Atomic Scientist, Science Fiction Films, and Paranoia," *Journal of American Culture* Vol. 20, No. 1 (Spring 1997): 31.

8. See Chapter 4 for a more in depth discussion.

9. Kevin Heffernan, *Ghouls, Gimmicks, and Gold: Horror Films and the American Movie Business, 1953–1968* (Durham: Duke University Press, 2004), 9.

10. See the previous chapter for a more in depth view of Hammer Horror.

11. Heffernan, 13.

12. Fred Botting, *Limits of Horror: Technology, Bodies, Gothic* (Manchester: Manchester University Press, 2008), 52.

13. Heffernan, 5.

14. Skal, *The Monster Show*, 172.

15. Cyndy Hendershot, "The Cold War Horror Film: Taboo and Transgression in *The Bad Seed*, *The Fly*, and *Psycho*," *Journal of Popular Film and Television* 29, no. 1 (2001): 20–31.

16. Often referred to simply as *The Thing* until the 1982 John Carpenter remake.

17. This contradicts a popular refrain of the war day: "Loose lips sink ships." Though many Americans were in the dark concerning the technologies of the war effort, the military was often reminded of the sensitivity of information. Scott champions the public right to information.

18. Originally published serially in *Colliers* in 1954. Not to be confused with Robert Wise's adaptation of Robert Louis Stevenson's *The Body Snatcher* (1945), which explored grave robbing as a method for medical advancement in lieu of available cadavers. For a more in depth examination of cadaver usage in modern science, see Mary Roach's *Stiff*.

19. Remade in 1978, 1993, and 2007.

20. M. Keith Booker, *Alternate Americas: Science Fiction Film and American Culture* (Westport, CT: Greenwood Press, 2006), 66–7.

21. Danny Peary, *Cult Movies: The Classics, the Sleepers, the Weird, and the Wonderful* (New York: Delacorte, 1981), 157.

22. Amid the growing anti–Communist mentality, Senator Joseph McCarthy (Wisconsin) unleashed a series of Senate hearings, ultimately leading to a witch-hunt that rooted out suspected Communist and Communist sympathizers. His accusations led to a further investigation by the United States House of Representatives by the House Un-American Activities Committee (HUAC), which created the notorious Hollywood blacklist. Among those targeted were Charlie Chaplin and Orson Welles. For more information, see Victor S. Navasky's *Naming Names*.

23. Booker, 64.

24. Henriksen, 7.

25. *Gojira* in the original Japanese.

26. Producer Shogo Tomiyama equates the monster to Shinto, "God of Destruction": "He totally destroys everything and then there is a rebirth. Something new and fresh can begin." Interview, www.pennyblood.com, February 3, 2005.

27. First discovered by geneticist Hermann Joseph Muller in 1926.

28. Cyndy Hendershot, *I Was a Cold War Monster: Horror Films, Eroticism and the Cold War Imagination* (Bowling Green, OH: Bowling Green State University Popular Press, 2001), 24.

29. Ironically, this was the very source of horror in Tim Burton's *Edward Scissorhands* (1990).

30. Cyndy Hendershot, "The Atomic Scientist, Science Fiction Films, and Paranoia," in *Paranoia, the Bomb and 1950s Science-Fiction Films* (Bowling Green, OH: Bowling Green State University Popular Press, 1999), 39.

Chapter 4

1. Charles Derry, *Dark Dreams 2.0: A Psychological History of the Modern Horror Film from the 1950s to the 21st Century* (Jefferson, NC: McFarland, 2009), 22.

2. Ibid., 24.

3. Pindedo, 91.

4. Kendall R. Phillips, *Projected Fears: Horror Films and American Culture* (Westport, CT: Praeger, 2005), 66.

5. Isserman and Kazin, 141.

6. Skal, *The Monster Show*, 259.

7. Derry, 29.

8. Ibid., 30.

9. Skal, *The Monster Show*, 293.

10. Matt Singer, "A New Kind of Monster," *The Dissolve*. August 19, 2013. www.thedissolve.com.

11. Ibid., p. .

12. Jason Zinoman, *Shock Value: How a Few Eccentric Outsiders Gave Us Nightmares, Conquered Hollywood, and Invented Modern Horror* (New York: Penguin, 2011), 47.

13. These lines, and the film being screened, are taken from Roger Corman's film *The Terror* (1963) starring Boris Karloff as Baron Victor Frederick Von Leppe and Jack Nicholson as Lt. Andre Duvalier. Karloff agreed to work for Corman for six days; however he completed his scenes in four days. When it came time to make his film, Bogdanovich sought out Corman, who acted as producer. Corman told Bogdanovich that he was allowed to make any film he

chose, providing that he use Karloff in the film, thus gaining back the two days Karloff owed him.
14. Phillips, 100.
15. Zinoman, 83.
16. Phillips, 98.
17. Ibid., 99.

Chapter 5

1. David Konow, *Reel Terror: The Scary, Bloody, Gory, Hundred-Year History of Classic Horror Films* (New York: St. Martin's Press, 2012), 41.
2. In a statement before the Senate subcommittee on juvenile delinquency, which sought to ban severe reading in light of Dr. Fredric Wertham's book *Seduction of the Innocent*, Gaines states his company philosophy as follows: "Pleasure is what we sell, entertainment, reading enjoyment. Entertaining reading has never harmed anyone. Men of good will, free men should be very grateful for one sentence in the statement made by Federal Judge John M. Woolsey when he lifted the ban on Ulysses. Judge Woolsey said: 'It is only with the normal person that the law is concerned.' May I repeat, he said, 'It is only with the normal person that the law is concerned.' Our American children are for the most part normal children. They are bright children, but those who want to prohibit comic magazines seem to see dirty, sneaky, perverted monsters who use the comics as a blueprint for action. 'Perverted little monsters are few and far between. They don't read comics.'"
3. David Hajdu, *The Ten-Cent Plague: The Great Comic-Book Scare and How It Changed America* (New York: Farrar, Straus and Giroux, 2008), 291.
4. Bradford W. Wright, *Comic Book Nation: The Transformation of Youth Culture in America* (Baltimore: Johns Hopkins University Press, 2001), 152.
5. Zinoman, 113.
6. The Hayes Code preceded the modern MPAA system for rating movies.
7. Wheeler Winston Dixon, *A History of Horror* (New Brunswick, NJ: Rutgers University Press, 2011), 125.

8. Heffernan, *Ghouls, Gimmicks, and Gold*, 7.
9. Phillips, 67–8.
10. Carroll, *The Philosophy of Horror*, 214.
11. Howard Brick, *Age of Contradiction* (Ithaca, NY: Twayne, 1998), 64.
12. Phillips, 85.
13. Michael Fanning, "Tom Savini Interview," [1982]. www.youtube.com/watch?v-tOsJq1ocvt0.
14. Ibid.
15. Savini interview.
16. Jesse Wente in *The Nightmare Factory*.
17. Phillips, 96.
18. *Scream Greats: Tom Savini Master of Horror FX* documentary (1986).
19. Skal, *The Monster Show*, 313.
20. David A. Cook, *Lost Illusions: History of the American Cinema 9* (Oakland: University of California Press, 2002), 5.
21. Stephen E. Bowles, "The Exorcist and Jaws," *Literature Film Quarterly* 4, no. 3 (Summer 1976): 199.
22. Zinoman, 219.
23. Richard Nowell, *Blood Money: A History of the First Teen Slasher Film Cycle* (New York: Continuum, 2011), 247.
24. Skal, *The Monster Show*, 245.
25. Zinoman, 188–9.
26. John Carpenter, citing Tobe Hooper, *Masters of Horror* documentary (see 37:35).
27. Skal, *The Monster Show*, 313.
28. Zinoman, 214.
29. Ibid., 215–16.
30. Also known as *A Nightmare on Elm Street 7*.

Chapter 6

1. Beth Bailey and David Farber, eds., *America in the Seventies* (Lawrence: University Press of Kansas, 2004), 209.
2. In his 1983 autobiography *Flashbacks*, Leary explains that the phrase has a definitive and identifiable goal behind it: "'Turn on' meant to go within to activate your neural and genetic equipment. Become sensitive to the many and vari-

ous levels of consciousness and the specific triggers that engage them. Drugs were one way to accomplish this end. 'Tune in' meant interact harmoniously with the world around you—externalize, materialize, express your new internal perspectives. 'Drop out' suggested an active, selective, graceful process of detachment from involuntary or unconscious commitments. 'Drop Out' meant self-reliance, a discovery of one's singularity, a commitment to mobility, choice, and change. Unhappily my explanations of this sequence of personal development were often misinterpreted to mean 'Get stoned and abandon all constructive activity.'"

3. Botting, 201.

4. Zinoman, 124.

5. Kim Newman, *Nightmare Movies: Horror on Screen Since the 1960s* (London: Bloomsbury, 2011), 272.

6. An adaptation of Bergman's *The Virgin Spring* (1960), which was an adaptation of a 13th century Swedish ballad.

7. Adam Rockoff, *Going to Pieces: The Rise and Fall of the Slasher Film, 1978–1986* (Jefferson, NC: McFarland, 2002), 11.

8. Orwell's 1949 novel prophesized a dystopian society that was under omnipresent government surveillance, where the superstate Oceania exists in a world that depends on revisionist history and propaganda in order to control society.

9. Phillips, 66.

10. Barbara Klinger, *Beyond the Multiplex: Cinema, New Technologies, and the Home* (Berkeley: University of California Press, 2006), 56.

11. Murray Leeder, "Forget Peter Vincent: Nostalgia, Self-Reflexivity, and the Genre Past in *Fright Night*," *Journal of Popular Film and Television* (2009): 193–4.

12. Ibid., 194.

13. Klinger, 242.

14. Derry, 331.

15. Linda Badley, "Bringing It All Back Home: Horror Cinema and Video Culture," in *The Horror Zone*. Ian Conrich, ed. (New York: I.B. Tauris, 2010), 58.

16. A.k.a. *Down*, a remake of the Dutch film *Lift*.

Chapter 7

1. Later retitled *Star Wars Episode IV: A New Hope*.

2. Shattuck, *Forbidden Knowledge*, 218.

3. Carroll, *The Philosophy of Horror*, 14.

4. Schattuck, 224.

5. Thomas Sipos, *Horror Film Aesthetics* (Jefferson, NC: McFarland, 2010), 11.

6. Gary Westfahl, *Science Fiction, Children's Literature, and Popular Culture* (Westport, CT: Greenwood, 2000), 121.

7. Ibid., 121.

8. An adaptation of William Shakespeare's *The Tempest* (ca. 1610).

9. The film takes its name from a general relativity, where the boundary in spacetime cannot affect an outside observer. Literally, it is the "point of no return."

10. Susan Sontag, "The Imagination of Disaster," *Commentary*, October 1965, 45.

11. Search for Extra-Terrestrial Intelligence.

12. Lars Schmeink, "DVD Review of *Splice*," *Science Fiction Film and Television* 5.1 (2012): 152.

13. Steven L. Goldman, "Images of Technology in Popular Films: Discussion and Filmography," *Science, Technology & Human Values* Vol. 14, No. 3 (Summer 1989): 286.

14. Andrew Feenberg, *Questioning Technology* (New York: Routledge, 1999), 131.

15. Hendershot, "The Atomic Scientist, Science Fiction Films, and Paranoia," 39.

16. A remake of the 2002 Japanese horror film of the same name.

17. This is the only version that changes the name of Matheson's original character.

18. Philip J. Kain, "Nietzsche, Eternal Recurrence, and the Horror of Exis-

tence," *The Journal of Nietzsche Studies* 33 (Spring 2007): 52.

19. Originally published May 1975 in *Cavalier*, and later included in the short story collection *Night Shift*.

20. The singularity is the theoretical moment when non-human intelligence supersedes that of human intellect.

21. Skal, *Screams of Reason*, 315.

22. The landmark Supreme Court decision of 1973 decided that, in a 7–2 ruling, the right to due process under the 14th Amendment extended to a woman's right to have an abortion of her own free will.

23. Westfahl, *Science Fiction, Children's Literature, and Popular Culture*, 89–90.

24. Carroll, *The Philosophy of Horror*, 150.

25. Eric S. Rabkin, "Science Fiction and the Future of Criticism," *PMLA* Vol. 119, No. 3 (May 2004): 462.

26. Asimov's three rules of robotics are adopted in the film as a creation of Dr. Lanning. They are, as Asimov postulated, as follows: 1) a robot may not injure a human being or, through inaction, allow a human being to come to harm; 2) a robot must obey the orders given to it by human beings, except where such orders would conflict with the First Law; and 3) a robot must protect its own existence as long as such protection does not conflict with the First or Second Law.

27. *A.I.* uses multiple references, blurring the demarcation between science fiction and fantasy as a way of looking at ingenuity of human ideas.

Chapter 8

1. The original French line is "L'enfer, c'est les autres," or "Hell is [the] others." The original French title of Sartre's work was *Huis clos*, first performed in 1944 at the Théâtre du Vieux-Colombier in Paris.

2. The novel was published in 1991 by Vintage Books after Ellis' original deal with Simon & Schuster fell through because of "aesthetic differences."

3. Newman, *Nightmare Movies*, 331.

4. First published in 1915, *Die Verwandlung* (German) is a title that has no English equivalent.

5. Botting, *Limits of Horror*, 130.

6. Portia Williams Weiskel, "On the Works of Franz Kafka," in *Franz Kafka*. Eds. Neil Hiens and Portia Williams Weiskel (New York: Infobase, 2009), 76.

7. Dave Cullen, *Columbine* (New York: Twelve, 2009), 175–6.

8. Ibid., 327.

9. Ibid., 327–8.

10. Pat Gill, "The Monstrous Years: Teens, Slasher Films and the Family," *Journal of Film and Video* Vol. 54, No. 4 (Winter 2002): 16.

11. Ibid., 17.

12. Sherry Turkle, *Alone Together: Why We Expect More from Technology and Less from Each Other* (New York: Basic Books, 2011), 243.

13. Charles Taylor, *Sources of the Self: The Making of the Modern Identity* (Cambridge, MA: Harvard University Press, 1989), 177.

14. David Deutsch, *The Beginning of Infinity* (New York: Penguin, 2012), 140.

15. Shattuck, *Forbidden Knowledge*, 46.

16. *Latin*: "passion (lust) for knowledge."

17. Shattuck, *Forbidden Knowledge*, 46. Shattuck cites the following passage from Augustine's *Confessions*: "There is also present in the soul, by means of these bodily senses, a kind of empty longing and curiosity, which aims not at taking pleasure in the flesh but any acquiring experience through the flesh, and this empty curiosity is dignified by the names of learning and science. Since this is in the appetite for knowing, and since the eyes are the chief of our senses for acquiring knowledge, it is called in the divine language *the lust of the eyes*."

18. Steven Bruhm, "Cell Phones from Hell," *The South Atlantic Quarterly* Vol. 111, No. 3 (Summer 2011): 605.

19. A remake of the Japanese film *Kairo* (2001), directed by Kiyoshi Kurosawa.

20. Chuck Tryon, "Video from the

Void: Video Spectatorship, Domestic Film Cultures, and Contemporary Horror Film," *Journal of Film and Video* Vol. 61, No. 3 (Autumn 1992): 40.

21. Derry, *Dark Dreams 2.0*, 345.

22. Through a ritual, the sin eater takes on the sins of others, absolving the soul of the sinner, thus transferring the sins to the new host.

23. The original Luddite movement was propagated by English textile manufacturers who protested machinery as a replacement for manual skilled labor in the nineteenth century.

24. A scene reminiscent of Michel Gondry and Charlie Kaufman's *Eternal Sunshine of the Spotless Mind* (2004), where Joel Barrish (Jim Carrey) erases the memory of his ex-girlfriend Clementine Kruczynski (Kate Winslet), only to find that one of the technicians (Elijah Wood) uses Clementine's memories of Joel in an attempt to win her over for himself.

25. Turkle, *Alone Together*, 264.

Chapter 9

1. Newman, *Nightmare Movies*, 441.
2. Ibid.
3. J. P. Telotte, "The *Blair Witch Project*: Film and the Internet," *Film Quarterly* Vol. 54, No. 3 (Spring 2001): 38.
4. Mary Beth Oliver and Meghan Sanders, "The Appeal of Horror and Suspense," in *The Horror Film*, ed. Stephen Prince (New Brunswick, NJ: Rutgers University Press, 2004), 255.
5. Charles Seife, *Virtual Unreality* (New York: Viking, 2014), 71.
6. www.blairwitch.com, which still is still an active domain. The website contains the same information, however there is now an option to buy the film online.
7. Leonard Maltin, ed. *Leonard Maltin's 2012 Movie Guide* (New York: Signet, 2012), 1308.
8. A.k.a. *Hidden*.
9. Sontag, "The Imagination of Disaster," 45.
10. Originally published in 1985 by Knopf, *The Vampire Lestat* is the second book of Rice's "Vampire Chronicles" series. Though the film deals with the storyline of the second book, the film takes its title from Rice's first novel in the series.
11. Jody Keisner, "Do You Want to Watch? A Study of the Visual Rhetoric of the Postmodern Horror Film," *Women's Studies* Vol. 37, No. 4 (2008): 420.
12. Ibid.
13. E. J. Westlake, "Friend Me If You Facebook: Generation Y and Performative Surveillance," *TDR* [The Drama Review] Vol. 52, No. 4 (Winter 2008): 33–4.
14. Hiawatha Bray, *You Are Here: From the Compass to GPS, the History and Future of How We Find Ourselves* (New York: Basic Books, 2014), 210.
15. Ibid., 38.
16. Fred Botting, "Future Horror: (The Redundancy of Gothic)," *Gothic Studies* Vol. 1, No. 2 (1999): 149.
17. Skal, *The Monster Show*, 303.
18. Mark Jancovich, "'Two Ways of Looking': The Critical Reception of 1940s Horror," *Cinema Journal* Vol. 49, No. 3 (Spring 2010): 61.
19. Zinoman, *Shock Value*, 9.

Chapter 10

1. Zinoman, *Shock Value*, 223.
2. Maltin, ed., 1295.

Bibliography

Ashby, LeRoy. *With Amusement for All: A History of American Popular Culture Since 1830.* Lexington: University of Kentucky Press, 2006.

Badley, Linda. "Bringing It All Back Home: Horror Cinema and Video Culture." *The Horror Zone.* Ed. Ian Conrich. New York: I. B. Tauris, 2010. P. 45–66.

Baldick, Chris. *In Frankenstein's Shadow: Myth, Monstrosity, and Nineteenth-Century Writing.* Oxford: Clarendon Press, 1987.

Baldwin, Neil. *Edison: Inventing the Century.* New York: Hyperion, 1995.

Booker, M. Keith. *Alternate Americas: Science Fiction Film and American Culture.* Westport, CT: Greenwood, 2006.

Borgmann, Albert. *Technology and the Character of Contemporary Life: A Philosophical Inquiry.* Chicago: University of Chicago Press, 1984.

Botting, Fred. "Future Horror (the Redundancy of Gothic)." *Gothic Studies* Vol. 1, No. 2 (1999): 139–155.

____. *Limits of Horror: Technology, Bodies, Gothic.* Manchester, UK: Manchester University Press, 2008.

Boulenger, Giles. *John Carpenter: The Prince of Darkness.* Los Angeles, CA: Silman-James Press, 2001.

Bourke, Joanna. *Fear: A Cultural History.* Emeryville, CA: Shoemaker & Hoard, 2006.

Bowles, Stephen E. "The Exorcist and Jaws." *Literature Film Quarterly* Vol. 4, No. 3 (Summer 1976): 196–214.

Brand, H. W. *American Dreams: The United States Since 1945.* New York: Penguin, 2010.

Bray, Hiawatha. *You Are Here: From the Compass to GPS, the History and Future of How we Find Ourselves.* New York: Basic Books, 2014.

Brick, Howard. *Age of Contradiction: American Thought and Culture in the 1960s.* Ithaca, NY: Twayne, 1998.

Briefel, Aviva. "Monster and Critics." *Film Quarterly* Vol. 61, No. 3. (Spring 2008): 92–93.

____. "Monster Pains: Masochism, Menstruation, and Identification in the Horror Film." *Film Quarterly* Vol. 58, No. 3 (Spring 2005): 16–27.

Briefel, Aviva, and Sam J. Miller, eds. *Horror After 9/11: World of Fear, Cinema of Terror.* Austin: University of Texas Press, 2011.

Bruhm, Steven. "Cell Phones from Hell." *The South Atlantic Quarterly* Vol. 111, No. 3. (Summer 2011): 601–620.

Brunas, Michael, John Brunas, and Tom Weaver. *Universal Horrors: The Studio's Classic Films, 1931–1946.* Jefferson, NC: McFarland, 1990.

Cameron, Allan. "Zombie Media: Transmission, Reproduction, and the Digital Dead." *Cinema Journal* Vol. 52, No. 1 (Fall 2012): 66–89.

Bibliography

Carroll, Noël. "Horror and Humor." *The Journal of Aesthetics and Art Criticism* Vol. 57, No. 2: Aesthetics and Popular Culture (Spring 1999): 145–160.

_____. "Nightmare and the Horror Film: The Symbolic Biology of Fantastic Beings." *Film Quarterly:* Vol. 34, No. 3 (Spring 1981): 16–25.

_____. *The Philosophy of Horror, or Paradoxes of the Heart.* New York: Routledge, 2010.

Castle, Terry. "Phantasmagoria: Spectral Technology and the Metaphorics of Modern Reverie." *Critical Inquiry* Vol. 15, No. 1 (Autumn 1988): 26–61.

Cheney, Margaret. *Tesla: Man Out of Time.* Englewood Cliffs, NJ: Prentice-Hall, 1981.

Chien, Irene. "Playing Undead." *Film Quarterly* Vol. 61, No. 2 (Winter 2007): 64–65.

Clover, Carol J. "Her Body, Himself: Gender in the Slasher Film." *Representations* No. 20 Special Issue: Misogyny, Misandry, and Misanthropy (Autumn 1987): 187–228.

Conrich, Ian, ed. *Horror Zone: The Cultural Experience of Contemporary Horror Cinema.* New York: I. B. Tauris, 2010.

Cook, David A. *Lost Illusions: American Cinema in the Shadow of Watergate and Vietnam, 1970–1979.* History of the American Cinema 9. Oakland: University of California Press, 2002.

Cullen, Dave. *Columbine.* New York: Twelve, 2009.

De Graff, John, David Wann and Thomas H. Naylor. *Affluenza: The All-Consuming Epidemic.* San Francisco: Berrett-Koehler Publishers, 2001.

Derry, Charles. *Dark Dreams 2.0: A Psychological History of the Modern Horror Film from the 1950s to the 21st Century.* Jefferson, NC: McFarland, 2009.

Deutsch, David. *The Beginning of Infinity: Explanations That Transform the World.* New York: Penguin, 2012.

Dixon, Wheeler Winston. *A History of Horror.* New Brunswick, NJ: Rutgers University Press, 2011.

Egan, Ken. "Edgar Allan Poe and the Horror of Technology." *ESQ* Vol. 49, No. 3 (2002): 187–208.

Eisner, Lotte. *The Haunted Screen.* Berkeley: University of California Press, 1952.

Ellul, Jacques. *The Technological Society.* Trans. John Wilkinson. New York: Knopf, 1964.

Evans, Arthur B. "Jules Verne's Dream Machines: Technology and Transcendence." *Extrapolation* Vol. 54, No. 2 (2013): 129–146.

Fahy, Thomas, ed. *The Philosophy of Horror.* Lexington: University of Kentucky Press, 2010.

Fanning, Michael. *Tom Savini Interview* [1982]. July 21, 2011. www.youtube.com/watch?v-tOsJqlocVt0

Feenberg, Andrew. *Questioning Technology.* New York: Routledge, 1999.

Fisher, Dennis. *Horror Film Directors, 1931–1990.* Jefferson, NC: McFarland, 1991.

Freud, Sigmund. *The Uncanny.* New York: Penguin, 2003.

Gallagher, Leigh. *The End of the Suburbs: Where the American Dream Is Moving.* New York: Penguin, 2013.

Gaut, Berys. "The Paradox of Horror." *Arguing About Art: Contemporary Philosophical Debates.* 3d ed. Eds. Alex Neill and Aaron Ridley. New York: Routledge, 2008, 317–329.

Gill, Pat. "The Monstrous Years: Teens, Slasher Films and the Family." *Journal of Film and Video* Vol. 54, No. 4 (Winter 2002): 16–30.

Glover, Jonathan. *Humanity: A Moral History of the Twentieth Century.* New Haven, CT: Yale University Press, 2000.

Goldman, Steven L. "Images of Technology in Popular Films: Discussion and Filmography." *Science, Technology, & Human Values* Vol. 14, No. 3 (Summer, 1989): 275–301.

Gonder, Patrick. "Like a Monstrous Jigsaw Puzzle: Genetics and Race in Horror Films of the 1950s." *The Velvet Light Trap* No. 52 (Fall 2003): 34–44.

Grant, Barry Keith, and Christopher Sharrett. *Planks of Reason: Essays on the Horror Film*. 2d. ed. Lanham, MD: Scarecrow, 2004.

Grant, Michael. *Modern Fantastic: The Films of David Cronenberg*. London: Praeger, 2000.

Grixti, Joseph. *Terrors of Uncertainty: the Cultural Contexts of Horror Fiction*. London: Routledge, 1989.

Gunn, Timothy. "The Effects of New Technologies on Independent Film and Video Artists." *Leonardo* Vol. 29, No. 4 (1996): 319–321.

Hajdu, David. *The Ten-Cent Plague: The Great Comic-Book Scare and How It Changed*. New York: Farrar, Straus and Giroux, 2008.

Halberstam, Judith. *Skin Shows: Gothic Horror and the Technology of Monsters*. Durham, NC: Duke University Press, 1995.

Hanscomb, Stuart. "Existentialism and Art-Horror." *Sartre Studies International* Vol. 16, No. 1 (2010): 1–23.

Hantke, Steffen, Ed. *Horror Film: Creating and Marketing Fear*. Jackson: University of Mississippi Press, 2004.

Harrington, Curtis. "Ghoulies and Ghosties." *The Quarterly of Film Radio and Television* Vol. 7, No. 2 (Winter 1952): 191–202.

Hayes, Edward Cary. "The Horrors of Respectability." *American Journal of Sociology* Vol. 23, No. 1 (July 1917): 117–120.

Heffernan, James A. W. "Looking at the Monster: Frankenstein and Film." *Critical Inquiry* No. 24 (Autumn 1997): 133–158.

Heffernan, Kevin. *Ghouls, Gimmicks, and Gold: Horror Films and the American Movie Business, 1953–1968*. Durham, NC: Duke University Press, 2004.

Heller, Terry. *The Delights of Terror: An Aesthetics of the Tale of Terror*. Urbana: University of Illinois Press, 1987.

Hendershot, Cyndy. "The Atomic Scientist, Science Fiction Films and Paranoia: *The Day the Earth Stood Still, This Island Earth*, and *Killers from Space*." *Journal of American Culture* Vol. 20, No. 1 (Spring 1997): 31–41.

_____. "The Cold War Horror Film: Taboo and Transgression in *The Bad Seed, The Fly*, and *Psycho*." *Journal of Popular Film and Television* Vol. 29, No. 1 (2001): 20–31.

_____. *I Was a Cold War Monster: Horror Films, Eroticism and the Cold War Imagination*. Bowling Green, OH: Bowling Green State University Popular Press, 2001.

_____. *Paranoia, the Bomb and 1950s Science-Fiction Films*. Bowling Green, OH: Bowling Green State University Popular Press, 1999.

Henriksen, Margot. *Dr. Strangelove's America: Society and Culture in the Atomic Age*. Berkeley: University of California Press, 1997.

Hitchcock, Susan Tyler. *Frankenstein: A Cultural History*. New York: Norton, 2007.

Hogle, Jerrold E. *The Cambridge Companion to Gothic Fiction*. Cambridge: Cambridge University Press, 2002.

Holland-Toll, Linda J. *As American as Mom, Baseball, and Apple Pie: Constructing Community in Contemporary American Horror Fiction*. Bowling Green, OH: Bowling Green State University Popular Press, 2001.

Huyssen, Andreas. "The Vamp and the Machine: Technology and Sexuality in Fritz Lang's *Metropolis*." *New German Critique* No. 24/25 Special Double Issue on New German Cinema (Autumn 1981–Winter 1982): 221–237.

Israel, Paul. *Edison: A Life of Invention*. New York: John Wiley and Sons, 1998.

Isserman, Maurice, and Michael Kazin. *America Divided: The Civil War of the 1960s*. 4th ed. New York: Oxford University Press, 2011.

Jackson, Kimberly. "The Contagion of the Image in William Malone's *feardotcom*." *Post Script* Vol. 30, No. 1 (Fall 2010): 55–65.

Jancovich, Mark. *Rational Fears: American Horror in the 1950s*. Manchester, UK: Manchester University Press, 1996.

_____. "'Two Ways of Looking': The Critical Reception of 1940s Horror." *Cinema Journal* Vol. 49, No. 3 (Spring 2010): 45–66.

Bibliography

Jensen, Paul M. *The Men Who Made the Monsters.* New York: Twayne, 1996.

Jones, E. Michael. *Monsters from the Id.* Dallas, TX: Spence, 2000.

Joseph, Branden W., and Cary Loren. "Son of the Creature: An Interview with Cary Loren." *Grey Room* No. 12 (Summer 2003): 116–125.

Kain, Philip J. "Nietzsche, Eternal Recurrence, and the Horror of Existence." *The Journal of Nietzsche Studies* Vol. 33 (Spring 2007): 49–63.

Keisner, Jody. "Do You Want to Watch? A Study of the Visual Rhetoric of the Postmodern Horror Film." *Women's Studies* Vol. 37, No. 4 (2008): 411–427.

Kinnard, Roy. *Horror in Silent Films.* Jefferson, NC: McFarland, 1995.

Kirby, David. "The Future Is Now: Diegetic Prototypes and the Role of Popular Films in Generating Real-World Technological Development." *Social Studies of Science* Vol. 40, No. 1 (February 2010): 41–70.

_____. "Science Consultants, Fictional Films, and Scientific Practice." *Social Studies of Science* Vol. 33, No. 2 (April 2003): 231–268.

Klinger, Barbara. *Beyond the Multiplex: Cinema, New Technologies, and the Home.* Berkeley: University of California Press, 2006.

Konow, David. *Reel Terror: The Scary, Bloody, Gory, Hundred-Year History of Classic Horror Films.* New York: St. Martin's Press, 2012.

Kracauer, Seigfried. *From Caligari to Hitler: A Psychological History of the German Film.* Princeton, NJ: Princeton University Press, 1969.

_____. "Hollywood's Terror Films: Do They Reflect an American State of Mind?" *New German Critique* No. 89, Film and Exile (Spring–Summer 2003): 105–111.

Leeder, Murray. "Forget Peter Vincent: Nostalgia, Self-Reflexivity, and the Genre Past in *Fright Night.*" *The Journal of Popular Film and Television* Vol. 36, No. 4 (2009): 190–199.

Lerner, Neil, ed. *Music in the Horror Film: Listening to Fear.* Routledge Music and Screen Media Series. New York: Routledge, 2010.

Lightman, Alan, Sarewitz, Daniel, and Christina Desser. *Living with the Genie: Essays on Technology and the Quest for Human Mastery.* Washington, D.C.: Island Press, 2003.

Lowenstein, Adam. "Alone on Elm Street." *Film Quarterly* Vol. 64, No. 1 (Fall 210): 18–22.

Maltin, Leonard, ed. *Leonard Maltin's 2012 Movie Guide.* New York: Signet, 2012.

Martschukat, Jürgen. "'The Art of Killing by Electricity': The Sublime and the Electric Chair." *The Journal of American History* Vol. 89, No. 3 (December 2002): 900–921.

Massé, Michelle A. "Gothic Repetition: Husbands, Horrors, and Things That Go Bump in the Night." *Signs* Vol. 15, No. 4 (Summer 1990): 679–709.

McCarthy, John. *Movie Psychos and Madmen.* New York: Citadel Press, 1993.

McGinn, Colin. *The Power of Movies: How Screen and Mind Interact.* New York: Pantheon, 2005.

Meikle, Denis. *History of Horrors: The Rise and Fall of the House of Hammer.* Lanham, MD: Scarecrow, 1996.

Middleton, Jason. "The Subject of Torture: Regarding the Pain of Americans in *Hostel.*" *Cinema Journal* Vol. 49, No. 4 (Summer 2010): 1–24.

Moffat, Isabelle. "'A Horror of Abstract Thought': Postwar Britain and Hamilton's 1951 'Growth and Form' Exhibition." *October* Vol. 94 (Autumn 2000): 89–112.

Muir, John Kenneth. *Horror Films of the 1990s.* Jefferson, NC: McFarland, 2011.

Newman, Kim. *Nightmare Movies: Horror on Screen Since the 1960s.* London: Bloomsbury, 2011.

Niles, John De Witt. "Lamkin: The Motivation of Horror." *The Journal of American Folklore* Vol. 90, No. 355 (January–March 1977): 49–67.

Noriega, Chon. "Godzilla and the Japanese Nightmare: When 'Them!' Is U.S." *Cinema Journal* Vol. 27, No. 1 (Autumn 1987): 63–77.

Nowell, Richard. *Blood Money: A History of the First Teen Slasher Film Cycle*. New York: Continuum, 2011.
Packer, Sharon. *Movies and the Modern Psyche*. Westport, CT: Praeger, 2007.
Peary, Danny. *Cult Movies: The Classics, the Sleepers, the Weird, and the Wonderful*. New York: Delacorte, 1981.
Phillips, Kendall R. *Projected Fears: Horror Films and American Culture*. Westport, CT: Praeger, 2005.
Pratt-Smith, Stella. "The Poetic Science of Nineteenth-Century Electricity." *Nineteenth-Century Contexts* Vol. 34, No. 1. (February 2012): 31–62.
Prince, Stephen, ed. *The Horror Film*. New Brunswick, NJ: Rutgers, 2004.
_____, ed. *Screening Violence*. New Brunswick, NJ: Rutgers University Press, 2000.
Pursell, Carroll. *The Machine in America: A Social History of Technology*. Baltimore, MD: Johns Hopkins University Press, 2007.
Rabkin, Eric S. "Science Fiction and the Future of Criticism." *PMLA* Vol. 119, No. 3 Special Topics: Science Fiction and Literary Studies: The Next Millennium (May 2004): 457–473.
Radcliffe, Ann. "On the Supernatural in Poetry." *New Monthly Magazine* Vol. 16, No. 1 (1826): 145–152.
Rockoff, Adam. *Going to Pieces: The Rise and Fall of the Slasher Film, 1978–1986*. Jefferson, NC: McFarland, 2002.
Rothman, William. *Hitchcock: The Murderous Gaze*. Cambridge, MA: Harvard University Press, 1982.
Ruiz, Teofilo F. *The Terror of History: On the Uncertainties of Life in Western Civilization*. Princeton, NJ: Princeton University Press, 2011.
Russell, Bertrand. "The Science to Save Us from Science." *New York Times Magazine*, March 19, 1950.
Rutsky, R. L. "The Mediation of Technology and Gender: *Metropolis*, Nazism, Modernism." *New German Critique* No 60 Special Issue on German Film History (Autumn 1993): 3–32.
Salt, Barry. "Film Style and Technology in the Forties." *Film Quarterly* Vol. 31, No. 1 (Autumn 1977): 46–57.
_____. "Film Style and Technology in the Thirties." *Film Quarterly* Vol. 30, No. 1 (Autumn 1976): 19–32.
Scarry, Elaine. *The Body in Pain: The Making and Unmaking of the World*. Oxford: Oxford University Press, 1985.
Schmeink, Lars "*Splice*." *Science Fiction Film and Television* Vol. 5, No. 1 (2012): 153–57.
Schneider, Kirk J. *Horror and the Holy: Wisdom-Teachings of the Monster Tale*. Chicago: Open Court, 1993.
Schopenhauer, Arthur. "On Madness." *The World as Will and Representation*. Chapter XXXII. Trans E. F. J. Payne. Vol. II. New York: Dover, 1966. 399–402.
Sconce, Jeffrey. *Haunted Media: Electronic Presence from Telegraphy to Television*. Durham, NC: Duke University Press, 2000.
Seed, David. *American Science Fiction and the Cold War: Literature and Film*. Chicago: Fitzroy Dearborn, 1999.
Seife, Charles. *Virtual Unreality*. New York: Viking, 2014.
Sharrett, Christopher. "Fairy Tales for the Apocalypse: Wes Craven on the Horror Film." *Literature/Film Quarterly* Vol. 13 (1985): 139–147.
Shattuck, Roger. *Forbidden Knowledge: From Prometheus to Pornography*. New York: St. Martin's Press, 1996.
Shelly, Mary. *Frankenstein*. Ed J. Paul Hunter. New York: W. W. Norton, 1996.
Simon, Ed. *Necromomicon: 31st Anniversary Edition*. New York: Ibis Press, 2008.
Singer, Matt. "A New Kind of Monster." *The Dissolve*. August 19, 2013. www.thedissolve.com.
Sipos, Thomas. *Horror Film Aesthetics: Creating the Visual Language of Fear*. Jefferson, NC: McFarland, 2010.
Skal, David J. *The Monster Show: A Cultural History of Horror*. New York: Norton, 1993.
_____. *Screams of Reason: Mad Science and Modern Culture*. New York: Norton, 1998.
Smith, Andrew. *The Ghost Story, 1840–*

Bibliography

1920: A Cultural History. New York: Palgrave, 2010.

Smith, Caleb. "Bodies Electric: Gender, Technology, and the Limits of the Human, Circa 1900." *Mosaic* Vol. 41, No. 2 (June 2008): 111.

Sobchack, Vivian. *Carnal Thoughts: Embodiment and Moving Image Culture.* Berkeley: University of California Press, 2004.

Sontag, Susan. "The Imagination of Disaster." *Commentary.* October 1965. 42–48.

Soren, David. *The Rise and Fall of the Horror Film.* Revised Ed. Baltimore: Midnight Marquee, 1997.

Spadoni, Robert. *Uncanny Bodies: the Coming of Sound Film and the Origins of the Horror Genre.* Berkeley: University California Press, 2007.

Stewart, Susan. "The Epistemology of the Horror Story." *The Journal of American Folklore* Vol. 95, No. 375 (January–March 1982): 33–50.

Stoker, Bram. *Dracula.* Ed. David J. Skal. New York: W. W. Norton, 1997.

Takacs, Stacy. *Terrorism TV: Popular Entertainment in Post–9/11 America.* Lawrence: University of Kansas Press, 2012.

Taylor, Charles. *Sources of the Self: The Making of Modern Identity.* Cambridge, MA: Harvard University Press, 1989.

Telotte, J. P. "The *Blair Witch Project* Project: Film and the Internet." *Film Quarterly* Vol. 54, No. 3 (Spring 2001): 32–39.

Toumey, Christopher P. "The Moral Character of Mad Scientists: A Cultural Critique of Science." *Science, Technology, & Human Values* Vol. 17, No. 4 (Autumn 1992): 411–437.

Tryon, Chuck. "Video from the Void: Video Spectatorship, Domestic Film Cultures, and Contemporary Horror Film." *Journal of Film and Video* Vol. 61, No. 3 (Fall 2009): 40–51.

Turkle, Sherry. *Alone Together: Why We Expect More From Technology and Less from Each Other.* New York: Basic Books, 2011.

Twitchell, James B. *Dreadful Pleasures: an Anatomy of Modern Horror.* Oxford: Oxford University Press, 1985.

Underwood, Tim, and Chuck Miller, eds. *Fear Itself: The Horror Fiction of Stephen King.* Underwood-Miller: San Francisco, 1982.

_____, and Chuck Miller, eds. *Feasts of Fear: Conversations with Stephen King.* New York: Carroll & Graf, 1989.

Vieira, Mark A. *Hollywood Horror: From Gothic to Cosmic.* New York: Harry N. Abrams, 2003.

Virno, Paolo, and Alessia Ricciardi. "Familiar Horror." *Grey Room* No. 21 (Fall 2005): 13–16.

Warner, Marina. *Phantasmagoria: Spirit Visions, Metaphors, and Media Into the Twenty-First Century.* Oxford: Oxford University Press, 2006.

Wee, Valerie. "Resurrecting and Updating the Teen Slasher: The Case of *Scream*." *Journal of Popular Film and Television* Vol. 34, No. 2 (2006): 50–61.

Weiskel, Portia Williams. "On the Works of Franz Kafka." *Franz Kafka.* Eds. Neil Hiens and Portia Williams Weiskel. New York: Infobase, 2009.

Welsh, Tricia. "Foreign Exchange: German Expressionism and Its Legacy." *Cinema Journal* Vol. 38, No. 4 (Summer 1999): 98–102.

Westfahl, Gary. *Science Fiction, Children's Literature, and Popular Culture: Coming of Age in Fantasy Land.* Westport, CT: Greenwood, 2000.

Westlake, E.J. "Friend Me If You Facebook: Generation Y and Performative Surveillance." *TDR [The Drama Review]* Vol. 52, No. 4 (Winter 2008): 21–40.

Westmore, Kevin J., Jr. "Technoghosts and Culture Shocks: Sociocultural Shifts in American Remakes of J-Horror." *Post Script* Vol. 28, No. 2 (Winter–Spring 2009): 72.

White, Dennis L. "The Poetics of Horror: More than Meets the Eye." *Cinema Journal* Vol. 10, No. 2 (Spring 1971): 1–18.

Williams, Linda. "Film Bodies: Gender, Genre, and Excess." *Film Quarterly.* Vol. 44, No. 4 (Summer 1991). 2–13.

Bibliography

Wisker, Gina. *Horror Fiction: An Introduction.* New York: Continuum, 2005.

Wooley, John. *Wes Craven: The Man and His Nightmares.* Hoboken, NJ: John Wiley & Sons, 2011.

Workland, Rick. *The Horror Film: an Introduction.* Malden, MA: Blackwell, 2007.

Wright, Bradford W. *Comic Book Nation: The Transformation of Youth Culture in America.* Baltimore: Johns Hopkins University Press, 2001.

Wyrick, Laura. "Horror at Century's End: Where Have All the Slashers Gone?" *Pacific Coast Philology.* Vol. 33, No. 2. Convention Program Issue (1998). 122–126.

Zinoman, Jason. *Shock Value: How a Few Eccentric Outsiders Gave Us Nightmares, Conquered Hollywood, and Invented Modern Horror.* New York: Penguin, 2011.

Index

abjection 31, 33, 39
Aesop 99
Alien 92, 119, 120
alien invasion 43, 44, 55, 117, 118–121
Alighieri, Dante 12, 13
Amber Alert 166
American Dream 43, 59, 65–69, 96, 100, 106, 156, 175
American Psycho 137, 138–139, 142
anxiety 14, 36, 45, 78, 84, 91, 166, 168, 171
Apollo program 64
artificial intelligence 127–131, 132; see also *Demon Seed*
Artificial Intelligence: A.I. 115, 132
ATM 112
ATM 166
Atomic Age 42, 100, 115
atomic bomb 43–45, 56; bombing of Hiroshima and Nagasaki 3, 43, 55
atomic energy 53, 57–58, 59–60

B-movies 36, 47, 82, 89, 90
Bacon, Francis 87
Bacon, Kevin 4
Basement Tapes 140
Baudrillard, Jean 162–163
The Best Years of Our Lives 42
The Bible 15
Big Brother 71, 104
birth control 128
Black Christmas 104
Blackenstein 37
Blade Runner 132
Blair, Linda 94

The Blair Witch Project 3, 4, 39, 156–157, 160, 162
The Blob 18, 49
The Body 161
Body Parts 123
The Body Snatcher 42
The Body Snatchers (novel) 54
Bogdanovich, Peter 63
The Bourne Identity 3
Boyle, Peter 38
The Brain from Planet Arous 3
The Brain That Wouldn't Die 123
Brainscan 125
Branaugh, Kenneth 38
Bride of Frankenstein 36
Brooks, Mel 37
Brown v. Board of Education 48
Browning, Tod 30, 33
Bud Abbott and Lou Costello Meet Frankenstein 37
The 'Burbs 113
Burke, Edmund 17
Burgess, Anthony 97
Byron, Lord George Gordon 12

The Cabin in the Woods 173, 177–179
The Cabinet of Dr. Caligari 34–35, 43
cable (television) 172
Cache 161
cameras 3, 39–40, 70–72, 75, 85, 89, 152, 157, 161, 164
Cannibal Holocaust 158
Carpenter, John 80, 89, 151
Carrie 18, 90
Carroll, Noël 30, 84, 116–117

Index

Castle, William 46
The Cell 126
cellular phone 113, 138, 143, 145, 146, 150, 164, 165, 175, 179
Centers for Disease Control (CDC) 164
Chernobyl Diaries 167
Children Shouldn't Play with Dead Things 1
Child's Play 92
Chucky 91
A Clockwork Orange (film) 97
Close Encounters of the Third Kind 116
Cloverfield 147, 164
Cold War 43–48, 56–57, 81, 87, 109
Coleridge, Samuel Taylor 12
Columbine High School 140, 142
comics 6, 80–82, 87–88
Comics Code 80–81
Communism 64
computers 118, 126–131, 143, 146–148, 150–151
consumerism 100, 113
Contact 120–122
costumes 49, 85, 125
counter culture 67–68, 97, 99, 104
Craven, Wes 89, 92, 103, 169
Creature Double Feature 2, 83
Creature from the Black Lagoon 49, 83
Cronenberg, David 109–110, 127, 168

Dalí, Salvador 87
Dawley, J. Searle 28
Dawn of the Dead 87, 92, 100–101, 176
The Day the Earth Stood Still 52–54
Daybreakers 176
democracy 154
Demon Seed 127–131
De Niro, Robert 38
The Dentist 123
Department of Defense (DoD) 164
Descartes, René 140
Devil 113
Die, Monster, Die 2
District 9 147
Dr. Giggles 123
Dr. Jekyll and Mr. Hyde 139
Donovan's Brain 3
Don't Answer the Phone 104
Dracula (film) 21, 30, 33, 78, 90
Dracula (novel) 19–21
DVD 143, 155

EC Comics 80–81, 97
Eckhart, Aaron 40
Edison, Thomas 4, 28, 143
EEG 5
effects 2, 29, 89, 91, 143, 148, 158, 169, 177; and make up 84–87; *see also* costumes
electricity 22–23, 143
Elevator 113
Ellis, Brett Eason 138
e-mail 145
End of the Line 166
Englund, Robert 92, 94
The Epic of Gilgamesh 13
Event Horizon 120
EVP 147, 148
exhibitionism 163
existentialism 34
eXistenZ 127
The Exorcist 88, 90, 92, 94
The Eye 123
Eyes Without a Face 57

Facebook 126, 148, 154
Fade to Black 108
Farrow, Mia 73
Faust 25
FBI 126, 148
FDA 130
Fear 144
fear: perception of 16, 47–49, 103–104, 111, 147, 168–169; response to 5, 111, 166, 178; of science 37, 44–45, 55, 64; of society 7, 63–65, 98, 105, 111–112, 151, 164, 177
FearDotCom 149
Fiend Without a Face 3
film: exhibition 21, 23, 28–29, 43, 46, 89, 98, 110, 155, 168, 175; and home viewing 87, 108, 109; and innovation 47, 89, 91, 156; and lighting 2, 5, 103; and sound 29; *see also* Targets
The Final Cut 152–154, 162
Final Destination 167; as franchise 167
Finney, Jack 54–55
Flatliners 5, 123
Flesh for Frankenstein 37
The Fly (1958) 49, 57–59
The Fly (1986) 168
Forbidden Planet 49, 119
Forbidden World 120
found footage 156–164

202

Index

1408 111
The Fourth Kind 162
Frankenstein (film) 26, 28, 90; as franchise 35–41, 121, 166, 178
Frankenstein (novel) 11–13, 26, 31, 64
Frankenstein, Victor: creation of monster 32, 117; ethics 27, 122; name changed for film 29
Frankenstein Conquers the World 37
Frankenstein Created Woman 37
Frankenstein: 1970 37
The Frankenstein Theory 39–40
Frankenstein's monster: humanity 36; muteness 36; nature 26–27, 32, 38; symbol of change 41, 57, 104, 166; see also *The Rocky Horror Picture Show*
Freud, Sigmund 14, 22, 34
Friday the 13th 103–104, 170; as franchise 3–4, 101, 102, 111
Friday the 13th Part VIII: Jason Takes Manhattan 93
Fright Night 108–109
Frozen 167

Gaines, William 80–81
Germany: and film of 34
Godzilla 57, 83, 164
Godzilla vs. Mothra 2
gore 79, 82, 86, 88–89, 92, 103, 165, 171, 177
Gothic 3, 4–5, 6, 11, 13–14, 20, 23, 42, 46, 69, 91, 99, 141, 167
Grave Encounters 163
Great Depression 67
gun culture 76

Halloween 90, 93, 142, 146
Hammer Films 45–46, 64
The Happening 147
Harris, Eric 140, 142
Hawke, Ethan 176
Hawthorne, Nathaniel 15
Hayes Code 82
HBO 2, 109
Heidegger, Martin 34, 115
Hell 12
Hepburn, Audrey 72
Hitchcock, Alfred 2, 68–69, 90
Hollywood 34, 35, 42, 75, 77, 85, 88, 108, 173
home invasion 144
Homer 13

Hooper, Toby 87, 96
horror: aesthetics 16–19, 82, 157–159, 171; fans 13, 81, 155; perception 7, 16–18, 19–24, 25, 32, 108, 112–113, 121, 147, 149–150, 155–156, 158, 174–176; and psychology 13, 92, 118, 141–142, 145, 170–171; rules 159, 177; and sound 29, 77
horror film: dormancy 43–44; and franchises 36–37, 92–95, 147, 161, 168–170 (see also *Frankenstein*); marketing 30, 46–48, 158, 174; violence in 18, 23–24, 66, 74–77, 86–87, 88
Hostage 144
Hostel 147
Hotel Transylvania 38
House 113, 161
The Human Centipede (First Sequence) 123
human condition 12, 14–15, 16, 64
The Hunchback of Notre Dame 32
Hurricane Sandy 41
The Hurt Locker 175

I Am Legend 123, 124
I, Frankenstein 40
I, Robot 132
I Was a Teenage Frankenstein 37, 38
Immigration and Naturalization Act of 1952 48
iMurders 148
independent film 82–83, 89, 173
Inferno 12
Information Age 143
Instagram 126
The Internet, 113, 126, 137, 146–148, 152, 160, 163, 165
Interview with the Vampire: The Vampire Chronicles 163
Invasion of the Body Snatchers 49, 55–57, 58
The Invisible Man 31
iPad 146
Irving, Sir Henry 21
isolation 70, 72–73, 101–102, 103–104, 111, 143, 151, 154, 160, 165

Jacob's Ladder 113
Jaws 88, 89
Jesus Christ 15
Johnny Mnemonic 127
Julian, Rupert 32

203

Index

Kafka, Franz 139, 142
Kant, Immanuel 17
Karloff, Boris 27, 36, 37, 63, 75
Keaton, Michael 5, 148
Kemmler, William 22
Kennedy, Robert 76
Kierkegaard, Søren 34
Killer Klowns from Outer Space 167
kinetoscope 23
King, Stephen 101, 112, 125, 126, 161
King Kong 164
Klebold, Dylan 140, 142
Koontz, Dean 127
Kristeva, Julia 14, 30, 33
Krueger, Freddy 2, 92
Kubrick, Stanley 97, 101

Lady in a Cage 73, 113
Lang, Fritz 33, 35
The Last House on the Left (1972) 89, 96, 103, 112
The Last Man on Earth 124
The Lawnmower Man 125–126, 129
Leary, Timothy 97
Leigh, Janet 2, 68
Levin, Ira 174
Levittown, NY 58
Lewis, Herschell Gordon 83, 84–85
Life Without Soul 28
Live! 163
Logan's Run 115, 132
Lugosi, Bela 21

mad scientist 26, 35, 45, 56, 58, 82, 117, 121–123, 127–128, 174
Make Room! Make Room! 176
Manhattan 93, 104, 113, 138, 145
Manhattan Project 44, 48; see also atomic bomb
Marxism 33
Mary Shelley's Frankenstein 38
Matheson, Richard 123
The Matrix 127
May 38–39
McCarthy, Joseph R. 56
McCarthyism 44
McDowell, Malcolm 97
McNeil, Regan 94
Messages Deleted 149
"The Metamorphosis" 139
Metropolis 33–35
Milton, John 15
Monster Squad 38

monsters 26, 42, 48, 64, 72, 91, 109, 117, 145, 155–156, 166, 171, 173, 177–179; as construct of society 48, 98, 146, 164, 167, 179; as heroes 93
morality 15, 81, 149
MPAA 88, 89
MTV 109, 138
Murnau, F.W. 32
Myers, Michael 90, 91, 94
MySpace 126, 148

Netflix 172
New World Order 73
Nietzsche, Friedrich 124, 125
Night of the Living Dead 77, 85–86, 88, 100–101
night vision 164
A Nightmare on Elm Street 2, 18, 92, 93
9/11 113, 145, 147
976-EVIL 104
1984 104
No Country for Old Men 175
Nosferatu: A Symphony of Horrors 32

occult 12
The Odyssey 13, 16
Oedipus 12
The Omega Man 124
One Missed Call 149
Orwell, George 71, 104
The Other 25, 31, 33, 36, 39, 68, 98, 119, 141
Ott, Fred 21
Overlook Hotel 102, 141

Palidori, John 12
Pandora's Box 16
Panic Room 144
Paranormal Activity 162
Peeping Tom 70–72; and voyeurism 71
Perkins, Anthony 2, 68–69
Phantasmagoriana 12
The Phantom of the Opera 32
Phone Booth 104
The Picture of Dorian Gray 42
Pinocchio 133
Plan 9 from Outer Space 49
Playback 149
Poe, Edgar Allan 20
Poltergeist 96, 100, 105–107; and television 106–107
The Poughkeepsie Tapes 161

Index

Powell, Michael 70–72
privacy 154, 162; *see also* voyeurism
Prodigal Son 15
Production Code 47
Prometheus 16, 31–32
Prometheus 120, 122
Proteus 128–131
Psycho 2, 68–70, 77, 78, 79, 84, 88, 92, 103, 111
Pulse 150
The Purge 144–145

Quarantine 163–164

Radcliffe, Ann 19, 21
Ransom 141
Reanimator 123
REC 149
Return to Horror High 158–160
Rice, Anne 163
The Rime of the Ancient Mariner 12
The Ring 110
Ringu 110
Robby the Robot 119
The Rocky Horror Picture Show 104
Roe v. Wade 128
Romero, George 77–79, 85, 87, 100
Rosemary's Baby 73, 90, 98, 129

St. Augustine 149
Sartre, Jean-Paul 65, 137
Saving Private Ryan 3
Savini, Tom 85, 86
Saw franchise 5, 147, 170
Schindler's List 3
Schock Theater 83
science: and cinema 28; and progress 11–12, 60
science fiction 2, 25, 115–118, 119, 131–132; birth of 49–50
science fiction films 44, 48, 49–60, 115–116; Golden Age 55; as sources of horror 11–12, 45–46, 49, 60, 82, 116–118, 121, 122, 131–132, 133–134; as warnings to society 122–125, 128
Scott, Ridley 119, 120
Scream 18, 108, 146, 169; as franchise 158, 170, 178
Seconds 74
A Serbian Film 147
Sesame Street 20
Se7en 141
The Shaft 113

Shaun of the Dead 113–114
Shelley, Mary 11, 23, 25–28, 30–32; and fears 32, 40
Shelley, Percy Bysshe 12
The Shining 100, 101–102
shock value 6, 169
Shutter 149
The Signal 150–151
Signs 147
The Silence of the Lambs 3
Sing Sing Prison 22
singularity 127
Sinister 110
The Sirens 16
The Sixth Sense 4
slasher film 2–5, 89, 91–95, 103, 115, 118, 142, 145, 159, 169; and humor 95, 108, 151, 177; and predictability 93, 95, 108, 171; and weapons 105
Smith, Dick 85
Sneeze 21
social networks 144, 165
social progress 5–6, 100, 139
society: breakdown 112; escape from 4; fear of 6–7; norms 14
Son of Frankenstein 36
Sontag, Susan 44–45, 120, 162, 168
Sophocles 12
Soviet Union 44
Soylent Green 176
space 124
space race 121
special effects 82, 84–87, 92; and masks 85, 90
Spielberg, Steven 89, 132
Stand By Me 161
Star Wars 116
Steinbeck, John 42
The Stepford Wives 174
Stoker, Bram 19–21
Summer of Love 100
Super 8 161
supernatural beings 13
surveillance 162, 166
suspension of disbelief 2

taboo 6, 88, 163
Tales from the Crypt 80, 109
Targets 63, 74–77, 78, 98
telephone 104, 143, 146, 150
television 43, 59, 70, 83–84, 96, 105–107, 108, 111, 143, 145, 151, 161, 163, 166, 178

205

Index

Tesla, Nikola 4, 22–23, 58, 143
The Texas Chainsaw Massacre 87–88, 89, 92, 96, 103, 104–105
text messaging 144
They Live 151
The Thing from Another World 49, 50, 54
The Tingler 46
torture porn 147, 158
A Trip to the Moon 3
Tron 126
28 Days Later 164
Twitter 126

Universal (film studio) 36, 37–38, 45, 47, 171; Golden Age 49
the uncanny 14, 22, 30; *see also* Freud, Sigmund
Untraceable 148
urban legend 110, 111, 156, 177

Vacancy 110–111
The Vampire Lestat 163
The Vampyre 12
Van Helsing 38
VHS 1, 87, 88, 108, 138, 143, 151, 155, 172
video cameras 161, 162, 164
The Video Dead 110
Videodrome 109–110
Vietnam War 37, 74, 78–79, 83, 84–85, 98, 100, 105, 113, 161
Vile 174
virtual reality 125–126, 148, 156
Voorhees, Jason 91, 94, 103

voyeurism 71, 73, 96, 109, 151, 154, 165, 169

Wait Until Dark 72–73
Walkman 138
War of the Worlds 164, 168
Watergate 105
Weimar Republic 34
Weine, Robert 34–35
Wes Craven's New Nightmare 93
Westinghouse, George 22
Whale, James 27, 30, 34, 36, 41
Whedon, Joss 173
When a Stranger Calls 104, 146
White Noise 5, 147–148
Wi-Fi 165
Wilde, Oscar 1
Wilder, Gene 38
Williams, Robin 133, 152
Wise, Robert 52
World War I 43
World War II 34, 42–44, 48, 53, 59, 63, 67, 84, 147
Worsley, Wallace 32
Wyler, William 42

Young Frankenstein 37–38, 39
"Young Goodman Brown" 15
Yuppies 138

Zeus 32
Zombie Blood Nightmare 110
zombies 1, 77–79, 86, 100–101, 113, 150, 164, 177
Zombies on Broadway 42

www.ingramcontent.com/pod-product-compliance
Ingram Content Group UK Ltd.
Pitfield, Milton Keynes, MK11 3LW, UK
UKHW042003140426
5217IPUK00015B/954